ADVENTURES OF A
ZOO DIRECTOR

STEVE H. TAYLOR

Director Emeritus Cleveland Metroparks Zoo

outskirts
press

DEDICATION

This book is dedicated to my three "grandurchins," Shae, Hank, and Ainsley, and my two young nieces, Emma and Ava. After Hank's birthday in March 2013, the children were ages eight, nine, ten, eleven, and twelve. Don't ask me which is which! My advice for them is to follow the words of country music singer Lee Ann Womack.

"When you have a chance to sit it out or dance, I hope you dance."

Grandchildren and nieces
Emma, Shae, Hank, Ava, and Ainsley in 2012

Grandchildren and Nieces. Emma, Shae, Hank, Ava and Ainsley in 2012.

TABLE OF CONTENTS

CHAPTER 1

ADVENTURES IN GROWING UP

I WAS BORN on March 18, 1947, at Centinela Hospital in Inglewood, California, one month before Jackie Robinson took his first at bat for the Brooklyn Dodgers. I had two older sisters. Edith was seventeen years old, and Jean was fourteen years old. My brother, Ray, was seven years old. My father, Raymond Martin Taylor, was forty-four years old when I was born, and my mother, Ardath, was one week shy of her fortieth birthday, a fact she often mentioned with some pride. One can only imagine that my birth (and probably my brother's) was "unplanned."

My father worked for North American Aviation, later purchased by Rockwell Aviation. He retired in 1966 when he was sixty-two years old. He was a hard-working, intelligent man with a strong will and a great sense of humor. He and my mother were heavy smokers, and he died in 1970, a year after I graduated from college. The diagnosis was "acute bilateral bronchopneumonia." Translated: he smoked himself to death. While I was happy that he was there when my son was born, I always regretted that he was not around when I achieved my dream of becoming a zoo director.

My mother was a 1950s housewife, cleaning the house and cooking the meals. Nonetheless, she had a mind of her own, which she certainly displayed in 1956 when she surprised everyone by purchasing her own car with cash she saved from thirty years of grocery money and kept in a secret bank account. Supposedly Dad did not talk to her for several months after she purchased the car, but I was too young to remember. Mom lived until she was eighty-five, when I was director of the Sacramento Zoo, although her dementia probably never allowed her to fully understand any of my adulthood successes.

I grew up in Inglewood at 416 W. 64th Street. My sisters were out of the house for most of my childhood, and Ray and I shared a room until he left home after college in 1962. Ray and I were far enough apart in age that we had little in common. When he was home, our times together were mostly when he had to babysit me while Mom and Dad played bridge or visited friends. Ray had the type of high intelligence that allowed him to do well in school and become an engineer, a profession that I assumed pleased our father. Dad had never gone to high school, but he was intelligent enough to teach himself to be a toolmaker and supervisor/administrator. I was told that during World War II, while at North American Aviation, he had several thousand people working for him in his division.

As my brother and I got older, we grew closer. Now we see each other often, travel together, visit each other's homes, enjoy a bottle of wine or two, and generally enjoy being brothers.

In the 1950s and 1960s, Inglewood was what I would call a "Leave it to Beaver" neighborhood. There were many children my age on my block, and I grew up playing hide-and-go-seek, kick the can, and later, spin the bottle. It was as safe as most communities were in the 1950s. One now questions how any of us managed to survive secondhand smoke, BB guns, lead-based paints, smog, lawn darts, sitting or standing in the back seat of a car with no seat belts, flexi flyers, skateboards (they were three-foot long two-by-fours with an old roller skate nailed to the bottom) and living through the constant fear of a nuclear attack by the commies.

With brother Ray, sisters Edith and Jean in 1990.

In 1958 I was in the fifth grade when the Brooklyn Dodgers moved to Los Angeles and the New York Giants moved to San Francisco. My dad took my friend George Thompson and me to the Los Angeles Coliseum, built for the 1938 Olympics, to see our first major league baseball game. The Dodgers had to play in the coliseum for two years until Dodger Stadium was completed in Chavez Ravine. As the coliseum was not built with baseball in mind, the shallow left field was "guarded" by a huge vertical wall, maybe forty feet high. People called it the Moon Wall, as the Dodger outfielder Wally Moon became efficient at hitting pitches high enough to go over the wall. These hits would have been shallow fly outs in any other ballpark. Like many other fifth graders, I could name all the players on the everyday line-up. It included Gil Hodges, Charlie O'Neil, Pee Wee Reese, Wally Moon, Duke Snyder, John Roseboro, and pitchers Johnnie Padres, Don Drysdale, and Sandy Koufax. How I can remember those names today when I can't remember what I had for breakfast amazes me. I was one year too late to see Jackie Robinson and Roy Campanella, who died from cancer, play for the Dodgers. Another memory of my first major league baseball game was my dad at the ticket window asking for three good seats for two nearsighted young boys and himself.

With my father and brother in Newport Beach, California in the mid-fifties.

In those days, the only regular season games on TV in Los Angeles occurred when the Dodgers played the Giants in San Francisco. I guess it was not practical to televise games on the East Coast and show them in LA, and it wasn't economically feasible to televise home games, as the owners wanted to fill seats at the coliseum. I did listen to many games on the radio, though.

The racial makeup of my part of Inglewood, and indeed Inglewood

High, in the 1950s and 1960s was mostly white, with some Hispanics, mostly of Mexican descent, and some Asians. I never remember much racial tension between the white majority and the Hispanics or Asians, but certainly there was a fear that blacks (referred to as Negroes or worse, back then) would one day move into the neighborhood. Race never preoccupied my mind until later in high school and then in college. The Watts riots in the summer of 1965 certainly brought the matter of race to my attention.

I do not know how I developed my interest in animals and wildlife. I do not remember having an early mentor. In fact I cannot think of any early influence, although as long as I can remember, I liked having animals around. Mom and Dad did not think I was responsible enough to take care of a dog, so I had other pets in the house, such as fish in a small freshwater aquarium, a parakeet, and a hamster. Myrtle the turtle, actually a desert tortoise, was kept outside, behind the garage. There I also kept many small local native animals, such as alligator lizards, western toads, and one particularly long-lived horned toad I collected at an early age on a rare trip to the desert. The toads and lizards were collected in nearby fields, such as the oil fields on Baldwin Hills or an empty lot across LaCienga Boulevard. One day when my friend Alan Smith and I were catching bugs in an abandoned lot to feed my small collection of animals, a police car approached and opened the window. In a stern voice we were asked, "Are you kids looking for trouble?" I proudly held up my collection bag and answered, "No, just bugs."

The policeman chuckled and drove off. Perhaps my interest in wildlife is simply due to the fact that my parents would never let me have a dog, so I was forced to find other animals to amuse me.

While I cannot remember one person in my childhood who helped create my lifelong interest in wildlife, I do remember books, school reports, and TV shows. *ZooRama* was a show filmed at the San Diego Zoo wherein the moderator interviewed one of the curators, such as Clyde Hill, curator of mammals, or Chuck Shaw, curator of reptiles. The curators each talked about one of the animals in the zoo collection. I still remember an episode on the fossa, the largest carnivore, related to meerkats and civets, from the island of Madagascar. It was in a display in cat canyon, and the zoo had a giant four-feet-around "hamster wheel." I remember the fossa using that enrichment devise forty years before the word *enrichment* became a popular term in zoo animal husbandry. I have told that story several times, when a pair of fossa came to Cleveland Metroparks Zoo in 2003 and became popular zoo animals. At Cleveland Metroparks Zoo, we installed our own fossa wheel in 2005.

In sixth grade I gave a career-day report on being a zoologist. It was a difficult assignment, as everyone else had countless resources to study professions from doctor and lawyer to garbage collector, but little written information existed on becoming a zoologist. About this same time, I read my first Gerald Durrell book, *A Zoo in my Luggage*. I was hooked. Over the years I have spent many delightful hours reading and rereading all of Gerald Durrell's books. Those books, more than anything else, steered my life toward being a zoo director. Twice when I had an opportunity to meet Gerald Durrell, I thanked him for influencing my choice of careers.

I did have many adults who had a positive effect on my life as a manager and leader. In high school I was elected senior class president for the first semester. Even as early as 1964, there was an antiestablishment movement, and I was seen as that candidate, as the other candidate was the more popular choice—smarter and an athlete. The drama teacher, Mrs. Benedict, noticed my first attempt at public speaking. She searched me out and gave me private lessons, especially on projecting my voice. She didn't know me, but she realized that I could use her help. I am certain that most of us have had a teacher who took extra time to help us when we were students. By the way, projecting my voice has never been an issue for me after high school.

I stayed active in Student Council throughout my senior year. I was the campaign manager for my friend Mike Mahoney for second-semester student body president. He lost. I wanted to stay on student council, but since I supported the losing candidate, my options for an appointed seat were limited. Nonetheless, the student council advisor, Mr. Harvey, convinced the incoming student body president, Tom

La Briola, to appoint me commissioner of activities. I believe those early efforts at leadership were important in my future.

I also started to develop my public-speaking style and self-deprecating sense of humor. In one speech at a senior class banquet, a faculty member introduced me by saying that another staff member had asked him who that skinny guy was that was about to speak. He told her that it was Steve Taylor, first semester senior class president. When I got up to speak, I started by saying, "After that introduction, I hope you can all see me behind the microphone stand." I went on to tell everyone that it is very important to vote and further reported that I had won the election for senior class president by just one vote. I added, "Now I bet some of you wish you had voted." Well, maybe it wasn't that funny, but I did get a few laughs.

I graduated with a 3.3 grade average, seventy-sixth in my class of about five hundred. Mike Mahoney and I had the exact same grade average. In those days it was good enough to get me accepted to the new University of California, Irvine (UCI). It was my first choice for several reasons. First, it was close to Newport Beach, an area that was our family vacation spot for the previous fifteen years. Second, it was the only school with a bachelor's degree in biology that did not require a foreign language, a subject that was very difficult for me.

At UCI, I also had a wonderful field botany course that allowed my fellow classmates and me to spend time exploring what was then the vast wilderness of the Irvine Ranch, which is mostly housing now. The university also had access to the San Joaquin Marsh, a fantastic area for birding that included ducks, egrets, blue herons, coots, and other water birds. These water birds still make this place an oasis in the middle of urban Orange County, California. The area around the university was so natural that on my many hikes I saw cactus wrens and roadrunners and an occasional bobcat and golden eagle. I enjoyed my time in college and felt fortunate to be in the first four-year graduating class (1965–1969) from UCI.

One of the unique opportunities we had as the first four-year class at UCI was choosing the school mascot. One must remember that it was the 1960s, and anything that was thought of as "normal" was challenged, and I mean everything, so whatever mascot we chose had to be unusual or even bizarre. One idea brought forward was to become the Irvine anteaters. During the campaign some were critical of anteaters as not ferocious enough. The proponents countered with the fact that anteaters were ferocious to ants, and we would therefore make our opponents in sporting events the ants. One very clever part of the campaign showed a redrawn black and white Playboy bunny, a popular logo then, with a long anteater nose. The slogan was Vote for Anteaters, a Mascot for Real Men! Peter, the giant anteater, has been the UCI mascot ever since.

With Peter the Anteater at my 50th college reunion from University of California, Irvine.

I received a bachelor's degree in biology from UCI in 1969. Most biology majors at the university would go to medical school or a similar field. Few courses were geared toward becoming a naturalist, as E. O. Wilson would later call biologists like me. I did have a course in animal behavior that gave me one of my few A's. I should note that I took it in my last quarter, and I also received a D in biochemistry. I graduated with a 2.5 grade point average. When talking with young people, I often mention the fact that some people are successful without going to a famous college and earning high grades. There is more to life than high intelligence. One must work with what they have.

"No institution can possibly survive if it needs geniuses or supermen to manage it. It must be organized in such a way as to be able to get along under a leadership composed of average human beings." Peter Drucker

While my father had saved enough money for me to attend UCI, I did have summer and part-time jobs through college. After graduation from high school, I worked that summer at North American Aviation, my father's employer for more than thirty years. It was a factory job, and I worked directly with other factory workers who ranged in age from twenty to sixty. The job paid well, and I felt lucky to have that experience. The summer of 1965 was also the year of the famous Watts riots, which occurred about three miles from the North American plant. Many African American employees came into work very frightened for their homes and families.

Another summer job included working at Marina Del Rey Hardware, where I sold products, delivered goods, did some simple repair work, and mowed the owner's lawn. I often had to deliver supplies to a printing company in downtown Los Angeles owned by the son of the hardware store's owner. While I had never been trained to drive a stick shift, I did not admit that fact during the job interview. By trial and error I learned to drive the stick shift in the Volkswagen van with absolutely no training.

Other jobs I've held included working for the Planning Department in Newport Beach taking an inventory of red, yellow, and green curbs and traffic signs.

The year prior to my graduation, the UCI Medical School opened. I got a part-time job taking care of laboratory animals and later worked there full-time for a couple of years. All of my jobs were great learning experiences for me.

Before I graduated from college, I married my high school sweetheart and had a son, Travis. Travis was born in 1969, on my twenty-second birthday. After graduation I worked caring for the laboratory animals at the new UCI Medical School and attended graduate school at Long Beach State. At Long Beach State I was able to take many courses that were not offered at UCI, such as herpetology, ornithology, mammalogy, and more. These classes gave me an important educational background for my future in the zoo profession.

At the time I graduated from college, I thought that I might want to be a high school biology teacher, but then I realized I wanted to work in a zoo. I did not really know how to go about getting such a job, but I applied to the closest zoo, the recently relocated Los Angeles Zoo. Sometime in 1971, along with 1,200 other job applicants, I took a written civil service test in the auditorium of Hollywood High School in hopes to become an animal keeper at the Los Angeles Zoo. I believe I received the highest score on the test, as I was ranked number seven, and everyone with higher scores received ten extra points for serving in the military. I never had to serve in the military, because after I graduated from college in 1969, where I had a student exemption, on the first military draft lottery, I drew 334. As comedian Robin Williams said, "That would mean that the communists would have to attack Kansas City before I would be called." What can I say? At the time, I felt I was very lucky.

CHAPTER 2

ADVENTURES IN MY EARLY CAREER

I AM AN ANIMAL KEEPER

I started as an animal keeper at the Los Angeles Zoo in May 1972. By then I had already been divorced and was away on a weekend trip in San Francisco when my ex-mother-in-law called to tell me I was scheduled for an interview with Bill Turner, assistant director of the Los Angeles Zoo.

I must mention here that of the many wonderful people I have met in my life, I was fortunate in having two extraordinary mothers-in-law. I miss them both.

I drove back from San Francisco, interviewed, and reported to work at the children's zoo of the Los Angeles Zoo in May 1972. Claudia Collier, who later went on to direct the zoos in Santa Ana and Atascadero, California, was the nursery keeper, and she trained me my first day. I remember walking to the parking lot with Claudia that day, having to pinch myself to make certain it was real. I was now an animal keeper.

Things were different in the zoo world in the early 1970s. The modern environmental movement had just begun. The Endangered Species Act had just passed, and some people feared it might have a detrimental effect on animal acquisition in zoos. Now zoo professionals in the United States are doing everything possible to make certain the act is not weakened by anti-environmental legislation. The first Earth Day, which many consider the birth of the environmental movement, occurred on April 22, 1970. At that time, most Americans were oblivious to environmental concerns. Twenty years later, in 1990, on the twentieth anniversary of the first Earth Day, more than 200 million people in 141 countries celebrated the event. It was the first of Cleveland Metroparks Zoo's many successful Earth Day events, two of which attracted more than 30,000 participants.

In 1972 there were no women animal keepers at the Los Angeles Zoo, except in the children's zoo. They wore pink blouses and powder-blue jeans and were called children's zoo attendants. The men wore brown pants and khaki shirts. There were no registrars, no conservation or science departments, no animal-enrichment programs, and no professional zoo designers. The first gorilla born in a zoo was born in Columbus, Ohio, only seventeen years earlier. Many of the keepers were older and had little education. The director of the Los Angeles Zoo was Chester Hogan, a long-time city bureaucrat who became zoo director by default, when he did not get his dream job as head of the new Los Angeles Convention Center.

I was so excited about being a zookeeper that I constantly asked questions of the older keepers who often had a great amount of practical knowledge. I remember early on in my days at the children's zoo asking an older keeper who was busy preparing food in a rubber tub, "What are you feeding?" It looked very interesting with a large assortment of colorful fresh fruit and vegetables, various prepared foods, peanuts, and other things. I will never forget his answer, "I don't know what you call it. I just know what it eats." It was a paca, an interesting large rodent from the rain forests of South America.

As an animal keeper at a zoo, you are the envy of many. Many people think working outside with beautiful exotic animals must be a great job. And it is. At first, most people do not think about the hard work in less-than-perfect conditions. Some people do understand that caring for zoo animals is hard, dirty, and smelly work. Once while I was working in the aviary at the Los Angeles Zoo, a school group happened to pass while I was using a plumber's helper to unplug a clogged drain. No matter which zoo or which animal exhibit, from a bird aviary to an elephant exhibit, drains in the exhibits or night quarters are rarely large enough. A sweet female teacher suggested to her class that they might want to continue their education through college so that they could one day work with animals in a zoo. I distinctly heard one ten-year-old correct her by saying, "You don't have to go to college to be a plumber." Not all people are impressed with animal keepers.

During my years at Los Angeles Zoo, it had three different zoo directors. Chester Hogan was there when I started, and while he was probably a great civil servant, he did not have the background necessary to be zoo director. Dr. Charlie Schroeder, retired director of the San Diego Zoo and the San Diego Wild Animal Park, which was his dream and he was rightfully credited with its development, took over as interim director while the City of Los Angeles searched for a new director. The city eventually chose the controversial Dr. Warren Thomas, who had recently left his position as director of the Gladys Porter Zoo in Brownsville, Texas. Dr. Thomas had been director at the Oklahoma City Zoo and Omaha's Henry Doorly Zoo before building the zoo in Brownsville, Texas, for the JC Penney heiress, Gladys Porter. He had been a part-time zookeeper at the Columbus Zoo while in veterinary school at Ohio State. In fact, his early claim to fame was being the keeper on duty when Colo, the first-ever captive-bred gorilla was born. The Gladys Porter Zoo was a new state-of-the-art zoo with a second-to-none animal collection. Some of the controversy with Dr. Thomas concerned his methods of acquiring that collection of wildlife. I learned much from Dr. Thomas, as he was a brilliant zoologist and an interesting leader. He constantly competed with other zoo directors in the acquisition of animals, a practice that has now, for the most part, been replaced with cooperation. He was a captivating public speaker combining his encyclopedic knowledge of wildlife with sort of a folksy Will Rodgers-type sense of humor. I decided then that if I were to succeed, I would have to develop my own style of public speaking. I practiced whenever I could and tried to copy Dr. Thomas's speaking style.

I learned other lessons from Dr. Thomas. He once told me that "it's not enough to be right." While that truth was not what an idyllic young man wanted to hear, it proved to be much more important to me in later years. In my years as a zoo director, I had many great ideas, but they could not be realized until I convinced others that they were important. Sometimes I succeeded, but at other times I did not.

Another lesson learned from Dr. Thomas was always to do what your boss asks, no matter how small or petty. While I was serving as a six-month curator apprentice, one of my jobs was to set up a slide projector whenever Dr. Thomas was speaking. One day when Dr. Thomas needed me to set up a projector, I had left the zoo with Rick Rundle, curator of birds, to take some birds to the San Diego Zoo. I had either forgotten or did not think it was that important that Dr. Thomas was speaking to docents that afternoon and would need the projector. The next day he severely scolded me for neglecting my duty. While I thought someone else could do it or maybe he could set up his own projector, obviously I was wrong. For many years when employees complained that their bosses asked them to do things that they didn't feel important, I cautioned them that a few minutes spent pleasing their boss was not an unreasonable use of their time.

One fond memory I have of my curator apprenticeship was helping host members of the International Union of Zoological Gardens Directors (IUDZG, now World Association of Zoos and Aquariums, WAZA) on their visit to Los Angeles. One of my duties was taking several members to Disneyland. I asked the very distinguished aviculturist, Dr. Jean Delacour, who was then eighty-five, if he would like to go to Disneyland. He gave a rather lengthy response about Disneyland being just for kids. As he walked away from the group he mentioned, "I have been their many times."

With an International Union of Directors of Zoological Gardens delegation and senior staff from the Los Angeles Zoo in 1976.

While working at the Los Angeles Zoo, I continued attending Long Beach State College, slowly working on a master's degree in biology. My master thesis was to be titled "Mother/Infant Behavior in Scimitar-horned Oryx." I chose these animals because the zoo had a large breeding herd, and I knew there would always be calves of various ages. While the report was not completed, I did have enough data to present it at my first American Association of Zoological Parks and Aquariums (the AAZPA, now shortened to AZA) regional meeting in Monterey, California, in the spring of 1978. There I met the executive director of the San Francisco Zoological Society, who was looking for a new children's zoo manager. Landes Bell, a friend, was leaving the position to develop a deer park in Southern California. I guess the executive director was impressed enough with my presentation and background, because I was offered the job. For the first time in my life, I would be living somewhere other than Southern California.

LEAVING SOUTHERN CALIFORNIA

Taking the job in San Francisco was perfect for me. While the rest of the zoo was part of the City of San Francisco, the San Francisco Zoological Society operated the children's zoo. In some sense, I had my own small zoo. As with many children's zoos, a main component was the farm, complete with an old red barn full of sheep and goats. The rest of the five or six acres contained a mixture of animals, mostly native wildlife. There was an exhibit of a pair of coyotes that were donated by an older man whose first name was Dick, but I forgot his last name. He made a living writing jingles. He actually had keys to the children's zoo, and early every morning he came in and fed "his" coyotes. He told us his claim to fame was writing words to the children's poem, "Mares eat oats and does eat oats and little lambs eat ivy." While I could never verify his authorship, it does sound like something he would have written.

Very soon after arriving at the San Francisco Zoo, I had the opportunity to hand-raise a female orangutan. Sumara stayed in the children's zoo nursery for about three or four years. A young male orangutan, River Sydney, from the zoo in the "river city," Sacramento, later joined her. Throughout my years at the children's zoo we hand-raised many interesting animals, including a serval, a spider monkey, a Malayan tapir, a water buffalo, and several others.

Nature Trail, where young volunteers handled turtles, snakes, opossums, and other small native animals, was popular in the summer. After a few years, a small auditorium was converted to an insect zoo. The extra admission fee for the children's zoo paid for most of the operation. I had a wonderful time in San Francisco, both being children's zoo manager and exploring a beautiful city with many nearby natural areas, such as Muir Woods, Golden Gate National Recreation Area, the East Bay Regional Parks, and others. Uniquely

I lived in an apartment in the children's zoo that was connected to the baby animal nursery. While it meant I was never far from work, it was an experience I would not trade for anything. Living in a zoo. Wow! I had really made it.

To help with the care in hand-raising zoo animals, especially the two orangutans, I recruited two dozen volunteers to work three four-hour shifts every day. They were amazing, and they were very reliable. Of course because of the unique opportunity of hand-rearing infant orangs, I was able to pick only the very most dedicated volunteers to participate. Many of these volunteers became great friends. Occasionally my apartment and the children's zoo became the site of some great thank-you parties. Aside from food and drink, these parties also included a late-night ride on the carousel in the zoo.

With a young orang (River Sydney) in my office at the Children's Zoo in San Francisco.

After I had spent a couple of years at the children's zoo, a friend donated two female collies named Lassie and Shirley. They were very friendly dogs and added to the farm atmosphere. I also used them as watch dogs, and while they might bark at anyone entering the zoo at night, they certainly were not aggressive. In fact, the most they would do would be to walk up and lick the intruder's hands. However, they were big dogs, and people could initially be afraid of them. If there was someone in the zoo after closing, I always took the dogs with me, but never called them Lassie and Shirley. To keep up the farce that they were guard dogs, at night I always called them by stronger names, Rhino and Tank.

At the children's zoo we had a large collection of donated parrots that we used in various programs. One donated African Grey parrot named Tansy was a great talker and had learned to imitate my voice perfectly. The phone in the animal nursery was near Tansy's cage, and this parrot often heard me on the phone. I have never been one for long phone conversations. To the amusement of the staff and volunteers they often heard Tansy imitating me on the phone and say, "Hello? Okay. Okay. Bye."

Being a member of the management team of the San Francisco Zoological Society, I had a wonderful opportunity to learn about more than just animal care. In the zoo society staff meetings we discussed everything from fund-raising and events to concessions and education.

Soon after my arrival in San Francisco, Peggy Burks, the marketing director, was promoted to executive director of the San Francisco Zoological Society. She was an excellent one. She was smart, hardworking, and fair and always asked the right questions. Most importantly, she took the entire staff to an all-day seminar on Management by Objective. From that time forward, including in retirement, I always had both long-term and short term *written* goals.

I AM A ZOO DIRECTOR

In 1982 I was given the opportunity to become zoo superintendent—zoo director—for the twelve-acre Sacramento Zoo. Now I really had my own zoo. While the zoo was small, it had a good reputation. The collection of animals included two Asian elephants, giraffes, a hippo, Grévy's zebras, Addra gazelles, cheetahs, Amur tigers, a gorilla, chimps, orangutans, thick-billed parrots, mongoose lemurs, giant hornbills, American flamingoes, and a large collection of reptiles from around the world. It was a city zoo with a not-for-profit support group. The Sacramento Zoological Society had less than 1,500 members and no staff when I started in Sacramento.

I have always been proud of what we were able to accomplish in my years at Sacramento. There was never enough money. We had to be very innovative in creating a better zoo. I was fortunate to have a supportive boss. Bob Thomas was hired as director of community services—parks and recreation and the city-run museums—shortly after I was hired as zoo superintendent. He was as committed to a better zoo as much as I was; however, he needed to balance the demands of the entire department.

He was supportive of moving out less-productive employees—mostly transferred to other jobs in the department—and creating opportunities to hire better ones. He was supportive of my involvement in expanding the role of the zoo society and let me work out the details. I soon was director of both the zoo and the society. I have always believed that this unity-of-command approach to managing a government-run and society-supported organization was a great model. Unfortunately I was never able to convince the leadership in Cleveland of that concept.

Bob left the operation of the zoo to me, and while he stayed in touch with regular meetings, he was not involved in planning exhibits, management of the zoo society, organizing special events, or any animal acquisition or de-acquisition. He met with me "formally" each month in his office, and he would pull out a manila folder and go over issues that were important to the zoo and the city.

He reviewed what we had talked about at our previous meetings, and we would agree on actions. Since working with Bob, beginning in the early 1980s, I always used the same technique with my direct reports. By getting buy-in from employees and writing it down, I rarely had to worry that something would be forgotten or not done. This system also allowed me to delegate and not micromanage employees. I have always felt that employees needed to know what was expected of them, and then it was up to them to report their progress at the appropriate time, often at a monthly meeting.

By the end of my tenure at Sacramento we had completed three major exhibits: renovation of the lion and tiger exhibits, construction of a new exhibit for orangutans, and conversion of the old gorilla and orang moated exhibits to one large exhibit for chimpanzees. We started planning an exhibit for three species of South American cats. In-house staff made several improvements to many exhibits, including decorating many displays in the reptile house, the flamingo exhibit, and the small mammal house. The zoo also purchased a doublewide trailer for a classroom. Probably more important were the exhibits we deleted, because they were marginal at best. They included exhibits for penguins, seals, and llamas.

When I arrived at the zoo, the full-time staff consisted of a head keeper, an assistant head keeper, eleven keepers, two maintenance workers, and one cashier. The zoological society had no staff, and volunteers managed the membership program. A local concessionaire managed food service and souvenirs and did a poor job, with little of the funds going back to the zoo. In summary, the opportunities were endless. The challenge was that the City of Sacramento had limited resources, so other resources had to be found. By slowly increasing user fees, adding other revenue sources, expanding the zoological society, and self-operating the concessions, we were able to greatly expand the zoo programs.

FUTURE CHIMP

LOOK AT WHAT WE COULD

With Mayor Rudin (right) and Society Board member introducing plans for a new chimp habitat at the Sacramento Zoo.

For most of my time in Sacramento, completing a master plan for the twelve-acre zoo was one of my top priorities. With the Portico Group of Seattle, staff and the zoo society board of directors worked on several proposals to expand and improve the zoo. Several neighbors around the 250-acre William Land Park objected to the zoo's plans and formed a group they called Save Land Park. At public meetings they had their children carry signs that said things like, Don't Pave Paradise and Put Up a Parking Lot. One of our detractors moved out of town when President Ronald Reagan appointed him to the United States Supreme Court. Yes, that was Anthony Kennedy. Even without Anthony Kennedy, the group was very influential, and in the end the zoo was not able to expand or even provide more parking.

When I left at the end of 1988, the zoological society had quadrupled its membership to 6,000 members and the zoo doubled annual attendance to almost 600,000 guests. As entrance fees were increased, the zoo was able to use some of the new revenue to improve staffing.

The zoo added a curator position, a receptionist/secretary, and an administrative assistant. For the administrative assistant we were able to promote Maria Baker, a very talented primate keeper who had great potential for leadership. While her official city title was administrative assistant, she acted as assistant director. Maria eventually replaced me as zoo director when I moved on to Cleveland.

As the society grew, it was able to support growth. It funded an education curator and a public relations director. The zoological society was also able to acquire a contract with the city to manage the zoo's food service and merchandise operations, an additional source of funds for the zoo.

While I felt proud of the physical improvements during my years as zoo director, the building of the professional staff and creation of new programs were probably just as important.

A drawing presented to me when I left the Sacramento Zoo.

MOVING TO OHIO

For much of my six years in Sacramento, we worked on creating a master plan to expand and improve the twelve-acre zoo. It was a tremendous amount of work, and we produced a great plan. Because of the neighborhood opposition, the plan basically died. About the time that it became painfully obvious that no expansion would be allowed, I was offered the job as the director of the Cleveland Metroparks Zoo. It was a long way for a native Californian to move, but it was a large zoo of 165 acres, with a good animal collection. It had been poorly managed and under financed for several years. One could say it was undistinguished. I saw potential and decided I could go for a few years and attempt to turn the place around. I stayed in Cleveland for the rest of my zoo career.

The process of interviewing for the job as director of Cleveland Metroparks Zoo was extensive. It started with an interview at the annual AZA conference in Milwaukee on September 26, 1988. The new Cleveland Metroparks executive director, Vern Hartenburg, and David Lauderback, from the Cleveland office of Korn Ferry, an international search firm, interviewed me. I made the first cut and I flew to Cleveland on October 10, 1988, to continue to explore this opportunity. I had never been to Cleveland, and while I knew Cleveland was in Ohio, I didn't know it was on one of the Great Lakes. In Cleveland there were several interviews, and I toured the zoo. I noticed the zoo had only one computer, actually just a Wang word processor. It was incompatible with the new International Species Inventory System (ISIS). The zoo offices were not well kept and had dreadful furnishings. There was a need for additional qualified senior staff. There was no full-time veterinarian, no registrar, no marketing director, and no full-time guest-services staff. The new poorly conceived 85,000 square-foot tropical building in a converted foundry was under construction, and from the outside it looked more like a department store than a modern zoo exhibit. I felt the various interviews went well, and David told me I was the top candidate and a team wanted to come to Sacramento and see the zoo and talk to people in Sacramento, including my boss, Bob Thomas, and Mayor Anne Rudin. I was nervous, as I didn't really know if I wanted the job and leave my home state of California. I liked Sacramento and enjoyed the job. I took time to write down the pros and cons of the move. In the end I saw the move as a good one and a chance to direct a large American zoo. At the time it did not seem that the Sacramento Zoo was ever going to be able to expand beyond its twelve acres.

A four-member team came to Sacramento. Joining Vern Hartenburg and David Lauderback were Metroparks Commissioner Dan Corcoran and Jack Rupert, president of the Cleveland Zoological Society. Toward the end of their visit, I began to realize that there was a sincere interest in creating a world-class zoo in Cleveland. I flew back to Cleveland on October 30, 1988. I toured the zoo with Curator Don Kuenzer and met various people who had an interest in the zoo, including Harvey Webster of the Cleveland Museum of Natural History, Sandy Rowland from the Humane Society of the United States (HSUS), and the Cleveland Metroparks senior staff. I had dinner at the Watermark restaurant in the Flats—an area along the Cuyahoga with many restaurants and bars—with ten members of the zoological society. At a Board of Park Commissioner meeting on November 3, 1988, I was appointed zoo director and met briefly with the press. That afternoon I flew home to Sacramento, and the next day announced I was moving to Cleveland to become the director of Cleveland Metroparks Zoo starting on January 2, 1989. I couldn't start on January 1, as the board didn't want to pay me for the holiday.

Appointed by the Board of Park Commissioners as Director of Cleveland Metroparks Zoo in the Fall of 1998.

During the press conference in Cleveland, I inadvertently made a statement that was later taken out of context and reported in *Cleveland Magazine*. I started the news conference by saying, "I have good news and bad news. The good news is that I finally got to have a larger zoo." I was referring to our efforts to expand the Sacramento Zoo. "The bad news is it is Cleveland." I was referring to the fact it was not to be in Sacramento, and my supporters would not be happy, but *Cleveland Magazine* and many in Cleveland who were tired of Cleveland jokes took my statement as a put-down of Cleveland. I certainly did not mean it that way. I learned the hard way to be a little more aware of people's feelings when talking about my new home.

There were many reasons that I stayed in Cleveland. One of the most important had to do with a chance meeting on the United Airline's flight number 943 from Cleveland to Chicago on my way back from my first interview in October 1988. Sarah Margaret Young sat next to me on the flight. The young woman was single, an accountant with

Ernst & Young, and had moved from Columbus to Cleveland about two years prior to my arrival. In the hour flight I asked her about a million questions about living and working in Cleveland. To make a long story short, we were married in May 1993.

Coming from California, it took me a while to adjust to so many changes. One snowy day in December 1988 when I was in Cleveland looking for housing and making other arrangements, I passed a Christmas tree lot. For a quick couple of seconds I thought, "That's different. In Cleveland they flock every tree in the lot." I definitely had a lot to learn about Ohio.

As of 2021, I have spent thirty-two years in Cleveland, Ohio. I have had so many wonderful experiences that I would not have had if I had left to go to another community. First of all, Cleveland in the 1990s was a "comeback city." I have already mentioned the zoo was part of Cleveland Metroparks, probably the finest regional park district in the United States. When I arrived in 1989, a beautiful new office tower, the Society Center (now Key Bank) with an adjacent Marriott Hotel was about to be constructed downtown. Tower City, a downtown shopping center with an adjacent Ritz-Carlton was about to be opened. In 1994 the Gateway Complex opened with Jacob's Field, later Progressive Field, for the Cleveland Indians baseball team and the Gund Arena, later Rocket Mortgage Field House, for the basketball team, the Cleveland Cavaliers. Sarah and I attended the opening of Jacob's Field where President Clinton threw out the first pitch. As we were walking to the ballpark, we stopped at a crosswalk next to a man in a dark suit with an earphone, obviously Secret Service. He smiled at Sarah, and she asked if the president was coming, and without saying a thing, he pointed his finger to the curb, motioning her to stay put. A minute or so later the president's limo drove right by us.

Having a new ballpark and bringing the Cleveland Cavaliers back to the city changed the whole dynamic of downtown Cleveland. In 1995 I attended the opening ceremony of the Rock and Roll Hall of Fame, and the next year Sarah and I went to the gala for the opening of the Great Lakes Science Center.

As things were happening in the city, Sarah and I had opportunities to attend many great sporting events, including many World Series games. We should have won both in 1997 and 2016. We were so close. We also attended All-Star games for both baseball and basketball and the last game at the old Cleveland Browns Stadium. When the Browns returned in 2000, we didn't renew our season tickets. In Akron, Ohio, we regularly attended the World Series of Golf, which became the Bridgestone Invitational, until it lost its sponsorship and moved to Memphis. We also attended the Champions Tour PGA Championship at Canterbury Country Club on the east side of Cleveland, as well as a couple of LPGA tournaments in Toledo. And for Sarah's sake, I must mention that we attended the National Figure Skating Championships. I brought a book to read.

Cultural offerings in Cleveland are of high quality and widely accessible. Cleveland has one of the best art museums in the world, and in 2010 through 2013 the museum completed a 350-million-dollar renovation. The Cleveland Orchestra has been called the best band in the land, and it is not just a slogan. We were at the opening of the renovated Cleveland Botanical Garden in 2001. A huge glass house with a Costa Rican rain forest and a Madagascan spiny forest were built, and while they were not a huge hit with the public, they were well done. Interestingly, live animals in these two large walk-through exhibits made these exhibits more successful than if they were just plant collections. The cultural institutions were all part of University Circle that also includes the History Museum and the Cleveland Museum of Natural History.

The largest playhouse district between New York and Chicago is in Cleveland, and it's a great one. It was well led by Art Falco, who retired 2019 and whose entrepreneurial strategies have made it very successful. The Cleveland Playhouse District has five renovated theaters that attract national shows, such as *Lion King*, as well as local programming. The theater district bought many of the surrounding buildings, and they have become an income stream for the theater district. The district formed partnerships with Public TV and Public Radio, now called Idea Stream. A few years ago, the Playhouse formed a partnership with Cleveland State University. Art has always been one of my heroes in Cleveland. I viewed the success of the Playhouse District as one of Cleveland's greatest modern-day accomplishments.

While others may be lucky to get concert tickets in Los Angeles or New York for many popular artists and then spend hours in traffic getting to and from the various venues, Sarah and I were easily able to attend many great concerts and were home within a half hour of the last number. We saw artists such as Jimmy Buffet, Sheryl Crow, Carol King, James Taylor, and Carol King with James Taylor together, Three Dog Night, Shania Twain, Rod Stewart, Joan Baez, and many others. Our favorite concert of all time was a Carol King concert, as we were in the seventh row, and it was like she was singing to us. Thanks to my friend Terry Stewart, president/CEO of the Rock and Roll Hall of Fame, we attended the induction ceremony for the Rock and Roll Hall of Fame in 2009. We felt like royalty when we walked up the red carpet.

In the spring of 2016, Sarah announced her retirement as controller of the Cleveland Indians Baseball Team. That fall the Indians and the Chicago Cubs were in the World Series. Of course we went to most of the games, including one at Rigley Field in Chicago. The Indians chartered an airplane and flew all the front office staff to Chicago to see one away game. As a parting gift to Sarah, we had business-class seats. At the airport we loaded into four buses and drove to lunch in the city and then to Wrigley Field. We were wearing our Cleveland Indians logo clothes, and Sarah asked a policeman if we could go visit a friend of hers at a local bar. He said, "absolutely not in those clothes." In the ballpark we were two of a very few Indians fans. The Indians won that game. We left the game, and the police guided us to our buses right near the entrance. We had a police escort with sirens blaring all the way back to O'Hare Airport, and at times we even drove on the opposite side of the street. A few fans even gave us a one-finger salute. Unfortunately for us, the Indians lost in game seven.

Sarah and I felt fortunate to have had all these opportunities, and its one reason we chose not to leave Cleveland. While some still call it "the mistake on the lake," they are wrong. While it experiences harsh winters, it is a most livable city, with much to offer and all of it is accessible to all.

CHAPTER 3

ADVENTURES IN MANAGEMENT AND LEADERSHIP

CLEVELAND METROPARKS ZOO

Always the planner, I laid out my plans for Cleveland Metroparks Zoo at my official swearing in at the Board of Park Commissioners meeting on January 9,1989. I presented the board with the following six goals:

1. Review and implement a new zoo staff organization structure that maximizes the contributions of each staff member
2. Begin a comprehensive long-range plan that will take the zoo into the twenty-first century
3. Improve the operational efficiency and self-support level of the zoo
4. Complete the RainForest exhibit and other projects that had been initiated previously
5. Improve community relations and the community perception of the zoo
6. Seek methods of constantly improving animal husbandry, exhibits, diets, and veterinary care

These goals were also reported in my first contribution to the Zoological Society's magazine, *Zoo News,* in the winter of 1989. I must say that we were successful in accomplishing all these goals, although they were not as easy as I naively thought during my first few weeks in Cleveland.

My first year at Cleveland was not an easy one. At times I felt that I made the wrong decision, coming to Cleveland. There were differences between the Metroparks Board of Park Commissioners and the Cleveland Zoological Society. The staff needed major reorganization and some new people to fill major openings. While most current staff members accepted their roles, several were not happy about the reorganization. It made my job difficult. The RainForest, an 85,000-square-foot indoor tropical house, was about 50 percent complete. It had several problems. It had to be redesigned, and several expensive changes were required. Initially the RainForest was to cost about ten million dollars, although by the time I joined the staff, it was already estimated to cost twenty to twenty-five million. The final cost was almost thirty-five million dollars. *The Cleveland Plain Dealer* kept the zoo in the news with constant stories of the controversies, mostly concerning the costs, surrounding the RainForest. In addition to these challenges, there was the death of three sea lions that a staff member drove to the Memphis Zoo without properly cooling the animals. I also quickly realized that I would not have the decision-making authority that I enjoyed in Sacramento. The Metroparks administration and Board of Park Commissioners did not delegate much decision-making to the zoo director. In Sacramento, I was used to making decisions in regard to food and gift concessions, supervision of capital projects, hiring and firing, and so forth, but it was not to be in Cleveland.

As I am about to give advice on leadership, I think it is only fair to share my flaws. Throughout my career I took various classes and seminars and analyzed my strengths and weaknesses as a leader. I took the Myers-Briggs test, another test from Nerren-Cooper Partners, and another called True Colors. I was a little disappointed that the various analyses showed that despite my best efforts and a certain amount of self-awareness, I did not change much over my thirty-plus years as a zoo director. Sure, I did make small changes, like trying harder to listen. Early in my career, I could also easily lose my temper at work, but over the years I was able to control my temper most of the time.

All the tests showed that I was a frank and decisive leader who enjoyed comprehensive systems when solving problems. They also indicated that I could be argumentative at times. While I saw myself as a good planner and goal oriented, others probably saw me as autocratic, controlling, and opinionated. One search firm described me as a pragmatic dreamer, and it is true that I could be a realist. Others may not be so complimentary and saw me as predictable and unimaginative. Good or bad, in many respects I suppose I was basically the same person at the end of my days as a full-time zoo director as I was in 1980.

Despite the challenges, I felt very fortunate to have been employed for so many years by Cleveland Metroparks. For almost my entire career at Cleveland Metroparks Zoo I reported to Vern J. Hartenburg, executive director. Vern was a tremendously successful leader whose many accomplishments were the envy of others in similar positions around the United States. He retired in 2010 and was replaced by thirty-eight-year old Brian Zimmerman from Milwaukee County Parks, who continued to improve the park system.

The Cleveland Metropolitan Park District was an independent governmental agency governed by three park commissioners appointed by the senior probate judge of Cuyahoga County. The commissioners received no compensation and met twice a month throughout the entire year, although less in more recent times. It was a huge commitment of time for these dedicated citizens. Regional Park Districts in the State of Ohio were created at the beginning of the twentieth century to allow counties to form independent park districts. These districts were separate from city and county government. The Park Commission had the authority to place a property tax levy on the ballot to fund the district. I was involved in two ten-year levies. The first levy passed by 70 percent in favor, and the second passed by

60 percent in favor. In 2013 shortly after I retired, a levy passed 73 percent in favor. The citizens of greater Cleveland loved Cleveland Metroparks, and they loved the zoo. While the commissioners were appointed for three-year terms, there were no limits to the number of terms, and many served for ten to twenty years.

I was fortunate to be part of the Cleveland Metroparks system for many reasons. First, the zoo had steady and continuous funding through the park levy. The levy paid for between 20 and 60 percent of the operating budget. The levy funds also provided capital improvement and equipment dollars, but the amount varied every year. When funds for major capital improvement projects were matched with funds raised by the zoo society, the zoo had a substantial amount of resources. However, most of us at the zoo felt strongly that it was never enough. Many similar zoos, including Columbus, Toledo, and other large and successful zoos, spent much more on capital improvements.

Secondly, I felt fortunate that despite the few differences in management and leadership style, I had with my superiors, and who doesn't, if it was not for their tenacity there would not have been a thirty-five-million-dollar RainForest, nor would there have been a twenty-five-million-dollar African Elephant Crossing. Other leaders would have thought these projects too expensive and too complicated and would have either greatly limited their scope or eliminated them completely. I was very grateful to the leadership of the Park District and the Cleveland Zoological Society for sticking with me on these two important capital improvement projects at the zoo. In the end the Cleveland community was also grateful.

There were certainly challenges. I made my share of mistakes, and I believe there were times when the Park District should have done things differently. In most cases there was no right or wrong, just another way to accomplish something. In this chapter I share what I consider to be the successes and challenges we had during my years at Cleveland Metroparks Zoo. I hope these provide some insight into leadership and management as well as provide an entertaining read. After all, what could be more entertaining than running a zoo?

VISION, MISSION AND STRATEGY
VISION AND MISSION

In many planning sessions I participated in over the years, some of the most frustrating were ones where the group dove right in before defining the terms. If done correctly, creating a vision and mission for any institution is hard work and takes much time. However, once done and done correctly, there is a strong feeling of accomplishment. There are many definitions of vision, mission, goals, key result areas, values, objectives, and so forth, and it does not matter which definitions one uses, as long as everyone involved agrees and understands the definitions. In a planning session for the Smithsonian National Zoological Park in 2004, the group used the following definitions for vision and mission:

- Mission = our reason for being (what would be lost if we didn't exist)
- Vision = what we really want to achieve—an exciting, compelling, and attainable future state

The following statement by Marc Stefanski, CEO of the Cleveland-based Third Federal Savings and Loan Association, made the following statement that I believe further defines purpose or mission:

> "A human being needs to breathe air, but it isn't your sole existence to breathe air. It's the same thing for a corporation. A corporation needs to make money, but its purpose isn't necessarily to make money."

A meaningful mission statement can guide an institution in good times and bad and act as a moral compass. It can be a very valuable tool and should answer some basic questions that can be easy to ignore in the day-to-day routine of running any business, institution, or department. The Cleveland Metroparks Zoo's mission, adopted as part of the 1993 Zoo Master Plan, read as follows:

The mission of Cleveland Metroparks Zoo is to improve the future for wildlife by exhibiting animals and plants and providing education and conservation programs, which encourage respect and stewardship of the natural world and a better understanding of our place within it.

This mission statement served Cleveland Metroparks Zoo from 1993 until 2010. We often used only the tag line, "to improve the future for wildlife" or "improving the future for wildlife." From 2009 to 2011, toward the end of my career at Cleveland Metroparks Zoo, a new Strategic Plan/Master Plan was created. I felt it was important to leave the zoo with a revised plan. While I did not want to dictate to future leaders what they would need to do, I wanted to give them some background for their decision-making. The new mission read as follows:

We create compelling experiences that connect people with wildlife and inspire personal responsibility for conserving the natural world.

The steering committee of the zoo, zoo society, Cleveland Metroparks staff, and Zoological Society board members wanted a new and different mission statement. This new mission statement had to work for both Cleveland Metroparks Zoo and the Cleveland Zoological Society, something I encouraged.

A poorly written or mission statement that lacks commitment by leadership has resulted in some believing the following:

"A mission statement is defined as a long, awkward sentence that demonstrates management's inability to think clearly. All good companies have one." Anonymous

Danny Woodley, a Kenyan of European descent and warden with the Kenyan Wildlife Service (KWS), told one of my favorite stories of distrust in a mission statement to Rick Ridgeway in the book, *In the Shadow of Kilimanjaro.* He and his brother Bongo were guiding author Rick Ridgeway on a walk from Mount Kilimanjaro to the Indian Ocean. They noticed the mission of KWS on the wall of a government office. It read as follows:

"We hold in trust, for now and tomorrow, the responsibility for protection and conservation of Kenya's extraordinary wealth, as represented by its fauna, flora, and natural beauty. KWS will manage these resources, which are of inestimable economic, socio-cultural, aesthetic, and scientific value. To fulfill this mission KWS will develop the required human resources, achieve financial self-sufficiency, and encourage support and participation of the people of Kenya."

Danny's version was different.

"We the willing, led by the unknowing, are doing the impossible for the ungrateful. We have done so much for so long with so little, we are now qualified to do anything with nothing."

While the difficulties in the conservation of wildlife in countries like Kenya with so many competing needs can at times seem unending, these quotes still can serve to illustrate skepticism in the direction of well-intentioned leaders.

It is important to have a vision, but these statements rarely are completely realized. Visions are something to work toward, like world peace, or in my case, a perfect world-class zoo. However, if you ever achieve them, it's time for a new vision.

"I was once asked if a big businessman ever reached his objectives. I replied that if a man ever reached his objective, he was not a big businessman." Charles M. Schwab

At Cleveland Metroparks Zoo, we did not have a formal vision statement until 2010. It was not part of the zoo's planning process in 1993. However, around 2000, I created a director's vision that was annually reviewed and was always part of the zoo's annual planning process. I believe the statement describes all the elements for a zoo to achieve greatness. That statement read as follows:

Cleveland Metroparks Zoo is a world-class zoo, and it's getting even better. With all our hearts, we deeply believe in our mission of saving the world's precious wildlife from extinction. And we know of no better weapon to use in our crusade to save wildlife and wild places than conservation education. To serve this purpose, we will continue to create and implement many wonderful programs and exhibits. In addition, we will accomplish our mission by championing exceptional guest services, creating world-class animal habitats, and fantastic landscapes, instigating significant animal-breeding programs, supporting superior animal welfare and veterinary health programs, participating in important in-situ conservation programs and scientific research, and much more.

We are a very proud, successful, and diverse staff. We are the leaders in our respective fields. At all levels of our organization, we are persistent and determined, resilient and resourceful, empathetic and enterprising, competent and creative. With enthusiasm, compassion, and good cheer, we are compulsive about working well together and are dedicated to orderliness, functionality, and excellence. We set our standards high, and we aim to exceed expectations of our guests, our members and supporters, our governing board, and even ourselves.

The zoo's vision for the twenty-first century is clear. Together with other accredited zoos and aquariums, we accept the

challenge of being the most important proactive conserva-
tion organization in North America. We will be a resource
for others. We will sustain wildlife that is in danger of extinc-
tion. We will venture outside our walls and actively engage
in significant conservation programs and help create and re-
store parks and reserves. And we will continue to stimulate
the millions of primarily city dwellers and engage them in
our important work.

Yes, it is a lengthy statement and certainly not one for staff and others to memorize. However, I felt it did describe three components of being a first-class zoo, and except for the uniquely zoo language, it could have been adapted to any organization. The first paragraph defined Cleveland Metroparks Zoo and stated what we needed to accomplish to be a great zoo. The second paragraph stated what kind of people we were and the behaviors we expected of each other. And the third paragraph gave the zoo relevance in a global perspective.

In 2010, Cleveland Metroparks Zoo developed the following vision statement:

By being regularly engaged in the zoo's programs and activities
to conserve wildlife and wild places, the people of Northeast
Ohio will demonstrate their love for the natural world and
be the most informed and enlightened conservationists in the
United States.

The steering committee wanted a vision that not only inspired but also challenged. In addition, it wanted a statement that reflected our role in the Cleveland community. I believe that this vision achieved both those goals.

VALUES

"We need to adjust to changing times and still hold to un-changing principles." Jimmy Carter

In 2010-2011, the "new" Cleveland Metroparks Zoo and Cleveland Zoological Society strategic planning process developed the following set of values for the zoo:

1. Excellence
2. Accessibility
3. Teamwork and Diversity
4. Knowledge
5. Stewardship
6. Integrity and Accountability

While these values are similar to those of many other organizations and private companies, each one had a special meaning to the zoo.

For instance, *accessibility* was important, as Cleveland Metroparks Zoo had always been very accessible to all citizens, primarily because the zoo was financially supported by the Cleveland Metroparks property tax levy allowing the zoo to have a free day, operate a free school bus to bring local students to the zoo, offer free admission to all in-county students, and more.

Teamwork and diversity were important values. One department alone could accomplish very little, and the vast majority of accomplishments took several departments working together. Often this task was easier said than done. Diversity had been a stated governing value of Cleveland Metroparks for as long as I can remember. The zoo worked harder at diversity of staff and attendance than many other institutions and for these efforts received one of the first diversity awards from AZA. Nonetheless, diversity was certainly something that we could have done even better.

Knowledge was an important value for Cleveland Metroparks

Zoo. It meant that the zoo collection would be scientifically managed. It meant that the zoo programs would be science-based. As an example, the zoo would discuss climate change and evolution.

Integrity was extremely important to Cleveland Metroparks, as several other local government agencies, particularly the Cuyahoga County government, were deep in scandal. Cleveland Metroparks had a stellar reputation in the community, and it was important that the zoo do nothing to damage that reputation.

SETTING GOALS AND OBJECTIVES

After defining an organization's mission, describing a vision for the future, and listing values, the next step is to organize the workload to produce the desired result. Different strategic plans use differing terminology. Some plans include Key Result Areas, some use strategic pillars, and some use goals, objectives, tasks, and so forth. Whichever terms are used, they must be defined so everyone understands the process.

> *"Nothing is particularly hard if you divide it into small jobs."*
> *Henry Ford*

Having written goals is especially important in zoos and aquariums, as these institutions are uniquely multifaceted. I always believed that the only way to continually improve and to do everything that is necessary in this complicated world was to divide tasks into workable units. One can do only one thing at a time. In the case of managing a zoo, an example of a goal might be designing, funding, and constructing a new twenty-five-million-dollar elephant exhibit. The only way to accomplish this large task (pun intended) is to divide the project into doable tasks and assign responsibility for those tasks.

The African Elephant Crossing opened in May 2011.

What gets measured gets done!

While it is important to set goals and objectives, it is just as important to monitor them. As Louis Gerstner, CEO of IBM in the 1990s wrote, *"People do what you inspect, not what you expect."* I always used systems of informal and formal inspections. I often spent time in the zoo. I talked with all staff members. I asked what they were doing. I examined workmanship. In a more formal way, I met monthly with my direct reports and reviewed their annual work programs. Two or three times a year I formally reviewed their work. I did not believe it was micromanaging their work, only checking regular progress and seeing if I could help. It was important for me to know if there was anything I could do to be helpful. For our monthly meetings, staff members came prepared with their own reports that helped me understand their progress. I always gave them the opportunity to talk first. The best of the best always surprised me with how much they had accomplished. Again, I have to credit this system to Bob Thomas, the Sacramento Park and Community Services Department director for whom I worked when I was zoo director there in the 1980s.

"People with goals succeed because they know where they are going. It's as simple as that." Earl Nightingale

The two different strategic plans in1993 and 2011 for Cleveland Metroparks Zoo completed during my time at the zoo had slightly different goals statements. Historically most zoos and aquariums listed recreation, education, research, and conservation as goals. Over the years additional goals were needed to better measure success, and more descriptive terms became necessary. Concepts such as animal welfare, environmental sustainability, fiscal stability, and exceeding guest expectations became terms that better described important goals. Most planners suggest not having more than six to eight goals. More than eight diluted the importance of the core goals.

The Cleveland Metroparks Zoo and its zoo society's new goals, referred to as Strategic Focus Areas in the 2011 plan, were as follows:

1. The zoo will exceed industry standards and guidelines for species in its care and adopt a program of continual improvement. The zoo will strive to be recognized as a leader in creating high-quality, innovative animal exhibits.
2. The zoo will capitalize on the unique role of zoos in saving endangered species through *ex-situ* (in zoo) conservation efforts. The zoo will build on *in-situ* (in the wild) partnerships and forge strong links between our work in the zoo and our programs around the world.
3. The zoo will be a model in sustainability by developing and implementing zoo-wide green practices and promoting sustainability throughout Northeast Ohio.

4. The zoo will be the foremost provider of lifelong learning experiences in Northeast Ohio, a trusted voice for wildlife conservation, and an inspiration for conservation action.
5. The zoo will exceed guest expectations for services and amenities.
6. The zoo will be a greater civic priority for Northeast Ohio and strengthen the zoo's leadership role as one of the top destinations in the area; as a regional economic development driver, and as the wildlife, conservation, and sustainability expert.
7. The zoo will be a robust, fiscally sustainable organization modeling best business practices with a culture of collaboration, partnership, and continual professional development.

There were eighteen years between the zoo's strategic plans, so naturally there were changes in the list of goals. For instance, in 2011, the leadership of the zoo and the Zoological Society wanted to elevate sustainability to its own goal and not be a part of the conservation goal. Another example would be that recreation was not mentioned in the 2011 plan, as it was thought to be addressed in the statement that "the zoo will exceed guest expectations for services and amenities."

Work Plan and Day-to-Day Stuff

The next part of planning is setting actual tasks. Some people will call these objectives or goals. Whatever one calls these elements, they must be easily understood and agreed upon by all involved. They must be SMART.

1. S: Specific
2. M: Measurable
3. A: Attainable
4. R: Realistic
5. T: Time-Framed/Target Date

"The secret to productive goal setting is in establishing clearly defined goals, writing them down, and then focusing on them several times a day with words, pictures, and emotions as if we've already achieved them." Denis Waitley

Since my days as children's zoo manager in San Francisco, goal setting has always been part of my life, both personally and professionally. From simple to-do lists to lifetime values and goals, these written statements were very important to me.

In the 1980s, I began using a Franklin Planner. This system taught me one method of planning. I do not believe it matters how we plan, only that we do plan. The Franklin Planner taught me to use the written word to understand my values. When I reached my forties, I found this technique extremely helpful in living my life to the fullest. For the rest of my life I have continually evaluated what is important to me. I know what I want to accomplish, where I want to travel, and how I can improve myself and my relationships with others. These things are important to me. I have plans to stay healthy and plans to be financially secure. My personal plans have always been integrated with my work plans. Even now, in retirement, I use the same method of planning.

Some will say that life needs to be more relaxed, more spontaneous and less planned. Not so! I can relax. I can be spontaneous. I also can change directions. In fact, I believe it is very important in all facets of life to have alternatives. Even if you're extremely happy with your job, occasionally looking at alternatives is appropriate. It has always been important to me to make the most out of my time here on earth, and planning was the best way to make that happen.

When planning our day, week, or year, we cannot separate our personal life from our professional life. In a single day we have twenty-four hours minus sleep time. During the sixteen or so hours we are awake, it is important to act on priorities. Sometimes work has a priority and sometimes play has a priority. Sometimes relaxation is the top priority of the day.

I actually plan every day using an ABC and numbers system. Some days the purchase of a gift for my wife may have been an A1, and on other days dealing with a staff member may have been my A1. In the ideal world we make time for both work and play. Life is about doing what is important to you and then setting priorities so you accomplish the most important items.

No task is ever too small to make a difference in our overall success, in business or in our personal life. Often it is extremely important to focus on the little things.

"Success is not about doing one thing 100 percent better, but about doing one hundred things 1 percent better."
Warren Bennis

The analogy with baseball is a good one as Kevin Costner stated in the movie *Bull Durham*. "The difference between hitting .250 and .300 is twenty-five hits. With six months in the season, twenty-five weeks, it means just one more hit a week is the difference between the majors and the minors." True in baseball and true in business and in life. For instance, the work program for Cleveland Metroparks Zoo for 2010 contained a few biggies, such as completing the construction of the twenty-five-million-dollar African Elephant Crossing, but 90 percent of the tasks were much smaller.

John Wooden, the famous head basketball coach of UCLA, had a similar goal-setting philosophy. It is well known that throughout his coaching career at UCLA, where he guided his teams to ten national championships, he emphasized teamwork, fundamentals, work habits, and ethics and never discussed winning. In his book, *Wooden on Leadership,* he quoted Mother Teresa and added his own perspective.

"Mother Teresa once said, 'There are no big things, only little things done with love.' That sums it up very well. When you derive pleasure and pride in perfecting seemingly 'minor'

details—and teach those you lead to do the same—big things eventually start falling into place. This is what separates achievers from also-rans, the great from the good, and the do-ers from the dreamers."

In recent years I have heard much emphasis on the importance of BHAGs, or Big Hairy Audacious Goals. Some people think having huge, maybe even impossible goals serves to differentiate a great organization from those not so great. While big projects and game-changing programs could be important, I have never thought them as important as concentrating on the hundreds of smaller details in many departments that serve to make a zoo or aquarium complete. With that said Cleveland Metroparks Zoo probably completed several BHAGs, including The RainForest, the African Elephant Crossing, and the Strategic Plan of 2011. However, much of the staff's efforts were directed to hundreds of smaller projects.

PERSONAL MISSION AND VALUES

During my years at the Cleveland Metroparks Zoo, my written personal mission and governing values were as follows:

I will use all my abilities, including passion, commitment, tenacity, persistence, and a sense of humor, to excel at being a zoo director, creating a world with greater love and appreciation for wildlife and wild places.

I will do this within a life where I am at peace with myself because I remain an admirable husband, father, and friend.

- I will be a good husband and keep our relationship interesting, stable, and loving.
- I will be a leader in the zoo and aquarium field.
- I will be financially secure.
- I will be a good father/grandfather.
- I will contribute to the cause of wildlife conservation.

- I will maintain a strong and healthy body.
- I will maintain friendships and cultivate new ones.
- I will continue to improve intellectually.
- I will be charitable.
- I will be content (but not complacent) with my lifestyle.

Like the zoo's work plan, I had goals for each of these personal objectives. While I probably could have done more, like learn a foreign language, I did OK. Interestingly, my personal mission and accompanied values did not have to be changed very much when I retired, other than tweaking my role as a zoo director.

THE STAFF AND TEAMWORK

LEADING THE TEAM

"As Jesus said at the last supper, if you want to be in the picture, you better all get on the same side of the table." Anonymous

In my career I worked for leaders who were great at delegation and also for leaders who were micromanagers. I think anyone hopes to work for a leader who can delegate and trust your decision-making. No matter how much self-esteem one has, working for a micromanager zaps your initiative. In addition, it erodes your authority with your own staff. While I tried not to let the fact that I was being micromanaged adversely affect my ability to do my job, I must admit it did. If one has a great work record, it is often possible to change micromanager bosses by pointing out to them that it's not necessary and you would appreciate it if they would let you do your job. And if they think that you are not doing the job, they should hold you accountable.

"You give them the vision and the strategy, and then you let them run with it. The biggest thing then is to get out of their way." Bob Shearer

Most micromanaging bosses never considered themselves micromanagers. Micromanagers cannot stop themselves from directly involving themselves in the most trivial matters, like choosing paint colors, setting zoo food concession prices, rewriting documents, and such. My favorite story had nothing to do with the zoo but illustrates the point. A new service center in one park was about to open, and a colleague of mine noticed that the weed trimmers were in a pile on the floor. When this colleague asked the park supervisor why the equipment had not been hung on the wall, the very competent park supervisor stated that the boss had to show him how. Evidently the park manager had been told that his micromanaging boss had a special way he liked weed trimmers to be stored.

> *"You have to be willing sometimes to listen to some remarkably bad opinions. Because if you say to someone, 'That's the silliest thing I have ever heard; get out of here,' then you'll never get anything out of that person again, and you might as well have a puppet on a string or a robot." John Bryan*

Micromanaging is different from simply being there and observing the operation and giving advice on improving. While I did not consider myself a micromanager, I did keep track of what was happening in all zoo departments. I believed that people sometimes do not do what you expected, but they were more likely to do what you inspected. I had formal biweekly or monthly meetings with my direct reports wherein we talked about accomplishments, expectations, and issues, and they told me if there was anything I needed to do to help them. I also did a monthly inspection of the entire zoo with a checklist of each of the zoo's two hundred exhibits. I needed to know firsthand if anything needed to be done to the exhibits for the animals or for the guests. I was particularly concerned if too many exhibits were empty at the same time, because of maintenance, animal health, or some other issue. All staff members were aware of my checklists and while animal health and welfare were our primary concerns, staff members were diligent about not closing too many exhibits at once. If staff members had to close an exhibit, they told me ahead of time. This information was important, as even if only three or four exhibits out of two hundred were closed for any reason, visitors would complain.

"Let people accomplish your objectives their way." Carl Johnson

Trusting staff members is paramount but trusting them does not mean never questioning them. Sometimes there are surprises. I once got a phone call from Jeff Koscen, executive director of the Cleveland Animal Protection League and a good friend. He said he had gotten a report that we were feeding kittens to the birds of prey. I told him of course not; the idea was ridiculous. We certainly would not do something like that. First thing I did after hanging up the phone was to call the curator and ask if we were feeding kittens to the birds of prey. He said, "Of course not." I decided I also had better check, as I might find out why someone would report that we were feeding kittens to birds of prey. After looking at the exhibits, two possible explanations came to mind. First, we did feed dead rabbits and rats to these birds, and maybe someone saw a half-eaten rabbit or rat and thought it was a kitten. Secondly, we occasionally had feral cats in the zoo, and one of them may have entered the exhibit and been caught by one of our birds. In any case, with a clear conscience I was able to call Jeff back and confirm that we had not been feeding kittens to the zoo's birds of prey.

It is also important to share recognition. Ed McAlister, director of the Adelaide Zoo, after receiving recognition for his years of service stated, "One can do little without the support of staff, colleagues, friends, and family. In all four areas I have been extremely fortunate." Successful leaders continually thank all levels of staff, from the beginning of their careers to the point they go out the door. It is important that praise is sincere and not superficial. It should not be given just because it is something good leaders do. It does take some thought; however, if a leader does not have anything to thank someone about daily, that leader may want to spend more time observing and listening to staff. Believe me, the successes are out there.

Another example of Ed taking time to recognize people and thus encourage them occurred in an email to me concerning my having lost an election to the WAZA (World Association of Zoos and Aquariums) council. I was not upset about not having an opportunity to be part of the WAZA council, because the people elected were actually much more active with WAZA than I was, but the following email from Ed was still much appreciated.

Dear Steve,

Just a few words of commiseration on your not getting on to the council. I would have enjoyed working with you, but what can I say, that it speaks well for WAZA when someone as talented as you has to miss out. I trust even though you will not be part of my council, I can count on your support during my term as president. I have a few things I would like to see improved/changed, and I want to maintain the momentum we have achieved in recent years: your assistance would be of great value.

Unless your company or agency is a real dud, there is always more achievement than failure. It's always important to thank others for the successes and take the blame for the failures. I have always tried to thank people every day for something they have done. I even wrote down in my daily work list to thank three people today.

I never wanted to create a low-stress work environment. I always concentrated on continuous improvement and never was actually completely satisfied with a project or a program. OK, maybe for a moment I celebrated a success. I realized that little was accomplished in an environment with only small changes and little stress. Eventually that environment would lead to a disaster.

I knew there was a fine line between those who were change agents and those who were just agitators. Both could be difficult at times. Both could create some negative first reactions; however, change agents never attack on a personal level. They win people over by persuasion and reasoning. They use facts, never emotion. They stick to the issue. Change agents understand people, and they work with people, especially their bosses, to bring about change.

Early in my career I am not so sure I was following the above advice when as a keeper at the Los Angeles in 1973 several keepers, including me, questioned many of the animal husbandry and veterinary practices at the zoo. The Recreation and Parks Commission of the City of Los Angeles eventually heard our complaints and appointed a blue-ribbon panel of zoo experts to investigate. The members included Gary Clarke, Topeka Zoo; Don Davis, Cheyenne Mountain Zoo in Colorado Springs; and Dr. Charles Schroeder, former director of the San Diego Zoo. A *Los Angeles Times* article on December 18, 1973, by Mike Goodman reported many of the observations and recommendations of the blue-ribbon panel. Some included the zoo being bogged down with bureaucracy, inexperienced veterinarians, and the zoo's failure to retain good animal management personnel ("Zoo has a reputation in the zoo world as a professional graveyard."). The article said the panel had also stated, "The zoo looks good—and is good. The animal collection is excellent." While I don't remember exactly what happened, apparently several of us were at the Recreation and Parks Commission meeting, and our comments were reported in the *Los Angeles Times* article. Chris Bosley, a keeper colleague of mine, said the report was "unfair, uniformed, and hastily done." Dr. Schroeder stated that "Keepers were justified in many things they're saying, but the same problem exists in other zoos. If there is a crisis in the L.A. Zoo, there's a crisis in zoos across the country." The article ended with a statement from me, a keeper with a whole one-year of experience. "Steve Taylor, a keeper, told the commission, the zoos of the world are in bad shape … 100 years behind the times." The article also stated that the commission said that "some animal keepers are frustrated and overeducated for their job and probably should seek work elsewhere." I wonder to whom the commission was referring.

One of the most difficult things to teach people is working in teams. First of all, it's hard work. Secondly, it prevents people from doing it their own way. It's compromise.

Over the years I saw many dysfunctional teams, both in my own place of work and outside my workplace. I found that animal care divisions or departments in many zoos and aquariums often fell into this category. In one mid-west zoo a very public disagreement between the director and the veterinarian was reported in the local newspaper and it started a widespread investigation of everything from animal deaths to staff morale. In the end, the director, the veterinarian and a few others lost their jobs and the zoo took several years to return to its greatness.

At Cleveland Metroparks Zoo we had our share of dysfunctional teams, although they never resulted in anyone being terminated. Throughout my years in Cleveland, the zoo basically had six departments. The zoo could only be successful if all these departments worked well together. It was not always easy. These departments were as follows:

1. Zoological programs included animal keepers, curators, veterinarians, registrar (record keeper) and scientists/researchers.
2. Conservation education was responsible for the zoo's education programs, including graphics.
3. The marketing and public relations division was similar in function as any institution's marketing division; however, a large part of their workload was creating and implementing various events, such as Boo at the Zoo, ZooBlooms, Noon Year's Eve, etc. Many of these events required corporate sponsorships.
4. Guest services was responsible for all guest activities, including being the liaison with the food and gift concessionaires.
5. Facilities operations maintained the facilities and supervised capital improvements.
6. The sixth division was the zoo's not-for-profit support group,

the Cleveland Zoological Society. Their primary role was community support, including membership and fund-raising,

Administration functions, such as human resources, purchasing, and finance, were performed by either the Cleveland Metroparks or by my one administrative assistant and myself.

As I read this paragraph myself, I realized that I am defining an unusual organization and one where one could easily see where there would be conflict that could cause institutional paralysis. However, this organization was really not much different than other non-profits, or for that matter, for-profit companies. For instance, the zoo had animal exhibits and education programs that were similar to the operations division of many companies. The zoo had a guest services unit, which was similar to customer support. Like most other institutions, the zoo had a marketing and facilities division.

There were several areas over the years where staff at Cleveland Metroparks Zoo had a difficult time working as a functional team. At times there were turf conflicts between the zoo's marketing division and the Cleveland Zoological Society. Both dealt with the community and both worked at getting financial support from corporations. While the two leaders of these departments communicated well, there were some conflicts. There was also duplication of service. Each had their own advertising and design firm. The zoo and the zoological society produce two different annual reports and the publications of both organizations had two very different looks. Both Cleveland Metroparks Zoo and Cleveland Zoological Society events took a tremendous about of collaboration among all divisions to be successful. There were conflicts at times and to those involved felt they were a major concern. However, everyone in the zoo understood that collaboration was paramount to the zoo's overall success, staff usually resolved these conflicts.

Perhaps the challenges within the zoological programs staff were the most interesting, and in the zoo profession, were certainly the most common. Problems developed for all the usual reasons. Each person had an important function and their success depended on the others. Unfortunately, some did not understand that fact. At times there was little respect for others. Staff members were not always held accountable for their actions. There was a difference in educational level within the division. Members were passionate and opinionated.

In 2006, I felt this division was on the verge of dysfunction and I stepped in to help the general curator and to emphasize the importance of working as a team. After talking with all parties one on one, we developed the following operating norms.

Teamwork
- Support decisions made by the team and/or your supervisors.
- Be accessible to peers and subordinates.
- Provide recognition for a job well done and reward teamwork.
- Be part of a positive work environment.
- Provide support for co-workers and subordinates.
- Lead by example.
- Be prepared to coach others in accomplishing joint goals.

Respect/Professionalism
- Do not speak negatively about decisions or each other to others outside the team.
- Treat others as they wish to be treated. Do not demean or insult. Don't make purposely divisive statements.
- Respect ideas of others even if they differ from your own and agree to disagree when necessary.
- Remember that everything you do represents Cleveland Metroparks Zoo.
- Be respectful of others' time.
- Be respectful of others' job descriptions.
- Dress and behave in a professional manner. Be organized in work and in the office.

Accountability
- Take responsibility for your actions and how they affect others.

- Act with integrity.
- Focus on achieving results.
- Keep long term objectives in mind.
- Hold peers accountable for their actions.

Communications
- Encourage participation and sharing in group settings.
- Silence implies consent – speak up if you disagree.
- Use proper communications etiquette and methods. Check e-mail regularly. Don't utilize e-mail to argue.
- Be an active listener to others.
- Seek and accept opinions from others.
- Confirm instructions both given and received.

These statements seemed to make sense to me and I think they were helpful in making a small cultural change with the zoological programs staff. However, as is often the case, circumstances changed and it was no longer necessary for me to stay involved. First, Dr. Hugh Quinn, the general curator decided to retire. Hugh was a great general curator and did much to move Cleveland Metroparks Zoo forward, especially the establishment of the science and conservation department. Second, one of the zoo's longtime curators also retired. There was a new dynamic in zoological programs. A year later the zoo hired Geoff Hall as general curator and then Dr. Christopher Kuhar was hired as curator of primates and small mammals. In 2011, the zoo hired Andi Kornak as curator of large mammals. While there were still challenges, these three new leaders began to change the culture of that division using some of the operating norms I listed above.

I believe there are basically four types of employees. The first group of employees understand the company's values and are very productive workers. The second group understand the values but aren't as good at their jobs. These are people you can work with to improve. The third group are good at their jobs but have little understanding of the organization's values. They are inconsiderate of others. They lack respect for others and are running over others to put a feather in their own caps. These people need to change or find another place of employment. At the bottom are those that do not understand the company's values and are not very productive. They should not be working at your organization.

Throughout my career I think the majority of the staff I hired belonged in the first group. When I retired from Cleveland Metroparks Zoo, I had this group to thank for all the wonderful compliments I received. In my years as a zoo director, I also terminated a good number of employees, but more often I was able to counsel them out. I spent much time with those staff members that needed to improve performance and probably kept them even when I should have known they would not improve.

> *"I haven't the slightest idea how to change people, but still I keep a long list of prospective candidates just in case I should ever figure it out." David Sedari.*

In her book, the *Team of Rivals*, Doris Kearns Goodwin, described Abraham Lincoln as someone who was slow to fire folks. Lincoln let General McClellan continue to lead the Army of the Potomac, even when it was obvious to everyone else that the general was too slow to move on the Confederacy. Lincoln's cabinet was not a group of trusted allies, but a team of rivals. For instance, the Treasury Secretary, Salmon P. Chase, was constantly criticizing Lincoln behind his back and was even preparing to run against Lincoln in 1864. When those Lincoln trusted confronted him with this, he merely said he was aware of Chase's behavior, but he needed him in the cabinet because he was a great treasury secretary! If Lincoln could manage in such a manner, I guess my preference to work with folks was not the worst of employee strategies.

A CULTURE OF COMMUNICATIONS

Communication starts at the top with the zoo director. Face to face visibility with the director is imperative. You cannot communicate effectively from behind the desk, by e-mail or with countless text messages. An open-door policy should not just mean that everyone is welcome to come in and talk, but it also means that the director can go out the door!

> *"Leading means being out front. Create presence in the workplace. People want to see you."* Bruce Hyland and Merle Yost

Like many other leaders, I probably seemed outgoing at times, but I could also be shy. I had to make myself get out of the office and talk to staff. I also had to train myself to listen. I knew it was important, especially in my later years, to make a connection with staff. One thing I did do was to find employees on their birthday and wish them a happy birthday. I used that opportunity to let them tell me about their families and have a friendly conversation. Sometimes we talked about work, but not always. I gave employees a candy bar wrapped in a special Cleveland Metroparks Zoo wrapper. The wrapper had a photo of one of the zoo's animals and the message on the front was, Thank You – You're Appreciated. The back of the wrapper listed ingredients: 100% Dedication, Ambition, Commitment to Excellence, Positive Attitude and Success. Yes, it was kind of silly, but it was always appreciated. I also had a more selfish motive for this action. As I often had difficulty remembering names, by making an effort to connect with more than two-hundred full and part-time employees at least once a year, I kept each employee's name fresh in my mind.

PERFORMANCE REVIEWS

Performance reviews were a wonderful opportunity to work with staff at all levels and recognize their achievements as well as refocus them on the most important efforts. However, many managers do not spend enough time to do reviews properly.

The biggest mistake managers make is reviewing employees only one time a year. This is not productive and is often a disaster. Managers must formally review their direct reports on a regular basis. They must continually monitor their performance, while not micro-managing. There should be no surprises at the time of the year-end review.

Most performance reviews use similar language. The first part usually is a review of accomplishments and a list of future projects and expectations. As zoo staff members were always required to have detailed work programs, these were attached to their reviews and the list of accomplishments and expectations on their reviews were highlights of this document.

The length of a staff members work program was not necessarily an indicator of that staff member's worth. For instance, at Cleveland Metroparks Zoo, an administrative assistance's job and a veterinarian's job were not project driven. The expectations for these staff members were better described in their job description and thus their performance was based on those expectations.

There are always performance indicators that are obvious and might not even be in any staff manual. These include:

- Be at work and be there on time.
- Follow the rules such as smoking rule, computer use, cell phone use and more.
- Be sober and don't use drugs.
- Be respectful of others, even your boss.
- Be professional. Dress appropriate to your job and keep your work area neat and orderly.
- Don't steal.
- Support the organization.
- Pay attention to the customer.

At Cleveland Metroparks Zoo these obvious behaviors were important in all reviews, but even more so with the union employees. Like most organizations, Cleveland Metroparks Zoo had many over achievers, but supervisors spent a large proportion amount of time on the few employees that could not even manage to abide by these basic expectations.

While reviews are not a time for humor, I have always remembered a few well-publicized tongue and cheek quotes from actual federal government employee performance reviews. Here are some of my favorites:

1. "This young lady has delusions of adequacy."
2. "This employee is depriving a village somewhere of an idiot."
3. "He brings a lot of joy whenever he leaves the room."
4. "Works well when under constant supervision and cornered like a rat in a trap."
5. "He sets low personal standards and then consistently fails to achieve them."

There were a few times in my career I wished that I could use one or more of the above quotes. Certainly, some were appropriate.

In any organization, there needs to be time for an employee and their supervisor to have open and honest conversation. Because of our legalistic society, performance reviews have become so complicated that they have lost some of their value. Many organizations are now overly cautious and even the simplest review must be reviewed by several layers of management plus staff in the human resources department. In addition, many organizations have complicated one-size-fits-all review forms that attempt to standardize reviews, but this often makes it difficult to truly assess a staff members pros and cons.

In my entire career, I personally never found a perfect compensation plan. Companies find consultants that look at external comparisons, which are very important in recruitment. It's difficult to attract great staff if your compensation package is below market. Consultants are often asked to do internal comparisons, which are important in fairly managing the entire staff. Let's face it, there were no secrets in our government-run zoo where all records could be reviewed because of open records laws. In my opinion, compensation is one of those items where one can only attempt to be fair.

WORK HABITS

"Nothing can stop a man with the right mental attitude from achieving a goal: Nothing on earth can help the man with the wrong mental attitude." Thomas Jefferson

PERSISTENCE

Any success I had professionally was mostly due to persistence and planning. During my career, I found that successful planning (see earlier parts of this chapter) was the first step in creating great work habits. Persistence was tremendously important in working for government-run organizations. All government jobs from street cleaner to the President of the United States require a great deal of persistence. Leaders that are not persistent and give up early usually fail. Those that see roadblocks and bureaucracy but persist and find legal means to get around them, not once, but many times, eventually prevail.

"Nothing in the world will take the place of persistence. Talent will not: nothing is more common than the unsuccessful person with talent. Genius will not; unrewarded genius is almost a proverb. Education will not; the world is full of educated derelicts. Persistence and determination alone are omnipotent. The slogan "press on" has solved and always will solve the problems of the human race." Calvin Coolidge

I can remember several examples of persistence in my own career. For my first four years as director of Cleveland Metroparks

Zoo, my main focus was completing the RainForest. Construction started on this thirty-five million indoor tropical exhibit about two years prior to my arrival. It was obvious that the zoo could not afford to open a new blockbuster exhibit every year so we struggled with finding something new to promote every summer season. While the RainForest was being built the zoo did simple and inexpensive promotions around adding new species to the animal collection, such as Bactrian camels and bongo antelopes. The bongo is an African forest antelope that had once been at Cleveland but had not been displayed there since the sixties. In fact, the Cleveland Zoo was the first zoo to ever display a pair of bongos.

Every year I suggested that robotic dinosaurs would be a wonderful seasonal promotion and other zoos had tremendous success promoting these as a seasonal attraction. Every year the idea was rejected as it was thought to be too expensive and that robotic dinosaurs had been done so much that people were not really interested anymore. Every year, I would counter that there is always a new crop of five-year-old boys and girls that will force their parents to come and see them. In 2003 after ten or twelve years of the same conversation, the idea was accepted. I was shocked! After all these years, I now hoped I was right! As it turned out, 2003 was the second highest attended year ever at Cleveland Metroparks Zoo.

Another example of persistence would be the creation of a new African elephant exhibit at Cleveland Metroparks Zoo. From the time I started as zoo director, I wanted a new elephant exhibit. The fifties-style exhibit at the front of the zoo was inadequate for the animals and was not very attractive to zoo guests. A new exhibit was part of the zoo's 1993 master plan and continued to be my choice for the next large project after the RainForest opened in 1993. My journal on August 25, 1994 mentioned that the Board of Park Commissioners decided to move ahead on a wolf exhibit and then make improvements to the children's farm. I wrote the following in my journal, "I think we could open wolves in 1996 and the children's farm in 1998. Obviously, my concern is little thought was given to one of the zoo's greatest needs, the elephants." It was not until almost ten years later, on July 25, 2003, after much planning, studies completed and visitor's surveys read that the Board of Park Commissioners, agreed the zoo should move forward with a new elephant exhibit. It was a very complicated project with many stakeholders, often with differing views. It took six years to design and raise funds and two and half years to construct. When it finally opened in May 2011, it was a tremendous success. That's persistence!

As I stated at the beginning of this chapter, I owe much to the leadership of Cleveland Metroparks. If it were not for the persistence and focus of the Board of Park Commissioners, there would have been no thirty-five-million-dollar RainForest. They were not as concerned about the eventual cost as much as they were concerned with the quality of the experience for both the guests and the animals. They felt that if it were a high-quality addition to the zoo, everyone would forget about the cost and other controversies. They were absolutely right and when it opened it was a tremendous success. And, to this day, no one ever mentions the perceived very high unanticipated cost of the RainForest.

Working for Cleveland Metroparks taught me to never get worked up trying to influence matters that were beyond my reach. I am certain that all zoo directors have had differences with their boards of directors. I concentrated on pleasing the board, which actually took very little effort, as well as myself. I stayed involved with the Association of Zoos and Aquariums (AZA), the professional organization for North American zoos and aquariums. I planned and worked hard within the parameters available to me to create a good zoo. I worked getting community and state and federal support for the zoo. There was plenty that I could do, and do well, without worrying about what I could not do.

Keep Things in Order

If your workspace is a mess, all your colleagues and others observe it will pass judgment on you. Research shows that a disorganized office means that you are wasting time. Any totally chaotic office can be cleaned and organized in half of a day. To keep it clean, one may need some instruction or a tutor. But it can be done and should be done!

It really does not matter if you have a small or large office space, you need to work with the space you are given. In today's world, much can be kept on the computer and that takes very little space. During my working years, I must admit that I unfortunately kept lots of paper. The following are some thoughts on office orderliness:

- Always quit work with enough time to organize your office and especially what is on your desk. That is a must!
- I always used an in-box and an out-box. I never let the in-box pile up. I dealt with those items every day. Sometimes that meant not thoroughly reading some items. Much reading material is not important anyway. Some inner-office mail and certainly most e-mails were not very important.
- I kept a small three-inch high drawer where I could put things that I may need to refer to at a later date but did not necessarily have a place for in the file cabinet or desk.
- I believed that manila folders are your best friend. They are now replaced with computer folders. If I absolutely had to have a hard copy, then it was in a labeled manila folder. As an example, I had a folder for each business trip and as I got flights, hotel information, and made appointments, I put it in that folder. Some of this information was also on my computer and when I took my laptop everywhere and in later years I was able to keep almost everything on my computer.
- I constantly threw out stuff. At the end of every year, I threw out lots of stuff. If I thought I might need some materials, I kept them one year. If I did not use them in that year, I threw them out. That is also the same with computer files.
- I believed that the drawers in my desk were not for trash. Each one had a purpose. I did not keep junk in them. And in a zoo,

it was wise not to keep food in there either. Most zoo offices have some critters running around and having food in a desk makes pest control more difficult. The things one needs in a desk are obvious. I kept my most active files, one for each direct report. I kept phone books, until they became obsolete with goggle. I kept pens, paper clips, different types of paper and envelopes, stapler, tape, tape measure, scissor, computer accessories. You get the idea.

Don't be Late

For me, on time to meetings, was ten minutes early. I was always punctual and I always expected it in others. I was often disappointed. In my opinion, starting meetings late gave the appearance that those conducting the meeting had little respect for other people's time. Starting meetings on time is always very much appreciated by staff who also have a very busy schedule attending the meetings.

One might think that being punctual in a non-punctual world wasted lots of time. However, I was also a good time manager and never went anywhere without having work, often just important reading, with me at all times.

Other Interests Outside Work

I loved the zoo profession. Very few things took me away from thinking about the zoo. But I did have other interests. Golf was one and I tried to play regularly, mostly with my wife, Sarah. Golf was the only outside interest that actually took me out of the zoo. When I played golf I rarely thought about the zoo. I enjoyed traveling, running, and gardening, but during those activities, I passed the time thinking about the zoo.

"It is impossible to remember how tragic a place the world is when one is playing golf." – Robert Lynd

Integrity in golf is amazing and a great lesson for young people. This is one of the reasons that Sarah has stayed involved with the local chapter of the First Tee. I will never forget a few years ago when thirty-two-year old Mark Wilson won the Honda Classic after calling a two-stroke penalty on himself, even though no one else would have noticed. During the second round, Carilo Anthony, playing with Mark Wilson, asked his own caddie about the hybrid club Wilson had just hit to the green. Chris Jones, Wilson's caddie, overheard the conversation and responded that the hybrid had eighteen degree of loft. Wilson notified the rules official that a penalty may have occurred. The official agreed and Wilson accepted a two-stroke penalty. The rules of golf are clear: a player, and by extension his caddie, may not ask or give advice to a competitor. What a great story, especially since Wilson went on to win the tournament. Even though no one would have noticed the infraction, Wilson told reporters that the victory would have been tarnished had he not penalized himself.

Sarah and I enjoyed playing golf on some of our international vacations. We did claim to be the only two people on earth that have played golf in all of the following: Zimbabwe, Trinidad, Australia, New Zealand, Dominican Republic, Bermuda and Costa Rica! Each one of these rounds was a memorable experience, not because of a great round, but because of the surroundings. I have a great photo of Sarah hitting a lofted iron over a small family of warthogs in Zimbabwe. Warthogs have a habit of getting down on their front legs and routing in the dirt for food. The photo looks like the warthog is ducking to avoid being hit by a low iron shot!

Aside from golf, I had other interests although I must admit that many of these had some relationship to my job. Sarah and I loved to travel and we took every opportunity we could to go to two or three new places each year. Many of the places had something to do with wildlife and the zoo supported much of my travel as we led various ecotourism trips sponsored by the Cleveland Zoological Society. Even when we went somewhere on our own, we managed to visit a zoo, botanical garden, or a natural area where I expanded my bird list. I have much more about travel in a later chapter.

I have never been fat, but as I got older my waistline certainly expanded and from fifty years of age on, like many folks, I had to work hard to keep myself in shape. Since my Sacramento days, I belonged to a health club and was a semi-regular attendee. I was never particularly athletic and in school was always the last one chosen for the team. I started running just after college and continue to this day. I am still able to make it to the finish line in a five-mile race, but I am embarrassed by the fact that those crossing the line with me are those ten years old, over seventy-five or overweight. A victory for me has always been to finish a run without stopping. In the past, occasional knee and shin problems kept me from running more than five miles. Now, my pace is so slow that injury is not an issue. I use the time to think and solve problems. It seemed that there was always some issue at the zoo that needed forty minutes of thought.

Like with golf, I remember some special runs. I remember a run under the Arch in St. Louis on September 11, 2001, one-half hour before the attack. I had several nice early morning runs with Mark Reed, director of the Sedgwick County Zoo, in Wichita, Kansas while we were attending a WAZA meeting in Adelaide, Australia in 2008. Sarah and I have had many wonderful runs in California at Christmas and other times when we visit my relatives. Actually, my regular run in warm weather is a three and a half mile run though my Rocky River, Ohio neighborhood.

None-the-less, my jogging can be described as John Schwartz described his efforts in an article in the *Wall Street Journal* in November 2011.

"...I will continue to plod through my town, apparently to the amusement of the neighbors. A friend says that when he sees me running in the mornings, I time you – with my calendar."

After retirement, I had a little more time to run and in 2017, at 70-years old, I trained all summer and ran my first, and likely my last, half-marathon on Kiawah Island, SC in December.

When I reached sixty, I started attending an evening yoga class. They called it practice and believe me I needed lots of practice. There is a wonderful yoga studio in Rocky River, not too far from our house. The beginner's session started at 7:30 PM and ended at 8:30 PM. I had no sense of balance and very little flexibility, but I enjoyed it because the people were so nice, both the instructors and participants. Having good-looking woman around me was also a plus! After about a year, the late evening hours became a pain as we then didn't eat dinner until 9 PM, so I stopped going. When I retired, I started again only this time I was able to attend during the day. Sarah found out that there was an all-male yoga class at a different studio and suggested that I might be more comfortable going there. I just laughed – why would I do that!

I have had a fairly healthy life with only a few aliments, mostly skin cancers from spending my first forty-two years in the California sun. Then in July 2018, I was diagnosed with HPV throat cancer. It was a shock and totally unexpected. Fortunately, this type of cancer was very treatable and while doctors never say it's cured, they do eventually say, no evidence of disease. It was very tough on Sarah as she did most of the worrying, but I knew what I had to do and just did it one step at time. By December, and after seven weeks of radiation, six chemo treatments and three months of recovery, I was pretty much back to normal. I even lost twenty pounds and kept it off. My blood pressure returned to normal after being high and controlled with daily medication. We were sad we missed a wonderful safari to South Africa with some great friends/clients. Fortunately, Jim Heck of EWT was able to step in to guide our group.

No matter what one values, I am certain that everyone should place personal health near the top of their list. Without good health nothing else we do is possible. It certainly should not be something that is done only when we have time.

COMMUNICATION

"Leaders identify, articulate and summarize concepts that mo-tivate others. Most importantly, they boil concepts down to an understandable idea." Laurie Beth Jones

WRITTEN COMMUNICATIONS

Like with work habits, good communications starts with good planning. Only when you have a well thought out plan that is clear-ly defined, can you have clear communications regarding mutually agreed upon expectations.

I like job profiles, not job descriptions. I would have had nothing against detailed job descriptions, if they did not take so much time, and in the end they did not really matter? They were also usually out-of-date as soon as they were printed. I thought that a short job profile was all that was important, especially when hiring a new employee and when benchmarking our institution's jobs with similar institu-tions. Other than that, lengthy job descriptions were of limited value.

That is not to say that we could operate the zoo without staff having a clear understanding of their job duties. In fact, that was ex-tremely important. The problem with the traditional job description was they tended to be both lengthy and inflexible. Length creates inflexibility. They were usually done during some exercise dictated by corporate human resources, filed away and forgotten.

I found there were other methods that insured that staff mem-bers understood their jobs. And most important, they needed to un-derstand their jobs were continually changing. They also needed to understand an important part of their success, and the zoo's success, was working with others outside their normal duties. I believed that planning documents such as three-year plans, annual work programs, regularly scheduled one-on-one meetings, and properly done per-formance evaluations were much more effective at describing a staff member's job, than the old and tired job description

Employee behavior emanates from conviction and belief, not

from procedures. Manuals and guidelines are very important in training and of some value in communications and coordination; however, they are of limited value in the heat of battle.

Unfortunately, all companies and agencies have so many written policies and procedures but no one can have them all memorized. It is only with training and constant communications can staff handle all situations appropriately. Cleveland Metroparks Zoo was not unlike any other large bureaucratic government agency. Cleveland Metroparks had a three-inch wide employee manual. Even I did not know what was contained in this document much of the time. For instance, I never remembered if Columbus Day was really a Cleveland Metroparks holiday, but I knew where to look. We also had a set of zoo guidelines containing procedures unique to the zoo, such as animal escape, animal acquisition and security. It was important that we had these and could use them in training and defining our culture, but no one in the zoo knew them by heart. Common sense and training got most staff members through the day.

Managing a zoo required having a well-written and well-understood dangerous animal escape plan. We discussed the plan at staff meetings, we had animal escape drills, and we modified the procedures when it seemed appropriate. However, when an escape happened no one went to the written policy, they just responded based on their intuition. In my forty years working in four different zoos, I never had to use the policy for an extremely dangerous escape. I was more fortunate in my career that some of my colleagues, but I was involved in several escapes when dangerous animals left their primary enclosure but not out of a building. Once a male gorilla left his night quarters and entered the back hallway. How this happened, I do not even remember. A staff member noticed him before any damage was done and an alert was announced with staff responding. While it was not written in any procedural manual, someone got a vehicle and parked it against the back door of the Primate, Cat, and Aquatics building preventing the animal from leaving the building. As required by law this exit had panic bars and a gorilla could have easily left the building. This was a classic example of using common sense. The gorilla was fairly calm, never tried to leave the building, and was successfully captured using a tranquilizer gun.

On a June morning in 2009 at the Riverbanks Zoo in Columbia, South Carolina, a male gorilla found some rain-soaked shoots of bamboo hanging over the containment wall in the exhibit and used it to escape. The gorilla walked past a couple of moms with strollers and then grabbed a concession stand worker, who had left his post to see if it was true that an animal had escaped. This was not a great idea. The concessions worker was not seriously injured and the gorilla, after being out of his exhibit for only five minutes, jumped back into the exhibit on his own. When asked why the concessions employees did not call for base for help as described in the policy, they stated that they did not know that base was the switchboard! It is impossible to think of everything and even having seemingly clear written instructions are not always enough.

The Dallas Zoo was not quite so lucky. They had had a series of tragic animal escapes in the late 90s and early 2000s. First, a gorilla got out of its overnight holding unit and into a keeper corridor. The gorilla got a hold of the keeper and seriously injured her. A short time later the chimps escaped from their outdoor enclosure and one animal climbed a power pole and was electrocuted. After those escapes, the Dallas Zoo developed one of the most elaborate sets of policies for animal escape in the industry. They did some things that other zoos had really not considered in their policies and training. One of those items was working with the local police force to make certain that when an animal was loose on the zoo grounds, it would be the zoo staff coordinating recapture, containment, or if necessary, disposal. This was important as the zoo staff understands the animals and has also trained itself in tranquilization, as well as shooting to kill. The Dallas Zoo even produced a video showing the zoo staff and the local police cooperating in an animal escape. I thought the video was so well done that I had it shown to our staff and asked them to set up a similar meeting with our local police department. The irony of this story is that the Dallas Zoo had another gorilla escape in 2003. This gorilla mysteriously escaped from the outdoor exhibit and instead of avoiding people, actually attacked several zoo guests. The local police who responded to cell phone calls from zoo guests rushed into the zoo, never communicated with the zoo's staff, and fatally shot the gorilla. While the outcome may not have been avoidable, the fact remains that the police and the zoo had a great policy, but it was ignored. The police on duty said they were unaware of all the coordination with the zoo, despite the fact that the Dallas Zoo was recognized throughout the United States as having excellent policies and procedures. The moral of the story is obviously, no policy will ever replace constant communications with the people most involved.

The Right Type of Communications

"I always feel like if my team can't have healthy debate, it's my fault." Walt Bettinger

Every new form of communication technology seems to get abused. It probably started with abuse of telegraph, pony express and then phones. Faxes were a great invention and allowed the written word to be reviewed and confirmed quickly. This was important as phone conversations could be misunderstood and could not be verified.

In my mind, the worst abuse came with e-mail and texting. Staff would e-mail or text others rather than pick up the phone or even walk ten feet to another office and discuss an issue. E-mail was great for setting up meetings and getting verification of various matters, but I felt it should never be used for lengthy discussions or debates. The Cleveland Metroparks Zoo's office was only twenty-thousand square feet and I constantly had to tell staff members to please go talk with the person.

MEETINGS

I knew that my general employee meetings (GEM) could be boring, but they were essential. It was an opportunity for everyone to get together as many had not seen each other for months. It was also a guaranteed time to see me and hopefully I imparted some important information. Rumors could be controlled. In 2009, when the executive director of Cleveland Metroparks announced his retirement, some assumed I would also retire. To the dismay of some, I put an end to that rumor and stated I would like to stay three to five more years. It was important that everyone heard about the state of the zoo firsthand, especially in times of uncertainty or major change. For me the most important general employee meeting came at the end of the year when I could summarize the zoo's successes and start the discussion on plans for the upcoming year. I also shared all the financial information. At Cleveland Metroparks Zoo, we held GEMs only every other month. They lasted one hour. While there was time for questions and comments, these meetings were basically to depart information. Other smaller meetings were better for sharing ideas and getting input.

Most organizations have some type of senior management meeting, sometimes as often as once a week or sometimes twice a month. In thirty years of senior manager meetings, I never felt I got them right. In the beginning they were mostly about sharing information, very important even in a small zoo like Sacramento Zoo. In later years with e-mails, texting, electronic newsletters and notices, I am not sure sharing of information in meetings was as necessary. The main purpose had to be to collectively solve problems and create new opportunities.

My meetings at Cleveland Metroparks Zoo with my direct reports were called Senior Management Meetings (SeMT). They were scheduled at least one month in advance. I would have liked to schedule them for the whole year, but for most of my tenure at Cleveland Metroparks Zoo, the Board of Park Commissioners did not schedule their meetings that far in advance so there would be potential conflicts if we scheduled SeMT meetings annually. We met for two hours at most, preferably in the morning, but more often in the afternoon. I did the agenda personally and got it out a few days in advance and was always open to additions. For ten years prior to my retirement from the zoo, senior staff did a written report and sent it out to all members of SeMT prior to the meeting. We were hopeful that this would cut the time for reporting and allow us more time for discussion. It didn't work as well as we wished, as everyone still wanted to take time to describe his or her division's activities. We even used an hourglass to time presentations, but even that didn't work. I understood that everyone was proud of their work and needed some time to talk about it.

LEADERSHIP

> *"Leadership is an active, living process. It is rooted in character forged by experience and communicated by example."*
> John Baldoni

> *"I want employees who will show me the possibilities. The goal of the gifted boss is to be worthy of exceptional talent."*
> *Dale Dauten*

PASSION

Passion is probably the single most important element of personal leadership. It is also contagious to staff, guests, donors, and board members. I always found that high job commitment served as an excellent antidote to stress. It was easy for me to be passionate about running a zoo, about working for the conservation of wildlife and wild places, and about educating children and adults about nature and the environment. I always loved my job. I was very fortunate in that regard. That is not to say there were not parts of the job that made me crazy. For instance, I never really enjoyed working in a teamster union environment. But because I loved my job and loved the zoo, I was able to do the parts of the job that I felt were less desirable.

Passion should not be confused with anger. As Benjamin Franklin stated: *"Anger is never without reason, but seldom a good one."*

Unfortunately, anger is a most human emotion and few have managed to go through life without showing anger on the job at one time or another. Most of the time it is very regrettable. If you're smart, you apologize to those present and move on. I have had to do that on occasion and each time I learned a valuable lesson.

WHO SHOULD LEAD?

It's always a little easier to lead, when you have a certain amount of technical expertise and experience. Lee Iacocca knew a lot about cars when he turned around Chrysler. Many great generals were great soldiers. I always found it a little easier being a zoo director because I had been an animal keeper. I always felt I had some empathy for those that did the hard work to make the zoo a great place for both the animals and people. In addition, the animal care staff members were less likely to bullshit me!

Like many organizations and businesses these days, there is always debate as to who would make a better CEO, an industry professional or someone with proven leadership ability. Obviously, it's great when you can get someone with both skill sets. With zoos and aquariums, it is difficult to find that perfect individual. Many zoo and aquarium professionals have no desire to move to the top spot. These professionals like being animal curators, veterinarians, educators, and/or scientists. They have had enough of management simply directing their own specialties. There certainly is no right or wrong here and many successful zoo and aquarium CEOs in the United States came from other professions, including being parks and recreation directors, military officers, business CEOs, and in leadership roles in various non-profits.

"People with small minds talk about other people. People with average minds talk about events. People with great minds talk about ideas." Anonymous

Seize the Opportunity

"While management is problem-oriented, leadership is opportunity oriented." Stephen Covey

Great leaders recognize opportunity and seldom let the naysayers keep them from the goal. Like the following story:

"Two shoe salesmen were sent to Africa to open up new markets. Three days after arriving, one salesperson called the office and said, I am returning on the next flight. Can't sell shoes here. Everyone goes barefoot. At the same time another salesperson sent an email to the factory, telling them, the prospects are unlimited. Nobody wears shoes here!"

As mentioned in chapter two, we needed to be very innovative in improving the Sacramento Zoo. The City of Sacramento was not going to come forward with increases from the general fund. Therefore, we needed to increase entrance fees and use some of the funds for increases in staffing and some increased funds went to the city's general fund. This was a win/win. We were able to expand the role of the Sacramento Zoological Society. The society began operating the food service and merchandising which gave the zoo additional resources for our programs. We knew what needed to be done and then collectively we found a way to accomplishment it.

One of the ways we improved our ability to continually improve Cleveland Metroparks Zoo was to take advantage of legal opportunities that allowed the zoo to use competent contractors that had had zoo or Cleveland Metroparks experience without the cumbersome and expensive process of going out to bid. Also, often with the Cleveland Metroparks bidding process the lowest bidder was not always that skilled, despite the park commission ability to choose lowest and best. If the zoo had hired a good painting contractor through the bidding process, we could expand their contract by change order. It that way we awarded competent contractors extra work. When we built the African Elephant Crossing in 2009/10, we added a two-hundred and fifty-thousand-dollar tram stop to the original contract. These were definitely examples of taking advantage of a legal opportunity.

Empowerment

"The function of leadership is to produce more leaders, not more followers". Ralph Nader

Leaders make empowerment felt throughout the organization. It's not an easy skill to develop. Most young leaders try to solve every problem themselves. They probably feel that their relatively high-level position requires them to solve all the problems since they were hired to manage. However, most good leaders evolve into teacher and rely on their direct reports to solve most of the problems.

At Cleveland Metroparks Zoo, I always felt that I empowered staff at all levels. Some might feel that I was just lazy, but I felt it was important to have those in charge of areas really take charge of those areas. Because of the zoo's planning process, as explained elsewhere, I believe all employees knew what I expected of them. The once-a-month formal meetings used to review the annual work programs was almost all I needed to keep track of everyone's progress.

Decision Making

The difficulty with decision-making is that one is wrong sometimes. Some people have difficulty being wrong and wait too long to make a decision.

"A good plan today is better than a great plan tomorrow."
George Patton

"Aim for success not perfection. Remember that fear always lurks behind perfectionism. Confronting your fears and allowing yourself the right to be human can, paradoxically, make you a far happier and more productive person." Dr. David Burns

These were lessons I had to constantly adhere to while I was director of Cleveland Metroparks Zoo. It would have been easy, and quite frankly was my style in the early days, to question almost every decision of the governing board. Sometimes I felt the governing board made some uninformed decisions.

Prior to my arrival at Cleveland Metroparks, management staff of the did cause embarrassment to the park system and the park commissioners by participating in several small, but none-the-less illegal acts. After those episodes, the Board of Park Commissioners were wary of staff even though most of us were new to Cleveland Metroparks. I learned very quickly to pick my battles. When the park commission refused to accept a plan that would have created a much more interesting themed main concession stand and one that would have provided viewing into several African animal areas, we let it go. However, when the park commission suggested the zoo locate the new veterinary hospital in a totally unacceptable location, we had to speak up. No one understood their reasoning for locating the veterinary hospital in the deepest part of the flood plain adjacent to the RainForest. While the RainForest was a strikingly interesting building from an architectural perspective, it would have been difficult and expensive to build an attractive veterinary hospital in the same vicinity. These discussions delayed the project for about a year, but finally we were able to negotiate a location for the hospital that was acceptable to everyone. One has to pick their battles.

One of the most complicated decision-making processes involved hiring staff. No candidate was ever perfect. The process at Cleveland Metroparks was lengthy and involved many people, from hiring supervisors, their supervisors, human resource staff members and often even the executive director. Cleveland Metroparks often utilized a search firm for certain senior staff members. For many jobs, Cleveland Metroparks required certain personality tests. They also did background checks and drug tests. I preferred to have many people involved in the interviews. All this was positive, but it took a very organized hiring manager to keep the process moving and fill a position in around six to eight months. With all this, we still managed to make some mistakes. No matter how much research one does, one always needs to make decisions with imperfect data.

If one tries to please everyone, somebody's not going to like it. When I arrived in Cleveland, the zoo had a single lone gorilla named Timmy. He had become a resident of the zoo in 1976, having been purchased from the Memphis Zoo for five-thousand dollars. At that time, he weighed only two-hundred and twenty pounds and was flown to Cleveland on a private plane for the cost of $642. In 1989 when I came to the zoo, he was literally a five-hundred-pound gorilla and he was a very handsome adult male gorilla. After announcing that the zoo would be sending this popular gorilla from Cleveland to New York over the objection to some ill informed people in the community, I received this note addressed Dear Scum:

> "I frequently read in the newspaper of your vicious attempts to ship Timmy to N. Y. I think you must be a homosexual. I fund many animal protection groups, and open cruelty like yours spurs me on to contribute more generously and also vote against any zoo levies or grants while you are a leech on the payroll. I would call you a swine, except they are really rather decent creatures. A Voter Watching You."

> "Being responsible sometimes means ticking people off."
> Colin Powell

At the time, Timmy was a thirty-three-year old male gorilla and Cleveland Metroparks Zoo exhibited him in a very dated facility that was not the best for housing a breeding troop of gorillas. AZA's go-rilla Species Survival Program (SSP) recommended sending Timmy to the Bronx Zoo in New York where he would have access to sev-eral females. While we hated seeing Timmy leave Cleveland, most of us agreed it would be best to follow the SSP recommendation. The move had been planned for several months before an animal rights group hired an attorney to stop the move based on the concept that it was inappropriate to separate Timmy from his new companion, Kribi Kate, a non-reproductive female at the zoo that I managed to obtain from another zoo so Timmy would not be alone.

The protests began and the zoo was taken to court over this is-sue. I was told that one protest sign read, Terminate Taylor the Timmy Tormentor! As lowland gorillas were a federally endangered species and thus protected under the Endangered Species Act of the Federal Government, the local court had to refer the case to the US District Federal Court. Judge Alice Batchelder already had a busy schedule, but she agreed to hear the case at 7 AM on October 31, 1991. The at-torneys representing Cleveland Metroparks were ready and I brought in the executive director of AZA, Bob Wagner, and the chair of the AZA gorilla SSP, Dr. Les Fisher, from the Lincoln Park Zoo as expert witness-es. After a brief introductory statement, the judge asked the attorneys to report to her chambers. After an hour or so Judge Batchelder reap-peared and reported her decision. She stated that while she personally might not want to send Timmy to the Bronx Zoo, the zoos had arranged the transfer under the federal endangered species act and therefore she would not prevent Cleveland Metroparks Zoo from moving Timmy to the Bronx Zoo. By noon that day Timmy was loaded in a crate and loaded on a truck. Several keepers, a curator, a veterinarian, and a mechanic accompanied him and two truck drivers as he headed to his new home with four fertile females at the Bronx Zoo.

This was one of the most significant court cases ever in American zoo history as the decision set a precedent allowing zoos to move endangered species across state lines for the purpose of creating self-sustaining populations of endangered species. The story had an unbelievable ending. Not only did Timmy make it to the Bronx Zoo safely, which we knew would happen, but he also integrated very well into a family of lowland gorillas. Prior to becoming a senior citizen, Timmy sired thirteen offspring so we achieved the goal of having his genes represented in the gorilla population in North America. After many years at the Bronx Zoo and after Timmy finished siring baby gorillas, he retired at the new gorilla facility at the Louisville Zoo in 2000. There he lived to be one of the oldest gorilla ever.

Like many curators and directors in the nineties, I realized that the only way zoos could maintain wildlife in their facilities was to cooperate. No one zoo could keep such a large and stable population of one species that would be genetically healthy enough to survive many generations. The AZA SSPs were established to manage our North American zoo populations. For instance, zoo curators and scientists created a plan that involved managing two-hundred and fifty Amur tigers in North American zoos for a hundred years and only losing about five percent of that population's genetic diversity. There are now several hundred similar AZA managed programs, and while they are all a little different, they are similar to the plan for the Amur tiger. Unfortunately, only a few, like the Amur tiger, are actually sustainable for even a hundred years. Creating sustainable animal collections does require zoos to move animals between institutions to preserve that genetic diversity. When the population reaches it goal, the SSP dictates that only certain animals should be bred.

Certainly no one always makes the right decision one-hundred percent of the time. Good leaders don't look back on mistakes, because they're always looking forward. They don't listen to the naysayers and those that don't participate in the process but are the quickest to criticize.

Innovation and Technology

Having graduated from college in 1969, I was one of the last classes of college students that had little knowledge of use for computers. I remember there were classes in computers, but no one took them except for a few strange physics students. I believe there was a computer room at UCI in the natural science building somewhere. I didn't know where. I believe it was about the size of New York City. However, I did have a slide rule! I wonder what I ever did with it.

I did not get my first computer at my desk until the early nineties, a year or so after becoming director of Cleveland Metroparks Zoo. From then on, I have always attempted to learn something new about my computer every day. It wasn't easy. Like foreign languages, computer use was not easy for me. I have never been one to be patient with any type of machine. However, I knew that I needed to be able to use the computer and to understand its usages, so I continually improved my skills. However, others, mostly younger staff members, made my computer acumen look pretty elementary. I always said that I strived to be on the "leading edge of middle tech."

WHY GOVERNMENTS SHOULDN'T RUN ZOOS

In my opinion, most government agencies are designed to minimize failure and avert scandal. When most energy is devoted to those two worthwhile endeavors, success becomes secondary. There are currently less than ten large government-run zoos in the United States. Many converted to non-profit management in the nineties and at the beginning of this century have been much more successful by any measure. Included in this group would be the Dallas Zoo, the Houston Zoo, the Pittsburgh Zoo, the San Francisco Zoo, the Detroit Zoo, the Tulsa Zoo and the Woodland Park Zoo in Seattle. While they all still receive tax support, and with some it is substantial, in the long run they were able to save the government entity money and were able to generate more private dollars. In addition, zoos operated by non-profit boards have a much greater chance of staying true to their conservation mission. Passionate zoo and aquarium board members are more likely to understand the zoos conservation mission than a government appointed or elected council that has so many other important responsibilities, such as police and fire.

One downside in all cases of privatization has been increased costs to visit a zoo or an aquarium and participate in their programs. In the past when many more zoos were run by government agencies, zoo admission fees were very low. However, in the fifties and early sixties, zoos were not what they are today. Animals were in barred cages or behind chain-link fences, grounds were unclean, graphics were simple plastic etched signs with very little information of interest. If there was a food stand, it had only hot dogs and stale popcorn. There were few veterinarians working full-time and many animal keepers did not even have a high school degree. So maybe the good old days were not so good after all!

While I realize that all large organizations have many restrictive policies created by corporate lawyers and others to protect the organization, government organizations have more. Working for the City of Sacramento, I received a memo that stated I was not allowed to ride in a helicopter on city business. Certainly, not riding in a helicopter as director of a twelve-acre zoo was not on my mind. Many years later in Cleveland the local chapter of the American Association of Zookeepers (AAZK) had an event titled Winos for Rhinos. After the second year they were told that they could not advertise the event in official zoo publications and websites as these communications tools could not advertise an event with alcohol in the title. OK, I get it. It was a great title for a great event and I doubted that some really up tight taxpayer going to complain. I doubt it and even if they did, so what!

Both government-run and non-profit governing board members often state the organization needs to run more business-like. While profit may not be the sole motive, zoos and aquariums must use good business methods. Like it or not, there is competition for the leisure dollar. Here are some basic business practices that even a government–run zoo need to consider:

- Create great customer service

- Conduct market research – continuous evaluation
- Planning - Do a master plan, a strategic plan and a three-year plan
- Adapt, change when looking at trends
- Balance the budget
- Eliminate deadwood – terminate non-productive and non-cooperative staff

Some good business practices are applicable and many I have already mentioned, but a zoo or aquarium cannot be totally run like a business. First, the skills required of the leader are different. While some zoo or aquarium CEO/executive directors may have considerable authority for decisions, most do not have the concentrated decision-making power of a corporate CEO. For instance, at Cleveland Metroparks Zoo, I could only sign for purchases up to one-thousand dollars and the executive director of Cleveland Metroparks could only sign for purchases up to twenty-thousand dollars. The government or non-profit CEO must rely on persuasion, politics, reputation and creditability and understanding of the needs of others, particularly members of the governing board, to create an environment to move the zoo or aquarium in the right direction. Even though a zoo or aquarium director may not have the total authority to get some things done, they are still responsible for seeing that the right decisions are eventually made on behalf of the institution.

LEADERSHIP SUMMARY

- Have a vision (dream) and a plan. Keep it simple.
- Communicate that vision and plan with passion.
- Be the best you can be. Be honest with yourself about both your good and bad qualities. Be authentic. Lead by example. Have great work habits.
- Be responsive to everyone. Tell the truth. Be transparent.
- Listen. Learn. Adapt when necessary. Mission above yourself.

- Delegate, really delegate. Teams. Trust the people you lead. Support them, even if they make a mistake. Be grateful.
- Enjoy

One Last Word on Leadership

In a January 2011 letter from Brigham Hill Consultancy, one of the many search firms I met with over the years, apologetically tried to discuss leadership in a short three-page newsletter. They stated most of the qualities I discussed above including passion for the mission, intellectual curiosity, collaboration, vision and more. They also mentioned a question they ask of every client organization once they have established the obvious, the need for a visionary leader. The question was: Are you looking for a General George Patton or Mother Theresa? After the startled clients thought about the statement for a while and a discussion followed, the organization's culture was better understood. Great leaders come in different forms and while they may have similar traits, they can also be very different.

CHAPTER 4

ADVENTURES AT THE ZOO – SAVING WILDLIFE AND WILD PLACES

IN MY JOURNAL in February of 1990 I wrote the following: "I am more dedicated to wildlife than I am to zoos, and I am more dedicated to zoos than to Cleveland Metroparks Zoo. In order to accomplish this grander mission, I must work to see Cleveland Metroparks Zoo become the best it can be."

Twenty-five years ago, Desmond Morris, the famous British zoologist, wrote several articles on the pluses and minuses of zoos and aquariums and he concluded that good zoos and aquariums were an important asset to conservation education and must be supported. He went on to write the following:

"If zoos disappear, I fear that our vast urban populations will become so physically remote from animal life, they will cease to care about it. Eventually someone will find the animal equivalent of the plastic flower and that will be that. As I watch a child today encounter a group of zoo elephants for the first time, I see the child's eyes open wider than one might think possible, as my own did years ago, I have no doubt in my mind. The zoo must stay."

I seriously believe that I have been involved in a noble cause. While some still see the primary role of a modern zoo and aquarium as providing a community with a worthwhile public attraction, zoo professionals and others, sincerely believe that zoos and aquariums have a much loftier mission. Modern zoos and aquariums are truly conservation agencies. That is the mission that kept me interested. While work at times could be frustrating, it was always rewarding. Most the time, it was even fun.

The mission of saving wildlife and wild places is what separates good zoos and aquariums from the many other museums, attractions and institutions that zoos and aquariums compete with on a daily basis for attendance and financial resources. I certainly do not have all the answers on what it takes to run a successful zoo or aquarium, but I do think some zoos and aquariums, including a few in AZA, have strayed from their mission. I do not believe that having revenue generating activities that families can enjoy are inappropriate in a modern zoo or aquarium. Carousels, water parks and zip lines have helped zoos and aquariums balance the budget. However, in my opinion, they should never be a distraction to the zoo or aquarium either by being tacky or a distraction to an adjacent naturalistic exhibit. Viewing the most majestic animals on earth, such as a giraffe, with a roller coaster in the background, is not my idea of a modern zoo exhibit.

I believe that using live animals in education shows is appropriate as long as those shows depict the animal's natural state and have a conservation message. I believe that shows that concentrate only on amusing tricks taught to intelligent wild animals distract from the zoo and aquarium's mission. While guests may enjoy a sea lion show called "Flippers Role in the American Revolution," it does nothing for conservation of wildlife, not to mention depicting a very confusing view of American history.

In my forty years working in four different zoos, I had a blast! No one-day was the same and some had me laughing and gave me an opportunity to share stories. With that said, like any job, there were frustrations. Some of them I have already discussed. People I met at cocktail parties or at similar events often remarked to me that they thought I had the best job ever. They thought that I got to play with animals and walk around the zoo anytime I wished. As my friend and colleague, Satch Krantz, once confessed and I agreed; "walking through the zoo is one of the most stressful and frustrating things I do." Like Satch, I always saw things that upset me, such as overflowing trash cans, temporary yellow plastic warning tape still in place even though the reason for the tape had long since been corrected, a label covered with snow and more. No place is perfect, no matter how much you want it to be!

CONSERVATION PROGRAMS

When asked what I considered were my greatest accomplishments during my years in Cleveland, I always mention the development of the conservation and science unit at Cleveland Metroparks Zoo. I really can't take the credit because it was Dr. Hugh Quinn, general curator, at the time that kept pushing for the program. Eventually we found a way to start the program by applying for a federal Institute of Museum and Library Services (IMLS) grant. After it was awarded in 1995, the zoo hired Dr. Patricia McDaniel as the zoo's first coordinator of scientific research. She created partnerships with Cleveland State University and the University of Andes in Venezuela. Working with these two Universities, Hugh and Patty created a three-week college level course in Venezuela on tropical ecology and conservation biology. The zoo created a field office in Merida, Venezuela and began working with the Chorros de Milla Zoo in Merida. With local Venezuelan partners, primarily BIOANDINA, Cleveland Metroparks Zoo staff developed field projects for both the Andean condor and the spectacle bear. Several Cleveland Metroparks Zoo animal keepers traveled to Venezuela and helped staff at the Chorros de Milla Zoo enrich the animal exhibits. Over the years, Vicki Davison, Cleveland Metroparks Zoo's curator of education, taught zoo education in the

Chorros de Milla Zoo and Stan Searles, curator of birds worked on the reintroduction of the Andean condor. They obviously enjoyed their experiences there, as in 2002 they were married in Merida, Venezuela.

Dr. Patricia McDaniel left the zoo in 1998 and she was replaced with Dr. Tammie Bettinger. Under Tammie's leadership, the zoo continued its efforts in Venezuela, and with Tammie's interest in chimpanzees, the zoo added programs in Uganda. At that point, the name of the zoo's conservation and research effort was changed to conservation and science. About that time the zoo started managing the Scott Neotropical Fund that supported scientists in Central and South America. The donor continued to send funds to the Cleveland Zoological Society for Neotropical conservation throughout my career. In 2001, the Cleveland Metroparks Zoo and the Cleveland Zoological Society spent two-hundred and sixty-five thousand dollar on conservation projects, not including staff salaries.

As the Zoo's Uganda program was rapidly expanding, especially with the potential of expanding various local education and awareness programs, we sent three staff members to Uganda to move these programs forward. Accompanying Tammie was Sue Allen, manager of marketing and public relations and Christine Kornak, senior education specialist. Tammie arranged for a Ugandan guide, Cliff, to be their driver and guide. At first Cliff thought he had died and gone to heaven as he got to spend time with three single attractive American women. After a week it was reported he changed his mind when he found out the American women don't clean, don't cook, don't obey their husbands and do not necessarily want to have children.

When Tammie left to join the research department at Disney's Animal Kingdom, the zoo was extremely lucky to recruit Dr. Kristen Lukas from the Lincoln Park Zoo in 2002. With grants to the Cleveland Zoological Society secured by Dr. Quinn, the zoo hired Doug Hendrie to work in Asia on fresh-water turtle conservation. By this time Kym Gopp had moved from the position as lead animal keeper to associate conservation curator and managed the zoo's worldwide conservation programs. Other staff members were added later. After a few years in Cleveland, Dr. Lukas was appointed by AZA as the chair of the Gorilla SSP. Of all the SSP programs in AZA, the gorilla SSP has always been the most difficult to manage. Gorillas are very popular in zoos and all zoo directors want to have family troops. However, genetically managing these popular primates requires some over-represented females not to breed. It also requires some institutions to manage all male troops or non-breeding troops. To get some zoo directors to take what they perceive as a lesser role in the gorilla SSP is not always easy. Kristen has done a fantastic job as chair.

In 2012, my last year as director of Cleveland Metroparks Zoo, the zoo and Cleveland Zoological Society spent a total over five-hundred and sixty-seven thousand dollars on field conservation programs. The Cleveland Zoological Society in the Spring 2020 Z Magazine reported that in 2019 the zoo and the society contributed over a million dollars to various conservation programs. That certainly represents phenomenal growth in this significant conservation effort. During the same year, AZA's zoos and aquariums contributed an amazing two-hundred and thirty-two million dollars to field conservation programs in one-hundred and twenty-seven different countries.

I was extremely honored upon my retirement when the Cleveland Zoological Society created the Steve H. Taylor Conservation Award. The award was created to make it possible for a conservation partner working in Africa to attend an AZA conference or other professional training that would enhance the long-term capacity of successful field conservation initiatives in Africa.

PROMOTING THE ZOO

In his Apple office in 1982, Steve Jobs was asked if he wanted to do market research and he said,

"No, because customers don't know what they want until we've shown them."

Then Jobs quoted, Henry Ford, who reportedly said the following:

"If I asked customers what they wanted, they would have told me, a faster horse."

That thinking was important in many of the zoo decisions, especially when choosing new species for the collection. Those decisions were complicated and involved many factors and customer input was only one part. More important factors were the appropriateness of the facility for the welfare of those animals and the importance of the species to the zoo's conservation effort. If left solely to customer input, Cleveland Metroparks Zoo should have acquired giant pandas and never would have acquired naked mole rats, onagers or fossa.

One of the most creative parts of being a zoo director was finding new ways to promote the zoo each season. It was easy when the zoo was opening a new exhibit and the zoo's marketing campaign could concentrate primarily on that event. Most new exhibits raised attendance and membership for an entire year after their opening. The RainForest, Wolf Wilderness, Australian Adventure and the African Elephant Crossing did just that for Cleveland Metroparks Zoo and the Cleveland Zoological Society. For the other twenty years of my career at Cleveland Metroparks Zoo, staff had to develop other ways to promote the zoo. As I mentioned previously in my discussion on persistence, for a half a dozen years we relied on a temporary display of twenty robotic dinosaurs. In fact, the Zoo's second-best year ever was 2003 the first year the Zoo exhibited robotic dinosaurs.

There are relatively few commercially available temporary/traveling exhibits available to zoos, unless a zoo had a large indoor space. Cleveland Metroparks Zoo had only one indoor space available for such exhibits and that was by combining the auditorium, which was used for many other functions, and a small, fifteen-hundred-square-foot exhibit hall. We only used this four-thousand square-foot space once for a seasonal exhibit and that was in 2010 when we hosted an unusual exhibit from Peeling Productions, entitled Scoop on Poop.

This very clever exhibit only had a couple live animals, including mice, a turtle and cockroaches, but the exhibits were interactive and educational. While it was very educational and did make guests smile, I don't believe it made a big difference in the zoo's attendance.

Of course, the main draw of any zoo is its animals. While most zoos and aquariums have fairly stable animal collections, new animals, like new exhibits, can renew enthusiasm. Gray Clarke, director of the World's Famous Topeka Zoo from 1963 – 1989, found many innovative ways to promote his zoo. First of all, it was a small zoo in a relatively small city, but it was always referred to as the World's Famous Topeka Zoo. Secondly, more than any other director, he knew how to use animal stories to promote his zoo. Many of the Topeka Zoo's (Sorry – the World's Famous Topeka Zoo's) promotions were similar to things zoos do today although a few may be a little outdated. He was one of the first to do a temporary loan of koalas from the San Diego Zoo. To obtain the koalas on temporary loan from San Diego he formed a K-team of several hundred Topeka citizens and businesses to raise funds for the display. Early on in his career he created Operations Noah where businesses created coupons to help their business and the zoo acquire animals. When he introduced his male gorilla, Max, to the new female, Tiffany, he promoted the event as Breakfast at Tiffany's! He loved naming animals from the boa named Julius Squeezer to the hippo named Submarie. My personal favorite was two wildebeest, also referred to as gnus, named Weather and Sports. He then could use the phrase, Gnus, Weather and Sports when referring to these animals. I have often recommended Gary Clarke's book, *Hey Mister – Your Alligator is Loose*, to anyone new to the zoo and aquarium profession that was interested in promoting his or her zoo or aquarium.

At Cleveland Metroparks Zoo, we did our share of acquiring unique animals on a temporary basis. These loans were potentially controversial, as some individuals were critical of wildlife being relocated just for a promotion. Never-the-less, when certain precautions were taken during transfer and exhibition, these promotions did not necessarily cause unnecessary stress. During my tenure we promoted white tigers, white alligators, Komodo dragons, and a wonderful interactive exhibit of stingrays and sharks, entitled, Touch.

Events are part of any zoo or aquarium's marketing strategy. Aside from fund-raising events sponsored by the Cleveland Zoological Society, Cleveland Metroparks Zoo had many different attendance generating events; some continued for years and some came and went. Boo at the Zoo, an eight-night Halloween event was always successful with attendance for the eight nights around 40,000 guests. So many American zoos and aquariums had similar Halloween events that Dennis Kelly, then director of the Smithsonian's National Zoo stated, "AZA zoos and aquariums own Halloween."

Many zoos have also been successful with events around the Christmas holiday, although not so with Cleveland. For approximately ten years the zoo hosted Holiday Lights, a twenty-evening event that never made a profit and never attracted more that seventy-thousand guests. Many zoos, including those zoos in Columbus, Cincinnati, Toledo, and Phoenix did very well and attracted over one-hundred and fifty-thousand guests annually to their holiday event. I was never certain why Cleveland Metroparks Zoo was not more successful. Staff felt that it was a combination of high labor costs for setting up the exhibit and staffing it with overtime in the evening. Other reasons may have been competition in the area during the holiday season and Cleveland's unpredictable and often rainy weather. Despite its financial failure, it was still a difficult decision and not a popular one with many staff and volunteers when I cancelled Holiday Lights. I felt like the Grinch that Stole Christmas. To make certain my mind wouldn't change, I immediately sold most of the zoo's strings of lights and displays.

A few years after I retired, the staff of the zoo brought back Holiday Lights using an outside contractor to install the lights, thus cutting labor costs. They also realized that they could charge much more than we had charged in the past. They created a successful and profitable event.

Over the years there were many one-day events that were a great success. They included Meet Your Best Friend at the Zoo where the zoo hosted local humane groups outside the entrance and guests could adopt domestic animals and learn about these organizations. In 2006, the zoo started Noon Year's Eve, a celebration of the New Year during the day on December 31 attracting five-thousand guests each year. Other ongoing events included Teddy Bear Day, Creature Comforts, highlighting the zoo's animal enrichment program, ZooBlooms, an event highlighting the horticultural aspects of the zoo, Photo Safari, Senior Safari, Thanksgiving at the Zoo and much more.

One of my favorite promotions at Cleveland Metroparks Zoo occurred in the summer of 2008 when the zoo showcased some of its new animals and called the event, Frogs, Hogs and Dogs. The zoo was able to accomplish several goals by providing this unique promotion. First, it allowed the zoo to add several new amphibian species in the RainForest and helped celebrate a national event, The Year of the Frog. Secondly, the zoo utilized its talented maintenance staff in constructing a New Guinea singing dog exhibit in Australia Adventure, a major addition to that eight-year old area of the zoo. And thirdly, mostly to make the promotion rhyme, the zoo acquired red river hogs on a short-term loan.

In 2012, one small zoo I know of tried to promote a non-event and I doubted that it was successful. This zoo in the middle of the country had many problems since it was first opened in the nineties. Most of its troubles were financial as it was a non-profit zoo with no government support in a relatively small town. It was accredited by AZA for a while (in fact I was chair of its inspection team) but lost its accreditation in 2011. The zoo seemed to have a new director every year. While the various directors tried their best, none were actually able to turn the zoo around. One newspaper article in fall of 2012 illustrated the point. The article, zoo confident its newest animal will be a big hit announced the acquisition of Fierca, a one-year old, twenty-five-pound playful Canada lynx. The article went on to suggest that Fierca could boost attendance, despite the loss of several of its most popular animals since the AZA pulled its accreditation in 2011. Those animals included grizzly bear cubs, two Siberian tigers and a wolverine. Aside from the one lynx, the article goes on to mention that the zoo also added a savannah monitor, green aracaris, an iguana, a gopher snake and several koi. Now I am a big fan of zoos and aquariums exhibiting more than just charismatic mega-vertebrates but replacing tigers and grizzly bears with a lynx and some reptiles and a pair of birds wasn't going to do a darn thing to boost attendance. After a few years, a new director was hired and he improved just about everything in the zoo and it regained its AZA accreditation.

THE ANIMALS

There are many great stories involving the amazingly clever orangutan. Jonathan, an orangutan at the Los Angeles Zoo, was a particular favorite of mine when I worked as an animal keeper in the Eurasian section of the zoo. During my first few years at the Los Angeles Zoo, I was involved in hand-raising young Jonathan prior to his move to the Eurasian section. One day when I was assigned to that section of the zoo, a guest called me over to tell me that Jonathan, who was about five or six years old, had a screw in his mouth. I immediately went behind the scenes and found some grapes to make a trade. Trading food items for other items is a common practice with keepers working with orangutans. When I entered Jonathan's exhibit, an orangutan that I knew quite well, it appeared that he was not in possession of any hardware. I was perplexed. Then I heard a tapping on the window of the exhibit. The guests that originally made me aware of the problem had the screw and were tapping it on the glass. When I asked how they now had the screw, they stated that Jonathan saw me coming and he threw the screw through the overhead mesh to the outside! I gave Jonathan a few grapes anyway. Jonathan eventually went to Topeka Zoo, then the Buffalo Zoo before, like me, ended up at Cleveland Metroparks Zoo. While I could never scientifically prove it, believe he recognized me when I would visit him in the RainForest.

Like Jonathan, all orangutans are famous for hiding things in their ample lips. One of the most famous zoo stories that I had been told concerned an orangutan at the Omaha Zoo in the sixties that used a wire from his lip to pick locks of his holding cage. The first night he left his night quarters and created quite a mess in the night quarters/equipment room area. Staff assumed that someone had left a door unlocked. After several nights of the same thing and the keepers taking extra precautions to assure that all doors were locked prior to leaving for the evening, the staff decided to stay quietly in the area and observed the clever orang at night. After the orang assumed the staff had vacated the building, he took a wire from his upper lip and proceeded to pick the lock on his holding cage. Amazing! By trading wire for grapes, the keepers managed to retrieve the wire tool and this male orang had to sleep through the night safely in his night quarters. Word spread of this amazing endeavor and it just so happened that there was a locksmith convention in town and this clever orang was given an honorary membership to the locksmith's association.

Dr. George Rabb, director of the Brookfield Zoo in Chicago, stopped by the Sacramento Zoo in August 1988 and I proudly showed him the zoo's relatively new exhibit for orangutans. He entertained the keepers with a story about early orangutan intelligence studies undertaken by the staff of the Brookfield Zoo. A female orang named, Ginger, was the subject and the test of intelligence was a shell game. The researcher put a banana under one of three different shaped cups and Ginger was very quick to recognize which shape gave her a reward of a banana. The next day Ginger took a short cut and just simply knocked all the cups off the table and grabbed the banana. On the third day the not so patient Ginger saw the keeper bringing in the bananas and simply walked over to the keeper, hit her on the side of the head, and grabbed the whole bunch of bananas!

By far my favorite orangutan story I heard concerned a female orang at the Louisville Zoo who truly enjoyed her new state-of-the art orangutan exhibit that was built around 2004. Like many newer exhibits it had a series of elaborate overhead passages in the holding area, giving the keeper maximum flexibility when moving animals from one area to another. One passage often utilized by the orangs had a clear view of the facility's washer and dryer where keepers would launder their own uniforms. After about two years in this new exhibit and watching keepers do laundry, this female orang escaped one night into the keeper area. This particular orang had only one interest and that was to do the laundry since she had observed the process so many times. She did everything perfectly, including opening the lid, putting laundry in the tub, turning the proper dials, closing the lid and starting the machine. There was only one thing she did not do correctly. She did not measure out the detergent. And as a matter of fact, she poured the whole box of powdered detergent into the washing machine! When staff came to work the next morning, suds were everywhere. Looking along the hall between cages above a couple of feet of suds was the head of one very cleaver female orangutan.

As a relief keeper at the Los Angeles Zoo, I spent many days in the animal nursery. As children's zoo manager at the San Francisco Zoo I was in charge of that animal nursery. So early in my career, I helped hand-raise many interesting animals. They included oryx, water buffalo, serval (African cat), tapir, camel, tiger, snow leopard, but none were more interesting than the great apes. At one point the Los Angeles Zoo animal nursery had an infant chimp, orangutan and gorilla all at one time. During the day all three were together in one exhibit. I learned much about the differences between the apes from watching these three delightful infant animals. Marilee Levin was the night keeper at the children's zoo and took care of all the hand-raised animals from 4 PM until midnight. She had an excellent observation concerning the differences between the three baby great apes. She stated that her observation was just for young great apes, but I felt it also works well for adult apes. Marilee's statement went like this, "A chimp looks at you and says, wow - you are a human being. An orangutan looks at you and says, you are not an orangutan. And a gorilla looks at you and says, I'm a gorilla!" I must admit that from my more than forty years working with all three great apes in four different zoos, the statement described these fascinating apes very well.

With two other animal keepers and a hand-raised gorilla, chimp and orangutan at the Los Angeles Zoo.

Lena was the first gorilla I ever worked with in a zoo. She was born at the Los Angeles Zoo in 1973, shortly after I started as an animal keeper. She was a special ape, the first gorilla born at the zoo and named after animal keeper, Bob Wolf's, wife. Bob was the gorilla keeper for his entire career at the zoo. On one March 18th I received a birthday gift for my son Travis from your friends at 357, the exhibit number for the zoo's gorilla troop. This was a very kind jester on Bob's behalf and it wasn't until I left the zoo that I realized that Bob shared Travis and my birthday, March 18. Lena was transferred to the Albuquerque Zoo in 1992 where she lived until she was thirty-nine-*years old*. She is mentioned in Betty White's, *Betty and Friends: My Life at the Zoo*. In the book, White says animals like Lena helped shape her life. I certainly had the same feeling from working with Lena for the first four years of her life.

I believe the most beautiful antelope in the world is the bongo and Cleveland Metroparks Zoo played an important role in the zoo world's history of exhibiting bongo. In 1959, a trustee of the Cleveland Zoological Society, Col. B. C. Goss, no relation to Dr. Leonard Goss, zoo director, was in Kenya and managed to purchase a young female Bongo. This orphaned bongo, later named Karen after a suburb outside Nairobi, was hand-raised by Alan Root, a young English nature photographer. Bongo Days were celebrated at the zoo on July 3,4, and 5, 1959 and the zoo received national press and Karen became a star attraction. In July 1963, a young male named Biff, after trustee Col. B. C. "Biff" Goss, joined Karen. While there had been a few bongos in zoos in the United States prior to Karen and Biff, this was the first time a pair had been seen together. Everyone was hopeful of a first breeding, but unfortunately it never happened. Karen passed away in October 1972 and Biff was sent to the Milwaukee Zoo to be with that zoo's female bongos.

Early in 1992, zoo staff members were looking for something to promote prior to opening the RainForest in the fall. I suggested the zoo bring bongos back to the Cleveland Metroparks Zoo and our promotion became, the Bongos are Back! The new pair of bongos were put in their old exhibit with an adjacent new barn built by the zoo's facilities staff. These bongos did quite well, producing several calves while at the zoo. To make room for the African Elephant Crossing, bongos had to be deleted from the collection. I was sorry to see one of my favorite animal species leave the zoo.

All four zoos in my career had koalas. While I was director of the Sacramento Zoo, the zoo had a successful temporary two-week koala exhibit. However, my first long-term experience with koalas occurred when Cleveland Metroparks Zoo decided that the zoo must have koalas in the new Australian Adventure exhibit that opened in

June 2000. I say the zoo decided but it was really the idea of commissioner Rzepka that the zoo built a koala exhibit. Koalas were not in the original plan. As a practical matter, koalas are one of the most expensive animals to house in a zoo, especially in a northern climate zoo where eucalyptus must be shipped to the zoo twice a week. The cost to feed each animal was approximately forty-thousand dollars a year! In addition, indoor/outdoor koala exhibits are expensive to construct. None-the-less, commission Rzepka felt if the zoo was to build a major exhibit of Australian animals, we must have koalas. Who was I to argue? Besides that, as usual, he was right!

Almost immediately the koala exhibit was a complete success. Zoo guests loved it and the animals were prolific. The only problem was that guests had trouble finding the heavily themed koala building as the only identification on the building was Gum Leaf Hideout. Guests wanted to know where to find the koalas. The problem was solved when the zoo added a couple of drawings of koalas on the outside. The building had two indoor exhibits, one for koalas and one for tree kangaroos. They both were beautiful exhibits with background murals of an eucalyptus forest and planted with Australian plants, including live eucalyptus trees that grew well under the skylights.

The zoo's one male, Ouraka age three, and two female koalas, Midgee and Colliet, both age two, were on loan from the San Diego Zoo. They began to breed almost immediately. It was not long before Cleveland Metroparks Zoo produced more koala joeys that any other zoo in the United States, except for the San Diego Zoo. By 2007, we had had eleven koala joeys, much to the delight of the zoo's staff and guests. This was a great success story and we decided it was worth an information item on the Board of Park Commissioners agenda. To make the koala success story even more memorable, I further explained that to sire eleven offspring, the male Ouraka, had only been with the females a total of about forty minutes! Males are quick when the females are in estrous and after mating, they need to be removed immediately as the happy couples would begin to fight. The story was of great interest to the commissioners and others at the board meeting! Also, this fact was fun to talk about on behind-the-scenes tours of the koala building.

Prior to my arrival as zoo director, Cleveland Metroparks Zoo opened a new rhino exhibit in 1985. Two white rhinos shared the exhibit with cheetahs. It was an outstanding example of a successful mixed species exhibit and I was always surprised that there were not similar exhibits elsewhere. However, black rhinos were more endangered as the entire wild population had been reduced from seventy thousand to less than three thousand from 1970 to 1989. The zoo made a decision to switch to black rhinos.

In 1994, the zoo acquired a male black rhino, Spike, from the Cincinnati Zoo. In July 1997, with the help of the International Rhino Foundation and AZA, the zoo received Inge, a female black rhino from South Africa's Addo Elephant National Park. Her journey to Cleveland took her from Johannesburg through Amsterdam and New York under the watchful eyes of the zoo's mammal curator, Alan Sironen and consulting veterinarian, Dr. Tony Lesh. South African veterinarian, Pete Morkel, also accompanied Inge to her new home in Cleveland. The entire move cost the zoo and the zoological society approximately seventy thousand dollars. Most of these funds went to the South African National Park System to improve their conservation efforts with southern black rhinos. Prior to the decline in the black rhino population throughout Africa, the South African National Park System relocated a number of eastern black rhinos from Tanzania to Addo for their protection. Over twenty years the population grew to over forty animals and the South African National Park System decided to concentrate only on southern black rhinos and sent the eastern black rhinos to zoos, back to Tanzania or other range countries.

The zoo's black rhino program was successful and eighty-pound Azizi was born on August 31, 2000. In 2003, Kabibi was born to the zoo's rhino pair. To prevent inbreeding, Spike was sent to another zoo and a male rhino, Jimma, came from Potter Park Zoo in Lansing, Michigan. This pair's first calf, Zuri, was born in 2007. In 2010, Zuri was sent to the Portland Zoo, while her mom, Inge, and

Kabibi, remained in Cleveland with male Jimma. Since that time, Inge became a grandmother when Juba was born in January 2011. The zoo continued to have a successful breeding program as a total of seven calves had been born by June 2020. The Daniel Maltz Rhino Reserve replaced the eighty-year old antiquated WPA constructed monkey island exhibit adjacent to the rhino exhibit. I believe that this was the last of many WPA constructed concrete monkey islands in the country! Utilizing the space made available with the demolition of monkey island, the zoo has more than doubled the outdoor space for the black rhinos. In addition, a much-needed bull barn was added.

For many people, zoos are all about lions and tigers and bears. By that I mean guests mostly want to see popular and well-known animals. However, zoo directors and curators get really excited about an unusual animal. In 2002, Cleveland Metroparks Zoo acquired on loan a two-year old male fossa from the San Antonio Zoo. Fossa is pronounced "foosh" as many children learned while watching the Disney movie Madagascar. At that time there were only six other zoos in North America with fossa on exhibit. Native to Madagascar, this endangered carnivore species is distantly related to mongoose and civets. At one point they were all in the same family, Viverridae. Since then this family of carnivores has been divided to three differ-ent families, one for civets, one for mongoose and a third, Eupleridae, includes eight species of mongoose-like animals all from Madagascar and includes the fossa. In the wild, these nocturnal predators feed on lemurs and other small animals. The staff at the zoo was extremely happy that four healthy fossa kits were born in 2004.

Early in my career I spent quite a bit of time in the Los Angeles Children's Zoo. It really wasn't so much of a children's zoo as a collec-tion of animals having no other home in other more themed areas of the zoo. One interesting animal was the echidna, an Australian egg-laying mammal that lives underground (eggs are placed in a pouch) and is related to the duck-billed platypus. They protect themselves with porcupine-type quills. They have to be one of the world's most bizarre animals. They are a little larger than a house cat and look like a cross between a porcupine and an anteater, with a bit of tortoise thrown in! They walk around the ground sticking their long nose in rotting logs and soil searching for termites. Their walk is somewhat comical, like much of what they do, because their rear feet appear to be put on backwards. Without a doubt, echidnas are one of the most bizarre creatures on earth.

Like many zoos in the United States, the Los Angeles Zoo had a successful adopt-an-animal program where supporters could donate various amounts of money and get the privilege of naming that animal. At the Los Angeles Zoo, donors received a bronze plaque on the exhibit of their adopted animal. Well who do you think would adopt the bizarre echidna? It was rocker Frank Zappa's children, Moon and Dweezil. Given their somewhat unusual names one would think that echidna would get the same. No, they named the echidna, Evelyn!

Years later Cleveland Metroparks Zoo acquired echidna for the new Australian Adventure that opened in 2000. I realized that these burrowing animals are very secretive, but still thought they would be a nice addition. In fact, Sue Allen, manager of public relations and marketing never saw one for ten years after their acquisition despite many calls to her office announcing that the echidnas were out of their shallow burrows in the koala building.

In 2011, when Cleveland Metroparks Zoo opened African Elephant Crossing, the indoor space had an exhibit for naked mole rats, certainly a mammal just as bazaar as the echidna. As with most zoos, Cleveland's exhibit looked like a giant ant farm as these fossorial (living underground) rodents could only be viewed in that manner. If their naked appearance with very small eyes and ears were not bazaar enough, their behaviors were. They live in large colonies of up to eighty individuals with only one breeding female, the queen, and she breeds with only two or three males. The rest of the colony members are workers, acquiring food of tubers and other roots. Their behaviors resemble colonial bees or ants. They are virtually cold blooded, similar to reptiles. What is most amazing is that they can live over twenty-five years, while a normal life span of other small rodents is only two or three years.

A favorite animal of mine has always been the giant anteater and I was very happy when Cleveland Metroparks Zoo opened the RainForest in 1992 with an exhibit for giant anteaters. As I mentioned previously, my interest in giant anteaters may have been due to Peter the anteater, the mascot for my Alma Mater, the University of California at Irvine. With their long snout, diagonal black and white shoulder stripe and long bushy tail, the giant anteater looks like no other animal on earth. Their twenty-four-inch sticky tongue can be pushed out one-hundred and fifty times a minute in order to gather up ants from nests they open up using their sharp powerful claws. While staff worked very hard to produce baby anteaters, none were born for the first twenty years of the RainForest. However, in December 2013, eleven months after my retirement, a baby anteater was born. While I had seen baby anteaters at the Santa Barbara Zoo, it was great to finally see one riding on its mother's back at Cleveland Metroparks Zoo.

One of Cleveland Metroparks Zoo's most unusual births was actually a blooming. After thirteen years of waiting, zoo horticulturists were very proud to announce the rare blooming of a corpse flower, (Titum arum), on July 23, 2007. The corpse flower is one of the largest flowering plants in the world and gets its name from its pungent odor. Despite the odor, seven thousand guests came to the RainForest to view the short-lived bloom of this very rare flower.

ELEPHANTS AND HIPPOS

Animals have senses we cannot completely understand. When I heard a story like this one, I was inclined to believe it. Meghan, one of our young female animal keepers had been told that she and her husband could not have children. She noticed one of the zoo's elephants, Moshi, was acting very strange towards her. Moshi seemed particularly unruly when Meghan wasn't near. When Meghan was working with Moshi, this female elephant wouldn't stop putting her trunk on Meghan's stomach. Shortly after this Meghan found out the joyous news, she was pregnant! The story doesn't end there. A couple years later, the elephant team noticed that the female elephant, Jo, kept touching Meghan's stomach. Mitch, the lead keeper, asked Meghan if she was pregnant and Meghan then went to her doctor and sure enough, she was once again pregnant. Coincidence – maybe!

During my entire career in four zoos, I had many experiences with elephants, some good and some not so good. The death of an elephant was always dramatic for everyone at the zoo. It was always of interest to media, especially in the last twenty years as the animal rights extremists increased their opposition to keeping elephants in zoos. In 1995, two of the three Cleveland Metroparks Zoo's African elephants died unexpectedly. Simba, a forty-two-year old elephant was brought to the zoo by Fred Crawford and Vernon Stouffer, members of the Zoological Society Board of Directors, in October 1955. She died of circulatory problems caused by tumors in her adrenal and thyroid glands. Less than a month later, eighteen-year old Tribby fell on exhibit and never got up. She died of a severe congestion in her lungs. The cause of this congestion was never determined. Zoo animal deaths when the cause is not determined, although common with zoo animals and not particularly uncommon in human medicine, are always the most difficult on staff. In addition, the necropsy, an autopsy for animals, of an elephant is just plain gross! There is no other word for it. I briefly watched four in my career, not something I will ever forget. I never forced any staff member to participate, but most felt it was their duty and did participate.

For two years, 1996 and 1997, Cleveland Metroparks Zoo did not have elephants on exhibit. Staff used the time to update the building by adding an Elephant Restraining Device (ERD). For years we called ERDs elephant squeezes but changed to the more universally accepted ERD! While guests understood that we needed to have elephants out of their facility during renovation, many guests complained about not being able to see the elephants during their visit to the zoo.

In January 2005, directors of AZA institutions housing elephants met at Disney's Animal Kingdom to discuss the future of elephants in

North American zoos. It was one of the most important AZA meetings I ever attended. A total of seventy-eight directors heard first-hand the status of the African and Asian elephants in North American zoos and then formulated a plan for their future.

Here is some of what we collectively knew at the time:

1. AZA zoos had about 300 animals about equally divided between the African and Asian species. Neither population was self-sustaining.
2. In 2004, the San Diego Zoo and the Lowry Park Zoo imported ten African elephants from Swaziland, Southern Africa. This was the first importation in over twenty-five years.
3. There were approximately another three hundred elephants kept in North America, outside AZA accredited zoos.
4. The European zoo population of elephants was more robust than the North American population since they had imported over one-hundred animals over the last twenty-five years.

Then, the group developed a plan of action and here are a few of the most important action steps developed during the meeting:

1. Conservation is the primary reason why AZA institutions care for elephants.
2. More institutions need to commit to holding males.
3. Investigate the potential of an elephant conservation center.
4. Increase the commitment to *in-situ* (in the wild) conservation programs and research.
5. Improve facilities, husbandry standards and staff training.
6. Explore working with non-AZA facilities.
7. Create a pro-active public relations campaign and speak with a consistent and unified voice.
8. AZA elephant facilities will continue to use "all the tools in the toolbox" in regard to caring for elephants, including protective contact, free contact and the combination of the two.

And finally, at that meeting the directors adopted a vision statement for keeping Asian and African elephants in North American zoos. That statement was as follows:

AZA is comprised of caring, trusted, experts committed to ensuring that elephants are a part of the world's future. Through our conservation, education, and research programs, elephants in our care play an essential role in the survival of the species in the wild. AZA advocates on behalf of all elephants with a unified and consistent voice and collaborates with others committed to the long-term survival of elephants.

Since that meeting, I believe that AZA zoos have made tremendous progress on all the action plans developed at the 2005 meeting. New training for everyone involved in elephant care from keepers to zoo directors became mandatory. Just about every AZA zoo made some renovations to their facilities to better care for their existing elephants including the addition of elephant restraining devices. Many zoos including those in Birmingham, Los Angeles, Tucson, Houston, Syracuse, Oklahoma, Pittsburgh, North Carolina, Dallas, Portland, Denver, San Diego and Cleveland made major improvements or created new exhibits for elephants. A few zoos decided not to make the huge investment and stopped exhibiting elephants. And several AZA members formed the independent National Elephant Center and after some false starts, opened a two-hundred and fifty-acre facility near Fellsmere in central Florida in 2013. This center along with all the AZA zoos with new facilities would hopefully allow for zoos to develop self-sustaining populations of both species of elephants. Unfortunately, the center was forced to close after a few years. While there are still challenges ahead, I believe the future for elephants in zoos is bright.

Despite improvements in facilities and care, there were still keeper injuries, and even deaths, of keepers in AZA institutions after the 2005 meeting. This reopened the discussion between those that advocated free-contact, contact with elephant with no barrier, and protective contact occurring behind a barrier. More and more zoos moved to protective contact and every AZA zoo was mandated to have facilities for protective contact. Still some felt that they were safe managing their elephants in free contact and some zoos still walked their elephants around their zoos. Currently, AZA requires accredited zoos to use protective contact, but allows for free contact in special cases when many safe-guards are in place. For example, during birth and veterinary care, some feel that free contact is very important. I believe that serious injuries and/or deaths of elephant keepers are now a thing of the past with AZA zoos.

I was very proud of Cleveland Metroparks Zoo and the Cleveland Zoological Society role in exhibiting elephants. Cleveland Metroparks Zoo has utilized protective contact in managing their elephants since 1997 and improved upon this method when the African Elephant Crossing (AEC) opened in 2011. Certainly, one of the highlights of my zoo career was the opening of African Elephant Crossing. The twenty-five-million-dollar exhibit opened with three large outdoor yards and seven indoor stalls with six elephants, one male and five females.

During planning for the AEC, it became apparent that the elephants could not stay at the zoo during construction as the Pachyderm building would need major renovation and the interior would be gutted. I talked with my friend and colleague, Jerry Borin, director of the Columbus Zoo as they had several exhibits that could handle elephants. While they only had Asian elephants at the time, at one time the zoo exhibited both species. Jerry and his staff agreed to do us a favor and made space available for Cleveland Metroparks Zoo's elephants, but we would have to care for them during their time in Columbus. Fortunately, two keepers very dedicated to the zoo's elephants, Mitch Zverina and June Madamba, agreed to move temporarily to Columbus to care for the three elephants. In the summer of 2008, I traveled to Columbus to make the final plans and rent an apartment for the zoo's keepers, not too far from the Columbus Zoo. After a while, the zoo hired Mike Zinter as a third elephant keeper and he worked his first year in Columbus. Ed Novak safely moved Jo, Moshi and Martika to the Columbus Zoo on September 2, 2008. As the truck could only move two elephants at a time, the entire operation took two trips back and forth. The three elephants and the staff stayed in Columbus until November 30, 2010 when they all returned to Cleveland (two years, two months and twenty-eight days). Cleveland Metroparks Zoo staff members were very appreciative that the Columbus Zoo allowed us to house the zoo's elephants at their zoo. It is another great example how AZA zoos and aquariums are often very cooperative with each other.

Until right before we moved elephants into the new exhibit, I was not certain that the zoo would have elephants. Yes, the zoo had three older African elephants in temporary facilities at the Columbus Zoo, but they were older and there was no guarantee that they would all be fine when we finished construction. For several years I let it be known that Cleveland Metroparks Zoo would like to have additional African elephants. Purchasing one of the few African elephants available from a private party was out of the question as the price could be as high as a million dollars. We had been talking to John Lehnhardt, then with Disney's Animal Kingdom and he thought that a non-breeding male, Willy, might be available, but could make no promises. In the end we successfully moved the zoo's three elephants back from Columbus and Willy came to Cleveland. Then the Henry Doorly Zoo in Omaha lost one of their two African elephants, so the remaining elephant, Shinga, came to Cleveland. After we opened, the Pittsburgh Zoo acquired three additional elephants and wanted to move one of their older females to Cleveland. Amazing, the Cleveland Metroparks Zoo had six African elephants!

While the original design for the AEC included an exhibit for Nile hippos, that exhibit proved too expensive for the zoo's budget, approximately another five million dollars. The staff then had to make a decision concerning Blackie, a male hippo that had been at the zoo since coming from Tanzania, then Tanganyika, on October 22, 1955, making him well over fifty years of age when the zoo started planning a new exhibit. It was obvious that no other zoo would take this old male hippo and staff members were also concerned that he would not survive a long move, as he could not stand for long periods of time. Blackie's life was very simple. In the morning he would come out of his indoor pool and either go to his outside exhibit (summer only) or go into an adjacent stall for breakfast. After eating he would go into a clean pool until the evening and then reverse the process, spending the night in his indoor pool using the steps for a pillow.

After considerable discussion and an unrelated decision to build an extension to the giraffe barn, it was decided to construct one stall in the new giraffe barn with a pool for Blackie. Staff felt that Blackie could retire to the giraffe barn. When he passed away, which could have been in a month or ten years, the pool would be demolished, a floor added and the stall would be used for giraffe. Now staff had a couple years to plan how to get Blackie out of the Pachyderm building to his new home in the giraffe barn. The zoo happened to have a very large crate that came with a new black rhino and it appeared to me to be more than adequate to move Blackie. Alan Sironen, the zoo's very knowledgeable, but often overly cautious curator of mammalogy (although I was always grateful for his caution) felt it was not quite large enough. We had our maintenance staff work for a week or two and enlarge this substantial crate. They did a great job and even Alan was satisfied. The very heavy crate was craned into the outside hippo yard and placed in front of the exit door. Food was placed in the crate so Blackie could get accustomed to being in the crate. The giraffe barn expansion project was completed just in time as demolition of the Pachyderm building started in the fall of 2008. On the morning of October 7, 2008, Blackie entered the crate for breakfast. On this day the door was dropped behind him. A huge rented crane lifted the heavy crate onto a nearby truck and the truck drove Blackie to his new home. The crane followed and when it reached the giraffe barn, cables from the crane were again attached to the crate and it was lowered to a position in front of the modified giraffe stall. Observing from an elevated deck in the barn, we all watched Blackie enter his new home and walk right into the pool. The only problem with his new home was that it was not viewable by the zoo's guests. However, Blackie was the star of many behind the scenes tours.

A few weeks after the successful move of Blackie to his new home in the giraffe barn in the very expensive custom metal crate, Alan told me a story about another zoo that transferred their hippo in a large dumpster. Wow! I hope we have a chance to use the crate again and then the expense in time and materials will make me feel better.

ZOO PEOPLE

I have met so many interesting people throughout my life I certainly cannot list them all. Some, such as my early teachers and bosses have already been mentioned. However, a few others should be mentioned here as they also had interesting stories.

Coming to Cleveland Metroparks Zoo in 1989, one thing was very apparent. The food and gift concessions were awful. Old-style carnival type concessionaires ran both with little interest in excellent service or quality of product.

Lenny Luxenburg operated the gift concession and was a wonderful character who eventually changed the way he did business by improving his product line and became a good friend of mine and many other staff. Early on I convinced him that cheap inflatable animals were not the type of merchandise that belonged in a fine zoo gift shop. He took the direction and before I knew it, a dumpster was full of tacky inflatable animals. Ironically, one of our own educators did not get the message that I was trying to change the zoo's image and she dug all these ugly inflatable animals out of the dumpster. When I came to the zoo to observe the zoo's Easter Bunny event, there was the Easter Bunny up on the stage of the auditorium surrounded by yellow, pale blue, pink and orange inflatable animals! All I could do was laugh and realize it would take more than a couple of months to change the culture at Cleveland Metroparks Zoo.

As I stated, Lenny stayed at the zoo for many years, forming a partnership with a younger associate. Lenny would never tell us his age, but he was certainly in his eighties when he formed the partnership in 1992. While occasionally we would have to go through his store and ask him to delete some of the tackiest merchandise, he upgraded the merchandise considerably and the zoo, Lenny and our guests all were pleased with the results. One of many items over the years I had him remove was a popgun packaged in a clear bag that had a target over a lion to illustrate its use. Even Lenny had to agree that was probably inappropriate!

Another gentleman operated the food concessions at Cleveland Metroparks Zoo when I arrived in 1989 and his best offering was a Tom Cat Burger. Many on the staff joked that it was an accurate description of the burger! On a busy day he operated the register himself yelling at guests to make up their mind or step aside. When we opened the RainForest in 1992 and bid out the food and gift concession, his contract was not renewed.

In 1992 Novelty Ventures, Lenny Luxenburg's company, was awarded the gift concession and Ogden, later they became Aramark, was awarded the food concession. Payments to the zoo went from a few hundred thousand dollars a year to over a million. After a few years, Event Network won the bid to be the zoo's gift concessionaire. Since that time, professional food and gift concessionaires have been an important part of Cleveland Metroparks Zoo's success. While some zoos and aquariums have been successful in operating their own food, catering and gift shops, zoos and aquariums that have used concessionaires like those above and Service Systems Associates have greatly improved their revenue.

As we were preparing to have new concession contracts and open the new thirty-five million-dollar RainForest exhibit in 1992, we discovered that the RainForest was actually in a dry ward of the City and we would not be able to sell alcohol, even for events, rentals or wedding receptions. That had to change. The only way to make the change was to have an election and hope voters in that ward would vote to allow alcohol sales in their ward. We worked hard by going door to door to educate the voters that we needed to have alcohol sales to have any kind of rental business at the zoo. I remember that most understood and one fellow even invited me in for a beer. A few people felt the zoo was for children and did not need an alcohol license, even for rentals. We eventually won so when the RainForest opened, we had a great opening party with adult beverages.

Ken Pekarek had several animal management roles at Cleveland Metroparks Zoo during my tenure. He came to the zoo to work with elephants, having worked at Sea World, Ohio right out of high school. While at Sea World he was involved in an animal show, featuring a young elephant being pulled through the water on water skies. Perfect training for the Zoo's elephant program in the seventies! After thirty-five years Ken retired from Cleveland Metroparks Zoo. We were all sad when he left as he had so much institutional knowledge that could not be replaced. He was also the "go to" guy when an animal had to be grabbed or moved without tranquilization. Few on the staff had his in-depth experience in grabbing animals.

When Ken retired, he told an amusing story of his first day on the job in 1977. This story illustrates some major differences between now, and 35 years ago in the zoo world. On his first day he was sent to the elephant house to work with a veteran keeper who had just put the elephants out on exhibit. Ken was told a little bit about the operation and then was told to clean the stalls. His mentor went to lunch around 11 AM, presumably to a local drinking establishment, and more significantly, never came back that day! Ken had to bring the elephants into the clean barn, chain them up, and clean the exhibit before he could leave at 5 PM. The next day, the older keeper didn't say much, but did say something like how did you do yesterday? He gave no apology or explanation. This probably was not that unusual of a story in the sixties or seventies.

Most people will understand that one of the most memorable people I ever had the pleasure to meet was Betty White, the TV star. During my years at the Los Angeles Zoo, I occasionally was assigned to take an animal somewhere for a public relations experience. As an example, before my first week had been completed, Claudia Collier assigned me to take an infant chimp to City Hall for a press conference. Frank Taylor, the public relations manager at the zoo, escorted me. I remember getting in the elevator and some public employee joked that I had little Sam with me (Sam Yorty was mayor then). Other times, I took animals to Betty White who would present them on a TV show. It was great publicity for the Los Angeles Zoo, something that Betty White has done for fifty years. Once I brought her a three-foot American crocodile, not one of the easiest animals to handle. As I struggled with the small crocodile I handed it to Betty and the reptile immediately went docile and she did five-minutes of running commentary while holding the respectful crocodile. From that moment on, I always believed that there were certain people, animal whisperers, who had something unexplainable about themselves that allowed them to have a calming effect on animals. Betty White is one, but I have met others throughout my career.

Dr. Leonard J. Goss was director of the Cleveland Zoo for twenty-one years from 1958 until February 1979. Prior to that he worked at the New York Zoological Society, operator of the Bronx Zoo, for nineteen years as veterinarian and assistant director. Dr. Goss received his veterinary degree from The Ohio State University in 1934 and a Ph.D. in pathology from Cornell University in 1938. I was privileged to meet Len on several occasions when he returned to Cleveland for a visit. I also did an interview with Len and his wife, Carol, at their retirement home in Asheville, North Carolina. Len was a well-respected zoo director, both nationally and internationally and I was glad I had the opportunity to get to know him.

During my interview, Len shared some amazing stories including the acquisition of bongo antelope and Timmy the gorilla. I asked Len what it was like graduating from veterinary school in the 30s? He responded that at twenty-one years of age, he was the youngest to graduate that year from veterinary school. He then stated that someone called him Dr. Goss for the first time and that scared him so much he decided to continue his education by studying pathology at Cornell University. He also told me something he learned from Lee S. Crandall, the famous curator at the Bronx Zoo. He stated, "Dr Crandall taught me very early on that you could learn a lot from the keepers if you kept your mouth shut and listened." He continued, "I think that's probably good advice for all zoo directors even to this day." So true!

Cleveland Metroparks Zoo was fortunate in having wonderful outdoor art by Viktor Schreckengost, a centurion and a distinguished artist in many different art forms. He has been called "the American Leonardo da Vinci." The Birds of the World building had five large and eight small ceramic bird tiles and the Pachyderm Building had two huge bas-reliefs of a mammoth and mastodon. These two very large pieces of art had to be carefully removed from the old Pachyderm Building when construction started on the African Elephant Crossing. In 2006, in conjunction with the centennial birthday celebration for Schreckengost, the zoo, zoological society and the Cleveland Museum of Art collaborated on a special exhibition, titled, Animals in Art: Clay Creatures by Viktor Schreckengost. This exhibit featured some of the artist's animal art sculptures, as well as the zoo's own aviary tiles that were saved prior to the demolition of the Birds of the World building. During that year, Viktor's hundredth birthday year, he received the prestigious National Medal of Arts from the President of the United States. In 2013, the zoo installed the bird sculptures on a new event center and the carousel building. While the zoo had plans to reinstall the life-sized mammoth and mastodon at the zoo's entrance, it lacked a final design and funding. All the pieces were restored and put in storage. Eventually these sculptures found an appropriate home in University Circle near the Cleveland Museum of Natural History.

In 1991, Sarah and I had the privilege of attending Frederick Crawford's hundredth birthday party at the Crawford Auto Museum, part of the History Museum in Cleveland. Fred was active with the Cleveland Zoological Society serving as chairman in the fifties and sixties. He was a true early pioneer in aviation leading his company, Thompson Products, to its greatest heights. Thompson Products merged with Ramo-Woolridge in the mid-fifties and became Thompson-Ramo-Woolridge or TRW. Fred was the first president of TRW until he retired in 1958. The guest of honor at his birthday party was chief justice of the Supreme Court, Sandra Day O'Connor. After dinner and a few speeches, I remember Fred and his wife, Kay, had the first dance. I remember thinking, that's the way to celebrate a hundreds birthday! Two years later several of us toured Fred and Kay through the zoo. Fred could still speak clearly on complex issues such as wildlife management, conservation and the role of zoos. He relayed the following to us that day when asked what he thought of zoos today? "I just admire the zoo staff for their loyalty to the zoo. Keep taking care of these animals and breed the scarce ones when you can. I think that's part of the inheritance we have in the world. I think we all agree that it's a precious inheritance and it's a shame to destroy any form of life because it never can come back. I guess with the study of animals, you learn things about life too."

To this day many zoo and aquarium professionals consider Dr. Murray Fowler to be the father of zoological medicine, especially since many current zoo veterinarians went through his program at the University of California at Davis. The Sacramento Zoo was fortunate to have him and his staff as the zoo's consulting veterinarians. I learned a tremendous amount about zoo biology and veterinary care from Dr. Fowler while I was director of the Sacramento Zoo. I occasionally took time to walk with him on his Tuesday rounds. I remember when I first started at the zoo we were talking and walking and as we neared the chimp cage and Murray immediately veered away. Zoo people do not like the word cage, but in this case the word is justified. Veterinarians rarely develop good rapport with zoo animals, similar to how many people feel about the dentist. Joey, the male chimp, had a special dislike for the good veterinarian and would make a real scene every time Dr. Fowler approached the cage, often throwing certain organic items at the doctor with amazing accuracy. When the zoo constructed its new exhibit for chimpanzees, it was glass-fronted which prevented the flinging of objects. However, it did not stop Joey from making a scene and jumping at the glass, frightening anyone near the exhibit. Dr. Fowler reported that even seven years after his retirement, Joey still recognized him and attacked the glass. After I moved to Cleveland, Dr. Fowler and I would occasionally cross paths. After Cleveland Metroparks Zoo opened the Sarah Allison Steffee Center for Zoological Medicine in 2004, I invited Dr. Fowler to give a presentation for the Cleveland Zoological Society's annual lecture for donors. It was a delightful presentation with many wonderful stories from his many years working with exotic animals, including the one about his relationship with Joey the chimp.

I met many interesting zoo and aquarium directors from around the world during my career. Clayton Freiheit, Director of the Denver Zoo, was certainly one. At first glance he seemed pompous and arrogant. He was a heavy smoker and drinker and ate way too much. He had an encyclopedic knowledge of wildlife and zoos and he never forgot a face. I considered him a friend and mentor. I got to know him when we were on the AZA Board of Directors together in the early nineties. He came to Cleveland early in my tenure and had dinner with Sarah, myself, and some of the zoo's staff. A few years later when I was the outgoing AZA president in Toronto, Canada, Sarah flew up to be with me for the occasion. She arrived at the hotel and went into the elevator and there was Clayton who had only met her on that one occasion. Clayton looked up, recognized her and said calmly, "Well Ms. Young, I see you are here for the de-throning."

If you wanted to find Clayton at the end of the day during a conference, you could be sure he was on a bar stool in the conference hotel, usually holding court. Often colleagues would come to seek his advice. One director asked him about a certain curator that this director thought he might like to hire. Clayton's only response was "sharp as a spoon." Another recently retired colleague was all excited about taking classes in meeting facilitation and thought it would be a good income source in retirement. Clayton took a puff on his cigarette, and commented, "You'll starve." His bad habits finally caught up with him and he passed away from lung cancer in 2007. When his friends go to conferences even to this day and pass the bar, we still expect to see him sitting there.

No matter if people liked Jack Hanna or felt that some of his antics were a little sophomoric, he was America's zookeeper. While I think he did educate people and promote wildlife conservation, some of his planned naivety did not present zoo directors or zookeepers in a positive manner. He believed strongly that we had to entertain people before we could get them to commit to saving wildlife. His various popular TV shows that have run for over thirty years do entertain viewers and have a conservation message. Another thing that is certain is Jack is truly a nice person.

Jack and I had some differences. When I was president of the AZA Board of Directors, Jack had his zoo's membership suspended by the AZA Board of Directors for bringing in giant pandas on a short-term loan, something our critics called rent-a-panda, and this was a program most of us wanted to stop. As I was president of the board, I believe Jack always blamed me. To tell the truth, I don't even know how or if I voted on the issue. I believe it was a close vote. Even with that disagreement, Jack did help me by coming to a fund-raiser at the Cleveland Metroparks Zoo. In fact, I do not believe Jack ever refused to donate his time to help any colleague when he was asked to participate in a program at their zoo or aquarium.

One can never have too many friends. Throughout my life I have always managed to have great friends. As a youngster in Inglewood, my first friends were neighborhood girls about my age. Later in elementary school some boys my age moved into the neighborhood. Alan Smith and I shared an interest in the outdoors, stamp collecting and civil war history as it was during the time of the centennial of the civil war. In high school Mike Mahoney and I shared an interest in student council and other interests typical of high school students of the time. Mike and I both went on to UCI in the biology program. I have always felt sorry that we lost touch after college. My girlfriend in my senior year of college, Shannon Lee Hennessey, and I stayed together through college despite going to different universities. We were married in 1968 and divorced a couple years later. Except for some difficult months after the divorce, we have remained friends for well over forty years. Going to the Los Angeles Zoo, my fellow animal keepers were my best friends, including Claudia Collier, Mike Dee, Bob Barnes and my roommate, Steve Wynn. In San Francisco, I met Kim Sturla, a young woman with a passion for animal welfare. She helped me understand the animal welfare and animal rights point of view. While some of these groups have been overly critical of zoos and aquariums, I believe I have always listened to their concerns because of what I learned from Kim. Becoming a zoo director at Sacramento, I immediately became a member of a very small unofficial fraternity with two hundred other zoo and aquarium directors. Many have been great friends, but none more than Satch Krantz, director of the Riverbanks Zoo and Botanical Garden in Columbia, South Carolina

I first met Satch over thirty-five years ago when Mike Sulak, curator at the San Francisco Zoo invited me to go the dinner with him and Satch at an AZA National Convention in Denver in 1978. I got to know him much better when we were both on the AZA Board together in the late eighties. At an AZA Board meeting in Columbia, Sarah joined me towards the end of the meeting and we spent time with Satch and his family. Since then I have visited Satch in Columbia and nearby Kiawah Island many times to play golf, kayak, bike ride and eat and drink. Sarah and I have traveled with Satch and Becky Krantz to France, the California wine country and Satch and Becky even drove me through North Carolina so I could visit three AZA accredited aquariums. And then there was our one-hundred and twenty-mile hike together across Tsavo National Park in Kenya, trips to Alaska, Galapagos and Europe. I will discuss some of these later in the book.

For much of my career at Cleveland Metroparks Zoo, Satch and I would talk almost daily. Seems like there was always a problem that one of us had that needed the other's counsel. Sometimes we took the other's advice and sometimes we did not. Whatever, we remained friends.

AZA's most prestigious award is the Marlin Perkins Award for Professional Excellence and has only been given about twenty times. I thought my friend Satch was deserving of this award and in 2013 I nominated him and got other colleagues to support the nomination. I wrote the following introduction for the presentation at the Annual AZA Convention in Kansas City. It was part roast and part serious. The only one I let review my short speech was Satch's wife Becky and she said it was perfect, as did many at the conference. Satch accepted the award in a sincere and humble manner. It was great that Becky and his sons Eric and David could join us for the ceremony.

Palmer E. Krantz III (Satch)
R. Marlin Perkins Award for Professional Excellence

This recipient and I are contemporaries and we both grew up and were in college at the same time in the sixties and early seventies. At that period in my life, I learned the difference between being an agitator and being a change agent. Throughout my career, I personally have always chosen the path of a change agent. This year's recipient could be a change agent, but often he has been an agitator.

When elected as President of his Rotary Club in the late eighties, he immediately fired the paid executive and restructured this long-standing traditional community group. It took a while for the Club to get over it, but his action did make the club much better.

His accomplishments are many and he has been recognized for them. The university he attended gave him a distinguished service award in 2012. He is has been mentioned for several years in local publications as one of the most influential leaders in his community. He was recognized for his accomplishments by the House of Representatives in his State and given the key to the city of his hometown.

He has been at his zoo for over forty years and director for thirty-seven of those years, longer than anyone in the profession. In the last year, his zoo set attendance records of 1,039,372. This is a community of only 600,000. And the attendance continues to grow.

He has a nickname that always has to be repeated when he is introduced to people for the first time. He has no idea how he got the name; his parents would never tell!

When I told this friend last year that I would retire at the end of 2012, he sincerely seemed sad that he had lost a valued colleague. When I told him, we would still talk regularly, he responded, "Why would I talk with you, you won't have any good gossip!"

I have known Palmer E. Krantz III (Satch) for over thirty-years and believe he is very deserving of this very prestigious honor. And, it is not because he is my friend, it's because I believe no one else in recent times has done more for AZA.

There is no question that Satch is one of the most well-respected leaders of our profession in both North America and worldwide. As evidence of this, Satch is one of only five Americans that has ever been President of the World Association of Zoos and Aquariums (WAZA). In addition, Satch was first president of AZA (now chairman) in 1988/89. Uniquely he again became chairman in 2007/08. He was the first member of

AZA to serve more than one term as president/chairman since Freeman Kelly served several terms during World War II.

Satch is a take charge person. In fact, he always has to be in charge. Years ago, I gave him a book to read, *In the Shadow of Kilimanjaro*, and we were talking about the book after a few glasses of wine with our wives in my backyard. It is a book about Tsavo National Park in Kenya and a walking safari. That's all he needed and he took the idea, contacted the safari company, got friends to accompany us and from then on it was always his safari.

Amazingly, during his second AZA chairmanship and his third term on the AZA board, Satch was not a quiet and complacent member. He could have sat back, give insightful advice and let others take the lead. Satch has always put animals in the forefront of his effort in running a first-class zoo and carried this passion to his various leadership roles within AZA. He has worked tirelessly to improve our cooperative endangered species breeding programs.

In summary, his accomplishments are many, at his zoo, in his community and on behalf of the zoo and aquarium community, particularly for what he has done for AZA. While at times it not always easy to be his employee, colleague, his friend or even his wife, in the end he always makes things better.

When I returned home from the conference, I received a heartfelt thank you note from my friend stating the I was his brother in spirit. I felt the same way. Despite my limited access to zoo gossip after retirement we still talk almost daily.

Satch Krantz and I celebrating the end of our 120-mile hike through Tsavo West and Tsavo East National Parks in February 2002.

THE GUESTS

Listening to the zoo's guests was always important to me as I wrote in the summer of 1990 *Zoo News*. "One guest noticed that we had a potential hazard next to the road from the greenhouse to the Big Creek area. A forty-foot sheer cliff above Big Creek had only a one-foot high fence to keep children from this hazard. In this case, the zoo staff added a much higher fence. Others have commented on the lack of directional signs around the zoo. After much discussion, the zoo has started a program of more complete signage within a three-mile radius of the zoo."

The reactions of guests, especially children, had to the zoo were especially rewarding for me. Almost any time of year, large Amish families visited the zoo. Everyone comes to the zoo, all ages, backgrounds, races, religions, ethnicities, and walks of life. Any day I could walk out of the administration building and see this incredible mix of Americana.

One time I observed a five or six-year-old little girl standing in front of the zoo's old elephant exhibit with her mother. She was clearly enjoying watching these magnificent creatures, but her mother was ready to move on. The mother continually urged her daughter to leave. She said, "come on let's go – you can see elephants anytime in your books or on TV." The little girl looked up at her mother and answered, "yes, but they are not this large." It's hard to replace seeing the real thing!

ENCOURAGING YOUNG PEOPLE

While I only had a few adults that counseled me concerning zoology and zoo management when I was growing up, I always took time to talk with young people who wanted career advice. I always told them the plusses and minuses of working in a zoo or aquarium. I told them that working in a zoo or aquarium often means working weekends and holidays. I told them that it was often difficult to work your way up in one zoo or aquarium and many have to move around the country to get promoted. I advised young people to stay in college and get any job they could at their local zoo or even volunteer. In that way they would get to know the zoo culture. I always told them that if you have a passion for wildlife, it's the greatest profession in the world and one I truly enjoyed.

I occasionally went to schools to talk to children about zoo and aquarium careers. Sarah and I had friends who had a young daughter who invited me to an elementary school in Bay Village for show and tell." Martha wrote the following report on me.

"I chose Steve Taylor who was born on March 18, 1947 in Inglewood, California. When he graduated from college, he got a degree in biology and became a zoo director. He came to Ohio when he was 41. His hobbies are traveling, bird

watching and golf. The most exciting international event in his life was the Berlin Wall falling down.

Mr. Taylor's first memory of helping others was when he was high school senior class president. He wanted to help others because he always liked people. He helps out in the community by being the zoo director because the zoo is part of the community. Mr. Taylor volunteers in the AAZPA. Mr. Taylor likes serving others because it helps animals and people. He goes to the school and talks about what it's like to do zoo work also. Mr. Taylor's most rewarding accomplishment was when he opened the RainForest because 1.5 million came that year. Mr. Taylor's family thinks that being a public figure is not always easy but can be fun. Mr. Taylor wants to become more involved in our city, our country and work as an advisor. Mr. Taylor thinks that people that do their job right, take care of their family and do something extra is what outstanding is. He is very glad and happy to be chosen for this honor.

I enjoyed interviewing and writing about Steve Taylor. I learned that it can be a lot of fun to be a zoo director but can be a lot of hard work. He taught me it is fun to help others too. I want to help others when I am older".

After Martha graduated from Wake Forest University, she joined the Peace Corps and was stationed in South Africa. I am sure her commitment to helping others was probably more due to her parents, not my short presentation at her elementary school. However, her note did show she was committed to helping others at an early age.

AZA – ASSOCIATION OF ZOOS AND AQUARIUMS

When I retired from Cleveland Metroparks Zoo on December 31, 2012, I had been a member of AZA for over forty years. There were only eight other AZA zoo directors who had been directors when I started as director of the Sacramento Zoo. They were Nancy Falasco, Brandywine Zoo, Phil Frost, Baton Rouge Zoo, Ron Forman, Audubon Zoo, Chuck Wikenhauser, Milwaukee Zoo, Troy Stump, Hershey Park Zoo, Satch Krantz, Riverbanks Zoo, Hayes Caldwell, Caldwell Zoo, Gary Geddes, Point Defiance Zoo and Clyde Peeling, Reptileland. In addition, I could find only four other names of zoo directors in the 1972/73 AZA directory who were members when I joined and were still employed by an AZA zoo. They were Pat Burchfield, Gladys Porter Zoo, Hayes Caldwell, Caldwell Zoo, Steve McCusker, San Antonio Zoo and Brian Hunt, African Safari Wildlife Park. In 1987 I was very pleased to be elected to the Board of Directors and was elected as president-elect in 1990, a four-year commitment as you also served as vice-president, president-elect, resident and finally, past-president. Bob Wagner, AAZPA's executive director, called me personally to give me the good news. Upon reflection, my notes show that I felt a little overwhelmed since at that time there was some amount of uncertainty at Cleveland Metroparks Zoo. Issues included finishing the then controversial RainForest, the uneasy relationship between Cleveland Metroparks and the Cleveland Zoological Society and the fate of the Fanner Building, a building being renovated as an education center when I arrived but was not a popular project with the Board of Park Commissioners.

I also felt uneasy, as I had lost my first election to be an officer running against two of my best friends; Steve Wylie, director of the Oklahoma City Zoo and Susan Engfer, director of the Cheyenne Mountain Zoo in Colorado Springs. Steve Wylie won that election. Susan played a great joke on Steve Wylie and me by creating buttons that had Steve with a red slash mark over it, no Steve's! Shortly after that first election, Dr. Paul Chaffee, who at the time was an officer, passed away. Susan and I were put together on another ballot and I won that election. I actually moved up to president-elect and Wylie, all of his friends called him by his last name, stayed as vice-president and therefore he would have a full four years as an officer.

At the time I was well aware of certain challenges facing the organization and they troubled me, especially since I would now be directly involved in solving them. First, the board was concerned that our current executive director was not the right leader to move us forward. Most of us realized that the organization needed to move from Wheeling, WV to Washington, DC if we were ever going to be taken seriously by government agencies and other conservation organizations. Secondly, there was controversy over short-term loans by the Chinese government of giant pandas. Several conservation and humane groups and felt that these loans might not be in the best interest of the individual animals and the loans were not doing anything for conservation of wildlife.

With all of this ahead of me, I did what I always did when faced with a challenge. I reduced my thoughts to writing and made a list of priorities. A few days later, on September 16, 1990, my apathy turned to excitement as I made a new list of all the great things in my life.

- I have been accepted as a member of IUDZG.
- I have been elected president-elect of AAZPA.
- My son is doing well at college and wants to be a zoo director. Note: he wised up later in life.
- The zoo has four major capital projects going on at once, including the RainForest.
- I am financially secure – Sarah balanced my checkbook and I have money in the bank.
- This summer I've been to St. Louis, Boston, Nantucket, Tulsa, D.C., N.Y., Toronto, Copenhagen, Detroit, Columbus and Indianapolis.
- My health is good.
- I love my job.
- I am in a stable relationship.
- By next spring the zoo will have a stable animal collection and a zoo organized in relatable sections (Africa, Rainforest, Northern Trek and two others.
- I do like Cleveland, but it's far away from home. Note: I suppose that is a feeling I continued to carry with me.

126

As I have mentioned before, whenever I felt down, I always found it helpful to sit down and write a list of things that made me happy.

I felt very fortunate to have done so many AZA accreditation inspections, probably around forty, mostly as the chair. The first one I did was in the early eighties. Karen Sausman, director of the Living Desert in Palm Desert, and I inspected the Micki Grove Zoo in Lodi, California. No matter how small or large the zoo or aquarium, I felt I always learned so much from each inspection and was able to bring new ideas back to my own zoo. I learned even more as I became a member, chair and then advisor on the accreditation commission.

By 1988, just before I left Sacramento, there were one-hundred and thirty-eight AZA accredited zoos and aquariums. By the time I retired from the Cleveland Metroparks Zoo at the end of 2012, there were two-hundred and twenty-three accredited zoos and aquariums. By 2021, there were two-hundred and forty-one accredited zoos and aquariums in AZA, including a good number of international members and I had visited two-hundred and twenty-five of them.

The involvement of zoos in wildlife conservation is not a new phenomenon, but one that only truly became commonplace in the last twenty years. While zoos have always bred endangered species, their motives were mostly self-preservation, or even financial. Conservation in zoos and aquariums in the last twenty years has evolved well beyond breeding endangered species in captivity. Now zoo and aquarium breeding programs are coordinated and done in conjunction with *in-situ* (in the wild) conservation programs.

"A man masters nature not by force but by understanding."
Jacob Bronowski

If ever there was a quote that explained why I was involved with zoos for so many years; that's it.

THE BEST ZOOS AND AQUARIUMS

First of all, there is no way to rank zoos and aquariums in a fair and unbiased manner. There is only opinion. Occasionally a newspaper or magazine will try and they usually do it in a very unscientific manner. Most newspapers and magazines create their lists of the best zoos and aquariums only considering the guest experience. There was an attempt to rate European zoos in the *International Zoo News* in 2008 and 2009. The author, Anthony Sheridan, did a good job of selecting criteria that included much of what is included in AZA's accreditation program. Mr. Sheridan then ranked some criteria higher than others; therefore, quality/quantity of the animal collection was worth almost four times as many points as marketing and publicity.

I am going to attempt to discuss the best zoos and aquariums and I am sure that if any zoo or aquarium professionals read this they would disagree with my results. Some might even be quite upset. I think that using the criteria from AZA accreditation, or any other regional accreditation program, is most appropriate. In AZA's program, the criteria are as follows:

- Animal Welfare & Management
- Veterinary Care
- Conservation
- Education and Interpretation
- Scientific Advancement
- Governing Authority
- Staff
- Support Organization
- Finance
- Physical Facilities
- Safety and Security
- Guest Services
- Strategic Planning

Now for a couple of disclaimers. I have no right to do this and nobody does. I haven't seen every zoo and aquarium in the world, although I have visited over three-hundred and sixty worldwide and over ninety-five percent of AZA accredited zoos and aquariums. I have conducted over forty AZA accreditation inspections, mostly as the chair. I am at a disadvantage as an aquarium evaluator since I have been a zoo director and not an aquarium director. I have only visited a few aquariums outside the United States so I only list the best aquariums in the United States. I have prejudices. I like natural looking zoos. I like zoos and aquariums that do not mix rides and animal exhibits where the ride distracts from the themed setting. I believe the best zoos and aquariums must have a substantial commitment to supporting conservation outside the walls of their institution. While I will discuss small and medium sized zoos and aquariums, the very best are large institutions. The larger institutions can do much more than smaller ones. This does not mean that medium and small institutions are inferior, it is just the larger institutions can do so much more.

My list of aquariums is short since I haven't visited that many aquariums worldwide. I know there are many great aquariums in Japan and I haven't visited any of them. I have visited many of the best zoos in the world, but very few smaller facilities. My favorite small zoo in the world is the Belize Zoo. The exhibits are natural and the zoo does not try to be something it is not. The labels are very clever poems. The zoo is a force in wildlife conservation in Belize. It is an attractive zoo with native wildlife.

Here are some general thoughts. Several of these top zoos are really several zoos, such as the San Diego Zoo and the San Diego Zoo Safari Park. Zoo Victoria in Melbourne has three facilities. In the United States, the San Diego Zoo, St. Louis Zoo and the Henry Doorly Zoo in Omaha, Nebraska have large and diverse animal collections. All of the top zoos and aquariums have excellent animal care, knowledgeable staff and state-of-the-art veterinary care. Even small, top quality zoos, like Buttonwood Park Zoo have a wonderful, well-equipped veterinary hospital. Staff members of the best institutions are accomplished and active in professional associations and have leadership positions in those associations. For instance, staff members at the St. Louis Zoo chair several AZA Taxon Advisory Groups (TAGS). Almost all the best zoos and aquariums are operated as non-profits but receive significant government funds. The best zoos that are still government-run, such as the Riverbanks Zoo, have considerable autonomy. Whichever governing model is used, all the best zoos and aquariums have stable financial resources.

All the best zoos and aquariums have over a million guests a year – some have many more. They have great facilities for their guests and guests are treated well by staff. No institution does it better than Disney's Animal Kingdom. At this facility there is a staff member at just about every exhibit interacting and educating guests. In the last few years, all great zoos and aquariums have learned from Disney on how to improve their guest services.

All great zoos and aquariums have major conservation programs, both with their managed animal collections, SSPs, TAGs, and support or conduct conservation programs in the wild. No zoo does more for conservation than the Bronx Zoo, and its parent organization, the Wildlife Conservation Society (WCS). This organization accounts for a third to a half of all the conservation programs of the two-hundred and forty-one AZA institutions. The Lincoln Park Zoo has thirty-two science and conservation staff members across five science centers, including hosting AZA's Population Management Center. Zoo Victoria's Healesville Sanctuary has an impressive on-site breeding program for endangered Australian wildlife including the Tasmanian devil (In 2012 they had about seventy animals), helmeted honeyeaters, pygmy possum and several others. The St. Louis Zoo's WildCare program along with the Zoo's outstanding group of researchers is very noteworthy. San Diego Zoo Global has long been a leader in conservation research and the Institute for Conservation Research is the largest zoo-based multidisciplinary research effort in the world with 200 dedicated scientists.

One zoo on my top-ten list is the Riverbanks Zoo and Garden in

Columbia South Carolina. While it's not a huge zoo or one with the largest research and conservation departments, it is overall a high-quality zoo. It opened on April 25, 1974. Being a relatively new zoo, it does not have any bad exhibits. Even the older exhibits are well maintained and interpreted. The collection is diverse and the staff members are fully engaged in AZA conservation programs. The zoo has continually improved since its inception and every addition is in the forefront of modern zoo design. It is extremely well supported by the Columbia community and receives financial support from two counties. While it's government-run by the Riverbanks Park Commission, in many ways it operates like a non-profit corporation. Its non-profit Riverbanks Zoological Society partner is integrated within the organization and directed by the zoo director. The zoo operates a wonderful botanical garden, connected by a bridge across the lower Saluda River.

Enough said concerning my thoughts on the best of the best zoos and aquariums. There are certainly many others that are noteworthy. And the best part about being involved in the wonderful profession is that zoos and aquariums continually improve and every day they find new ways to save wildlife and wild places.

My favorite zoo exhibits
- Sea World, Orlando - Sea Lion Exhibit
- Dallas Zoo - Giants of the African Savanna
- Audubon Zoo, New Orleans - Louisiana Swamp
- Bronx Zoo – Jungle World, Madagascar, Tiger Mountain, Congo Gorilla Forest and Himalayan Highlands, Baboon Reserve
- Denver Zoo - Predator Ridge
- St. Louis Zoo - River's Edge
- Woodland Park Zoo, Seattle, Washington – African Savanna, Northern Trail
- San Diego Zoo – East African Rock Kopje, Conrad Prebys African Rocks
- Fort Worth Zoo – Texas Exhibit

- Pt. Defiance Zoo, Tacoma, Washington – Polar Bear
- Toledo Zoo – Nature's Neighborhood, Aviary Renovation
- Minnesota Zoo – Minnesota Trail, Russian Grizzly Coast
- Detroit Zoo – Amphibiville, Polk Penguin Conservation Center
- Zoo Leipzig – Gondwanaland
- Zoo Hanover – Yukon Bay, Zambezi
- Binder Park Zoo, Battle Creek, Michigan - African Savanna
- Koln Zoo, Germany – Asian Elephants
- Healesville (Melbourne) – Entire Zoo (Australia Wildlife)
- Zoo Zurich – Masoala (Madagascar)
- Singapore – Night Zoo
- Disney's Animal Kingdom – Kilimanjaro Safaris
- Sedgwick County Zoo - Reed Family Elephants of Zambezi River Valley
- Oakland Zoo - California Trail

My favorite aquariums in the United States
- Monterey Bay Aquarium
- John G. Shedd Aquarium
- Georgia Aquarium
- National Aquarium in Baltimore
- Aquarium of the Pacific

My top ten best zoos in the United States
- San Diego Zoo
- Bronx Zoo
- St. Louis Zoo
- Denver Zoo
- Disney's Animal Kingdom
- Smithsonian National Zoological Park
- Riverbanks Zoo
- Oregon Zoo
- Woodland Park Zoological Garden, Seattle
- Henry Doorly Zoo, Omaha

My top ten best medium or small zoos in the United States
- Arizona Sonora Desert Museum
- The NEW Zoo (Northeastern Wisconsin Zoo)
- Santa Barbara Zoo
- Binder Park Zoo, Battle Creek
- Living Desert Museum, Palm Desert
- Akron Zoo
- Point Defiance Zoo, Tacoma
- Brevard Zoo, Melbourne, Florida
- Central Park Zoo
- Buttonwood Park Zoo, New Bedford, MA
- And Outside US – The Belize Zoo

My top ten best zoos in the World
- Singapore Zoological Garden (also Night Zoo)
- Melbourne Zoo (Zoo Victoria)
- San Diego Zoo (San Diego Zoo Wildlife Alliance)
- Bronx Zoo (WCS)
- Zoo Leipzig
- Schonbrunn Zoo, Vienna
- Zoo Hanover
- Zoo Zurich
- Chester Zoo
- Berlin Zoological Garden
- Prague Zoo

As I said, there is no agreement on the best zoos. In March 2014, *American Live Wire* listed the ten best zoos in America and only included four of mine – San Diego Zoo, Bronx Zoo, Henry Doorly Zoo, Omaha and St. Louis Zoo. In addition, they added Columbus Zoo, Phoenix Zoo, Memphis Zoo, Cheyenne Mountain Zoo in Colorado Springs, Brevard Zoo in Melbourne, Florida and the Minnesota Zoo. Everyone has an opinion!

ANIMAL RIGHTS

Despite what animal rights extremists want people to believe; zoo and aquarium people care more about the welfare of animals than anyone else. While the focus of zoos and aquariums is saving wildlife and wild places, the welfare of the animals in zoos and aquariums is forefront in the mind of every staff member.

I have no problem with people that feel that animals should not be in captivity. In the most simplistic way, it is hard to argue with that view, even though I differ. What I have a huge problem with is the untruthful statements that extremists use to publicize their own agenda. The following are some of the statements that extremists use to promote their anti-zoo and aquarium agenda:

1. While these groups do not always come directly out and say it, they would have people believe that zoos and aquariums yank animals out of the wild to populate their institutions. While zoos and aquariums get some animals from the wild, very few mammals come from the wild. It's not what zoos and aquariums are about. When animals do come to zoos from the wild, it is only after much scrutiny to assure that there would be no harm to the wild population. Lower vertebrates are more often imported for zoos and aquariums, mostly fish, but the same scrutiny applies.

2. Extremists rarely differentiate between AZA-accredited zoos and aquariums and non-accredited institutions, or international extremists between WAZA members and others. Accredited zoos and aquariums operate under strict guidelines and a detailed ethics code and are regularly inspected to make certain the guidelines and codes are followed.

3. Extremists state that zoo animals live in cages and they are robbed of their right to behave naturally. Yes, all zoo and aquarium exhibits restrict the space where animals live. In the wild, animals have territories and also live in restricted space dictated by food, access to water, presence of predators,

territorial behaviors of others and much more. Exhibits in modern zoos and aquariums, although usually smaller than an animals' wild territory, do provide for animals with space to move around freely and interact with others of their species, if that is natural and the animals are not by nature solitary. Zoo animals also have access to food and water, graze and look for food and more. It is true that zoos and aquariums do not let most predators kill their own food, but all predators are opportunistic and will eat carrion in the wild when it's encountered.

4. Extremists often state that wild animals are dangerous and have killed their keepers. While this is true, it is very infrequent, especially considering all the dangerous animals kept in zoos and aquariums worldwide. The number of deaths to staff due to dangerous animals held in accredited zoos and aquariums has declined over the years as these institutions have better facilities, better training of staff and have made changes in husbandry standards, such as protective contact when working with elephants.

5. Extremists state zoo animals often escape. Considering all the animals kept in zoos worldwide, the number of escapes in minuscule. Obviously, escape of aquarium animals in very unlikely.

6. Extremists mistakenly state that animals in zoos and aquariums die prematurely. Any comparison of median life span of animals has shown in just about every case that zoo and aquarium animals live longer than their wild counterparts. Good husbandry, veterinary care, balanced diets and lack of predators account for this fact. When extremists discuss premature deaths, they often mislead the public by using maximum lifespans, not median life expectancy. It would be like saying a person that dies in their eighties died prematurely as they could have lived to be over a hundred!

7. Extremists state that bad management causes death. I cannot deny that human error has caused the unfortunate deaths

of animals in even the best zoos and aquariums. Again, the number is very small compared to the large number of animals housed in institutions worldwide. A few years ago, there was a story about a Texas zoo that was sensationalized in the press. A male lion killed a lioness after they had been together for five years. Animal rights extremists were quick to blame it on stress caused by captivity. While it was unfortunate that it had to be observed by zoo guests, anyone who has studied lions in the wild knows that this is far from an unusual or unnatural experience. George Schaller's study of lions in the Serengeti National Park in the sixties showed that lions frequently kill one another for many different reasons.

8. Extremists feel that zoo animals should be placed back in the wild. Most zoo and aquarium animals have been in these institutions for many generations and cannot be released in the wild. It would be cruel and most would suffer terrible deaths. Aside from that there is no true wild left. Even animals in Yellowstone National Park and the Serengeti National Park in Tanzania must be managed.

Good zoos and aquariums will be around for a long time and will continue to provide the very best of care for wildlife and will continue to be major players in the fight to save endangered species.

THE FULTON ROAD BRIDGE

There are some things in the career of a zoo director that have nothing to do with animals or conservation or even running a first-class zoo. One of my greatest challenges and one I had little control over was the replacement of the Fulton Road bridge. Cleveland Metroparks Zoo is the only zoo I know of with a major highway going above its property. The Fulton Road bridge was constructed in 1932 and when I arrived in 1989 it was in need of replacement. The sidewalk on the south side was in such bad shape that it had been demolished in the eighties. Large pieces of cement would regularly fall a hundred and ten feet to the ground below and zoo guests could have been seriously hurt. As a solution, the county engineer suggested the zoo close its food concessions stand under the bridge. The county finally installed nets over the most dangerous areas to catch falling cement. When the nets understandably ripped, the county built heavy wooden platforms to protect zoo staff and guests. Sometime around 2000, the county installed large corrugated metal tunnels that stayed in place until the bridge was finally imploded on May 1. 2007. This was the second attempt at an implosion as the first try on April 28th was unsuccessful at bringing down the huge bridge.

The bridge was first closed to traffic on October 5, 2006 and not opened again until July 9, 2010, three years, seven months and four days later. During all that time, zoo staff had to deal with major inconveniences to guests, both getting to the zoo and routing them around construction within the zoo. It was not an easy time for Cleveland Metroparks Zoo, but somehow guests found their way to the zoo and didn't complain about the disruption during their visit. Guests often enjoyed watching the demolition and the construction. The original one cost one-million, one-hundred thousand dollars in 1932. The new bridge cost forty-nine million dollars and weighed a total of forty-nine thousand five-hundred tons, equal to the weight of nine-thousand three hundred female elephants.

When I was asked why it had taken so long to replace the bridge, I explained to people that it was a city bridge being designed by the county with state and federal funds on Cleveland Metroparks property. With that explanation, everyone understood.

CHAPTER 5

ADVENTURES TRAVELING THE WORLD

"Travel is fatal to prejudice, bigotry, narrow-mindedness and many people need it sorely on these accounts. Broad, wholesome, charitable views of men and things cannot be acquired by vegetating in one little corner of the earth all one's lifetime."
Mark Twain

OVER MY FORTY years in the zoo profession, I visited many zoos, both in the United States and around the world. Visiting other zoos and aquariums was always a hobby, but later in my career it became an obsession. That is when Mark Reed, director of the Sedgwick County Zoo in Wichita, Kansas, and I started competing to see which one could see the most AZA accredited zoos and aquariums by the time the first one of us retired. By my retirement, I had visited two-hundred and fifteen of the of the two-hundred and twenty-five AZA accredited institutions, ten more than Mark. Mark generously paid me the five dollars riding on the outcome.

1974 GREYHOUND BUS TRIP

My interest in visiting other zoos really began in August of 1974, a little over two years after I started as an animal keeper at the Los Angeles Zoo. During that month, I visited nineteen zoos in thirty days by traveling the country on a Greyhound bus. My notes show that I spent one-hundred and twenty-four hours on the bus and traveled five-thousand, four hundred miles. Not counting my bus ticket, which I believe cost three-hundred dollars, I spent a total of six-hundred dollars. Expenses were controlled as I spent some nights on the bus, some nights with newfound friends and a few nights in inexpensive motels. I started on August 3, 1974 with the bus leaving downtown Los Angeles at 1:45 AM after attending a Helen Reddy concert at the Universal Amphitheater.

In each zoo I visited, I documented some highlight or some animal that was new to me. In the following pages, I mention a few of these experiences.

"I arrived in Colorado Springs around noon on August 4th and rented a VW bug for seven dollars a day, plus mileage. Bill Argon, who was then Education Curator, showed me the zoo." Concerning the first zoo visited, I wrote, "Feline Building with an unbelievable collection including golden cats, Sumatran tigers, a jaguar pair, male black maned lion, Asiatic lions, and snow leopards." Back in those days many zoos were still stamp collections of animals.

My next stop was the Denver Zoo where Paul Linger, assistant director showed me the zoo. In my journal I wrote, "Probably the most encouraging thing I have seen so far has been the computer that is presently being used by the staff of the Denver Zoo. Except for a few problems, it is the zoo's answer to record keeping. Currently the zoo is renting the machine from a computer company. To buy one would cost eight-thousand dollars. A tape keeps records for the zoo from daily reports for about a month. Other tapes have form letters written on them, and a separate tape for the veterinary information and one for a complete inventory. Examples of its use – you might want to recall all mammals born for a certain period and the machine will print this out. Also, say you wanted all information available on kudu; the machine can print this out. It seems very simple to operate and retrieve information, even with a large collection." Little did I know that the creation of the International Species Inventory System (ISIS) was being developed at the same time in Minnesota. ISIS, now Species 360 as ISIS became an inappropriate term, with records on most zoo animals, is still used today. A few zoos around the world use other systems, including Denver.

I left Denver on August 6, 1974 at 7 PM and arrived at Omaha this morning at 6:45 AM and described my visit. "Called Ann (sleepy roommate answered the phone) who agreed to pick me up on the way to work. Arrived at the zoo around 8 AM and after talking with Ann for a while, made the rounds with Johnny Martinez, zoo super-intendent. Saw my first herd of gaur."

Since that first visit to Henry Doorly Zoo, I have visited several more times. Many new exhibits, including a rainforest, a desert pavilion, a major aquarium and more have created a first-class zoo that attracts two million guests annually, an amazing accomplishment for a relatively small market. Other than the zoo, I share Bill Bryson's view of Nebraska. In one book he opens a chapter with the following statement: "I am now driving into Nebraska. That's a statement I hope I never write again."

My journal contained some notes of interest on salaries of zoo-keepers. "Notes on salaries, the Colorado Springs Zoo's keepers have an hourly salary something less than three dollars an hour. Denver Zoo, one of the highest paid, has a top salary of nine-hundred and fifty dollars a month. Omaha Zoo salaries are similar to Colorado Springs."

I arrived in Chicago in the early evening of August 8th. In the bus station I looked around immediately for information that would get me to Brookfield Zoo. I ended up taking the B-Train through Chicago to an area near the zoo where I found a motel for the night. I thought I was living in style with a TV and my own shower. My journal had this entry about my visit, "This morning I left the motel at 9 AM and started walking towards the zoo. I was fortunate because on my way to the zoo I found a barber, a post office and a drug store that had large envelopes so I was able to mail home the information I had already collected. At the zoo I saw Ziggy's, famous male elephant. Pachyderm building old, but the zoo is doing work on the outside exhibits so the exhibits, as a whole, are pretty nice. Also in the building were hippos, tapirs, rhinos and Galapagos tortoise."

It was then on to the Lincoln Park Zoo. "Dewey Garvey took me through town and to Pat Sass's house where I am spending the night and then tomorrow Pat and I will visit the Lincoln Park Zoo. At 8 PM tonight, President Nixon resigned. That was all that was on television all night. Pat and I talked until about midnight and got to know each other a little. Sharing her house with her are four cats, one dog, a lemur, a spider monkey and a pigeon."

My journal for that day stated, "At 1:30 PM everyday Lincoln Park Zoo has a chimp tea party. This job is one of Pat's responsibilities, but since it was her day off today, others brought the three and four-year old chimps out of their enclosures for a milk mixture and a bowl of fruit. Very entertaining. About halfway through the show, the chimps noticed Pat in the audience and there was a noticeable change in their behavior."

At the Milwaukee Zoo I was impressed with the newer panorama-styled exhibits. I remember meeting the director, George Spiedel. After a short conversation he asked me for my parking receipt and then gave me $ 0.50 out of his pocket. I assume he wanted the receipt so he could be reimbursed.

After Milwaukee, I headed back through Chicago to the Fort Wayne Children's Zoo. There I saw, Amos, a male bonobo that director Earl Wells found in a local pet shop. My journal had this entry, "The zoo is staffed with a director, Earl Wells, a curator, Ralph Waterhouse, a supervisor, Jim McGowin, a maintenance man and a secretary, Lydia Luecke. All the rest of the staff members were two dollar an hour students. These keepers do everything, and well. This zoo is one of the cleanest I have ever seen." That evening, Ralph

Waterhouse took me to a party for all the staff as it was towards the end of the season. Then, as now, the Fort Wayne Children's Zoo closes in the winter.

On August 13th I visited the Toledo Zoo and remember being impressed by the architecture. Most of the buildings were old, but the interiors of the bird, reptile and aquarium buildings were beautiful. They looked like large dining halls of medieval castles – lots of dark wood and shiny painted red bricks. I had never seen anything like this in any other zoo. Years later these buildings were renovated, but still maintained their original charm.

I passed through Cleveland on the way to the Buffalo Zoo since no one I knew recommended a visit to the Cleveland Zoo. In retrospect, it would have been wonderful to have seen it a few years prior to it becoming Cleveland Metroparks Zoo and 15 years prior to me becoming its director.

After visiting the Buffalo Zoo and a wonderful side trip with the education curator to Niagara Falls and her family home in Canada on the shores of Lake Erie, I headed to New York City. I arrived at the bus station in New York City and the information desk had a card with written instructions on taking the subway to the Bronx Zoo. I purposely got to New York City early so I could spend the whole day at the zoo and leave that night to avoid spending an expensive night in New York.

I first toured the famous birds of the world exhibit and was very impressed by the clever graphics that were different than anything I had ever seen. They were large and colorful and each had a separate theme such as sexual dimorphism, brood parasitism, nest building, etc. Over at the older aquatic bird building I was much impressed with a breeding colony of northern boat-billed herons, a bird I had not seen previously.

Brad House, curator of mammals, toured me through the zoo in the afternoon. He showed me the new Asian area that was under construction

After a visit with my uncle and aunt in Philadelphia, they delivered me to the Philadelphia Zoo on August 18, 1974. There I saw two very old orangs, Guas and Guasrina, who arrived at the Zoo in 1931. Massa, the oldest gorilla in a zoo at that time, was in a very small heavily barred cage. Massa was estimated to be fifty-four years old when he died ten years later in December 1984. In my journal I wrote a quote from a sign on his cage which stated, "Some fat gorillas have weighed 670 pounds in captivity, but that is not normal." I should say that this certainly is not normal! Massa appeared to me to be a rather small male gorilla.

My journal on August 20th stated, "Three-hour bus ride from Philadelphia to Washington, DC. A city bus took me right to the back gate of the National Zoo." There I saw Ling Ling and Hsing Hsing, at that time the only two giant pandas in the United States.

I further wrote, "It's 7 PM and I'm in the National Zoo. Tonight, the zoo is having their equivalent to the Los Angeles Zoo's Zoobilee. All the exhibits are open and one keeper is assigned, at time and a half, to watch over the exhibits and answer questions. Many of the exhibits in the ape house and the small animal house are full of feral mice."

I returned to the Zoo the next day. While talking with Bill Xanten, his phone rang and he was informed that, Ham, the famous space chimp was loose outside his enclosure, but still within the great ape building! Everyone was cleared from the great ape building. Veterinarians responded and tranquilized this favorite large male chimp. Everyone was allowed back in the building but not in Ham's areas as he was out cold for some time."

At 5 AM on August 22nd, I arrived in Columbus, Ohio. Looking back, I find it interesting that I visited zoos in Toledo, Columbus and Cincinnati, but not Cleveland, a city I later called home for since 1989. I waited until 8 AM and rented a Ford Pinto and drove to Powell, Ohio where the Columbus Zoo was located. The first thing I did at the zoo was visit Colo, the first gorilla ever born in a zoo. By coincidence, Dr. Warren Thomas, the new director of the Los Angeles Zoo, was present when Colo was born in December 1956. A quote from the Columbus Dispatch was on the wall. I copied it in my journal and here is what it said:

> "It lay in its embryonic sac, the umbilical cord unsevered, when Warren Dean Thomas, Ohio State veterinary medical student, found the small bundle in the Ape House about 8:40 AM. Thomas performed the necessary midwifery, then breathed into the gorilla baby's month and administered artificial respiration."

I then visited one of the most unique reptile houses I had seen on this trip. Louis Pistoria was an ultimate collector and at the time of my visit, he had over eight-hundred specimens in the building. There was no attempt to make the exhibits natural looking. Aside from the specimen, each exhibit had indoor/outdoor carpet on the floor and a water bowl somewhere in the exhibit. Behind the scenes, many more specimens were in plastic shoeboxes stacked on top of each other.

At the time of my visit in 1974, the largest pachyderm building ever was under construction. This side on the zoo had not been yet developed and it was interesting to get a tour of a building where thirty-five years later it would temporarily hold the Cleveland Metroparks Zoo's three African elephants during construction of the African Elephant Crossing in 2009/2010.

My next stop was the Cincinnati Zoo and I arrived there at 11:30 AM on August 23rd and went to the administration office where I had a nice talk with Ed Maruska, director of the zoo. Robert Lotshaw, the general curator toured me through the zoo and treated me to lunch. My notes stated, "Lunch was excellent when compared with other zoo food services." I was especially interested in the zoo's large number of gorillas including eight animals born and hand-raised in the last five years.

I arrived in Louisville, Kentucky, on August 23rd. It was about 9:30 PM and I walked about six blocks up Walnut Street where I found the Seelback Hotel. It turned out to be one of the nicest places I stayed on my trip. The cost was minimal, only $10 a night and included a shower, TV, bed and air-conditioning. I felt I was living in high style!

The next morning, Red Bayer, the interim general curator, toured me through the zoo for about an hour and a half. My journal for that day stated, "Louisville is the second or third place where I was the second keeper there within the last month from California. An elephant keeper from the San Francisco Zoo was ahead of me to several zoos. His name is John Wolf and I will have to write him when I get back home." And I did meet John a few years later when I became children's zoo manager at the San Francisco Zoo and we became friends. At one point when I was in San Francisco, John and I drove a male sea lion to the Santa Barbara Zoo.

After Louisville I rode the bus two hours to Indianapolis. I arrived at 8:30 PM and walked into town. My journal reported, "The Downtowner Hotel was comfortable and clean, but way beyond my budget at sixteen dollars per night. Called the bus station and they couldn't tell me how to get to the Zoo, so a walked. Turned out to be about a six-mile walk."

The zoo I visited was the old zoo and in a different location than the one that opened in 1990. "Zoo architecture is basic ugly", I wrote in my journal. "The same kind of children's zoo approach that came close to spoiling Fort Wayne's Children's Zoo as it has the appearance of an amusement park, not a zoological garden."

I stayed at the zoo all day, not leaving until 8:30 PM, as the zoo was open late that evening. My journal stated the following, "Locking up the elephants was interesting. They lowered the drawbridge and walked the five-year-old female African elephant to its night quarters about one-hundred yards away. Pete got his training from a keeper at the Kansas City Zoo. Kansas City has a workable bull African elephant. I hope I have time to stop there."

On August 27th, I wrote extensive notes on my visit to the St. Louis Zoo. I noted that I thought it was wrong to have circus-type animal shows with chimps and elephants. "The zoo is famous for its animal shows. There was no chimp show yesterday because the chimps have

Monday and Tuesday off. I did see the elephant show. They all wore costumes and headgear with their names in large yellow letters. The elephants performed a number of skits including various dances, a barber shop number, plus all the basic elephant tricks."

Many things impressed me about the St. Louis Zoo including the bear grottos that were constructed in 1919 – 1921. I was especially impressed with the Atlantic walrus. "Huge animal in a small pool that is designed so he can come right up and be petted by the public. On the other side of the aquatic animal building was a much smaller Pacific walrus."

I was not so impressed with the primate house. "Zoo received an Edward H. Bean Award from AAZPA for breeding black lemurs. The primate house is about the most run down building in the zoo. Has a typical zoo design, cages around the outside and a large colobus cage in the center with a large skylight above." A few years later the zoo renovated all the older buildings in the zoo and each of the renovations are wonderful examples of excellence in zoo design.

On August 27th at 10 PM I arrived in Topeka, Kansas and was picked up at the bus depot by Gary Clarke, zoo director, and his family. Once at his house, Gary and I talked and he showed me slides until 1 AM.

When I visited the zoo the next day, I took extensive notes on every aspect of the new tropical rainforest exhibit, listing every animal in every exhibit. I did note that it was an especially attractive exhibit for the zoo's guests, but the small mammal exhibits were simple old-fashioned concrete pits. I mentioned that "most mammals have escaped at one time or another. The rough concrete has also helped mammals escape."

Touring the zoo on the 28th I saw how the zoo was doing so much with so little. They were well known for their breeding of golden eagles in exhibits made from combining two old baseball backstops together. I noted that the barrier fence of the elephant outdoor yard was so inadequate that staff had to be present anytime elephants were outside to prevent possible escapes. They actually had me ride one of the female Asian elephants, Sunda. I also commented on three small buildings – the Australian building, the creatures of the night building and the animal kingdom building. On the animal kingdom building I had the following observation: "This building could be the most dilapidated building in a U.S. zoo, but lack of funds prevented it from being abandoned and instead is used. From the visitor's side it is a very interesting exhibit. It is, however, difficult for the keepers to work and clean."

On August 29th, on my way to Oklahoma City, I wrote, "Last night I showed my slides to about thirty keepers and their guests. Gary Clarke seemed to be the most enthusiastic, but everyone was polite. No one fell asleep or even left early. It was a good show, but probably too long. In addition, I have a tendency to talk too fast and not leave time for much conversation. After the meeting we went to Straw Hat Pizza and drank beer. I drank too much and attempted to play fooz-ball hockey."

I visited the Oklahoma City Zoo, the last zoo on the trip, number 19, on August 30th and 31st. My best memory of the zoo was its huge collection of hoofed animals in large enclosures, including Pere David's deer, nyala, sitatunga, gaur, addax, sable, white-tailed gnu, Persian gazelle, saiga, chamois, Nubian ibex, Bukhara markhor and the only breeding herd of white-eared kob in the world. About the kob, I noted that the "male made a male blackbuck look dull." I also remember a children's zoo primate display that consisted of an ark surrounded by water. Also, in the children's zoo, I saw my first aardwolf. Years later I watched a wild aardwolf hunt for insects in Zimbabwe.

At the Oklahoma City Zoo, I spent a good deal of time watching three gorillas that at that time the zoo promoted them as mountain gorillas. If so, they would have been the only ones in the United States. A few years later they were eventually determined to be eastern lowland gorillas. Never-the-less, I reported that the male was over 600 pounds and one of the two females was 325 pounds. In my journal I made the following statement, "After some observations the massive size of these animals became apparent. The females looked particularly large in compared to the lowland variety. Head shape is very different as they have a larger crown. Limbs appeared stocky, but short." Maybe I was a victim of the hype!

Tired of bus travel, I changed my plans and flew home to Los Angeles on September 1st. Again, this was the start of my obsession of visiting zoos all over the world.

MORE ZOO VISITS

I continued to visit zoos throughout my career. In 1974, fellow keeper and friend, Mike Dee, and I traveled in my old beat-up Volkswagen to Arizona to see the Phoenix Zoo, Arizona Sonora Desert Museum and the Reid Park Zoo. It was amazing that car got us there and back. As Mike would comment years later when we would reminisce, we "went miles per hour!" To save money we stayed in some pretty awful motels, never paying more than twelve dollars per night! I was anxious to see the Arizona Sonora Desert Museum as I had heard so many good things about it. I wasn't disappointed. I also was interested in the Phoenix Zoo as they kept Arabian oryx and this zoo was probably most responsible for saving them from extinction. The Los Angeles Zoo had unrelated Arabian oryx and those two zoos, along with a few others, created a very successful breeding program. Much later this species did so well they were reestablished in several Middle Eastern Countries..

As I stated previously, for the last twelve years of my career at Cleveland Metroparks Zoo, I had a well-known competition with Mark Reed, director of the Sedgwick County Zoo in Wichita, Kansas to see the most AZA zoos. It became such an obsession with me that I stayed ahead of Mark for the entire time we competed. So, from 2000 until the day I retired, whenever I had an opportunity to see a new zoo, I took advantage of it. For instance, in 2009 when I went to a family wedding in North Adams, MA, I arrived two days early and rented a car in Albany so that I could visit the little zoos in

Millbrook, NY and in Binghamton, NY. The contest had no rules, so Mark was allowed to count the New York Aquarium, an institution he had not visited since he was six years old! However, he did not count Ocean Park in Hong Kong, one of several non-North American zoos in AZA, as he had no cash when he reached the gate and couldn't buy an admission ticket. The contest gave me the opportunity to take some amazing driving trips, such as driving across South Dakota from Sioux Falls to Rapid City or driving five-hundred miles in the state of North Dakota to visit all four of those zoos.

During my last year at Cleveland Metroparks Zoo, I had to be innovative to visit as many AZA accredited zoos and aquariums as possible. On the way to Miami for the annual AZA Director's Policy Conference, a title updated from the original title, Director's Retreat, to make it sound more professional and less like a party. I flew to Jackson, Mississippi to see that zoo and a couple more. Driving through Mississippi and Louisiana I saw a part of America that was very different from other regions of the country. I coined the following description of my drive: If it wasn't for Dollar General there would be no upscale retail and if it wasn't for the Waffle House, there would be no fine dining.

Even in retirement, I continued to visit zoos and aquariums, often as chair of AZA Accreditation Visiting Committees. Seeing zoos and aquariums new to me became difficult, although I did manage to see several of our international members such the SEAS Aquarium and Dolphin Island in Singapore, Cali Zoo in Colombia, Puebla Zoo in Mexico, Ripley's Aquarium in Canada and Tamaiken in Argentina. It is doubtful that I would ever see hundred percent of AZA accredited zoos and aquariums, as new ones are added each year, especially several new small for-profit SEALIFE aquariums. Also, there are additional International members and in 2020 AZA added two new members in South Korea. By the end of 2019, I had seen two-hundred and twenty-five of the two-hundred and forty zoos and aquariums accredited by AZA and three-hundred and seventy-six zoos and aquariums worldwide.

INTERNATIONAL TRAVEL

As zoo director at the Sacramento Zoo and Cleveland Metroparks Zoo, I had some wonderful opportunities to travel the world representing the zoo. By the time of my retirement, I had visited forty-five foreign counties, many representing the zoo at international conferences.

Probably my least favorite international trip was to China in April 1989 as part of a State of Ohio and Cleveland Metroparks delegation. The trip had already been on the agenda when I accepted the job as director of Cleveland Metroparks Zoo. This was a state delegation scheduled by the former Metroparks administration that had started a relationship with the Wuhan Zoo in Hubei Provence. The zoo had arranged for an animal exchange with the Wuhan Zoo, our sister zoo before my arrival. Cleveland Metroparks Zoo sent two chimps, two raccoons and two macaws in exchange for two clouded leopards, two red pandas, four pangolins and two Derby parakeets. Cleveland Metroparks Zoo also received two golden monkeys on a temporary loan in the summer of 1988.

Our delegation included Cleveland Metroparks Commissioners Fred Rzepka and Dan Corcoran, Metroparks executive director, Vern Hartenburg, Jack Rupert, president, Cleveland Zoological Society, and me as zoo director. Other members of the State of Ohio delegation were Thomas Zung, the architect for the RainForest, Richard Mosley, chief, Division of Natural Resources, State of Ohio and Dr. Stephen Still, director of the Horticulture Department, The Ohio State University.

Once in China, our delegation had at least twice as many Chinese counterparts. We were taken to the usual tourist attractions such as the great wall, summer palace and other sites. We also toured a dam and a sturgeon hatchery. We visited three zoos in China, those in Beijing, Shanghai and Wuhan. In Hubei province, where Wuhan was located, we drove for a day through the mountains supposedly to look for golden monkeys, which seemed to be always over on the next ridge. We never did see any monkeys. In fact, we never saw anything of significance on that drive. After two weeks in mainland China, we had a few days in Hong Kong before flying home to Cleveland. I enjoyed Hong Kong as we visited the small, but interesting, Hong Kong Zoo and the much larger Ocean Park. I suppose the previous administration may have had a plan for this trip, but since they were no longer part of the delegation, we were in the dark. For a year or two, I continued to correspond with the Wuhan Zoo, but after a while decided it was not a priority for our zoo. By that time, everyone else was willing to let it go as well.

With children in China in 1989. I was part of a
State of Ohio delegation visiting China.

During my first year at Cleveland Metroparks Zoo, I also had the opportunity to visit Lausanne, Switzerland as part of the AZA (then AAZPA) delegation to the Convention in Trade of Endangered Species (CITES). Each signatory country to this treaty had an official government delegation that voted on proposals. Many Non-Government Organizations (NGOs) that utilized wildlife or were interested in conservation of wildlife also attended, and in some instances, participated in discussions. This was my first international meeting and I was a little overwhelmed. Fortunately, Don Bruning from the New York Zoological Society and Kris Vehrs from AZA helped make sense out of the meeting. Anyone who studies elephant conservation will remember it was at the 1989 meeting of CITES that African elephants were placed on Appendix I, which severely limiting trade in elephants and their parts, including ivory. While I missed the first week of the convention and much of the debate on elephants, I was there for the final vote. My notes showed the final vote to be seventy-six countries voted yes, eleven voted no and four abstained.

It was interesting that in the main meeting hall, the NGOs were seated alphabetically so the AAZPA delegation was off to the right of the stage, a row or two from the front. What was more interesting was whom we were seated near. ACROPORO (no idea what initials stood for) was one member who had an interest in corals. There were several American Fur Industry (AFI) members as well as a group representing the British fur trade (BFI). In addition, right behind us were twelve delegates from the Japanese Association of Reptile Skin and Leather Industries (AJARSLI). It was important to remember that CITES is a trade treaty, and wildlife could only be protected under this treaty if they were endangered because of trade between countries.

Speaking of the Japanese, at that meeting their delegation actually issued a rather humorous statement in conjunction with the issue to allow for some trophy hunting of elephants, which they opposed. They stated that they opposed it as the Japanese possessed very few guns, but lots of cameras!

This was my first time spending much time with Kris Vehrs and from then on, I spent quite a bit of time with Kris and her husband, John, at various meetings and even taking time after meetings to visit the various sites. At the CITES meeting, I got to see Kris's ability to work with people from all over the world. After college, Kris worked as a tour guide in Europe so she could speak three or four languages and get by on a couple of others. She also had a great relationship with the United States government delegation and we had dinner with some of the members. Don Bruning used this dinner to talk frankly about a few issues about which he cared deeply. One was conservation of the Spix's macaw and the problems involved with the six to eight owners that held the last twenty birds. After a couple of drinks, the government folks mentioned how one zoo in the United State writes more importation permits than all the other US zoos combined. Don fueled the fire by stating that he felt that zoo often went around the permit process by going directly to a politician, instead of Fish and Wildlife. Again, it's an example of the only thing two zoo people agree on is what the third is doing wrong!

In 1990, I attended my first Conservation Breeding Specialist Group (CBSG) of the Species Survival Commission (SSC) of the International Union for Conservation of Nature (IUCN) and my first International Union of Directors of Zoological Gardens (IUGDG) in Copenhagen. IUDZG changed its name several times, but it is now known as the World Association of Zoos and Aquariums (WAZA). I guess conservationist really love acronyms! IUGDG started just before World War II and was reestablished after the war in 1946. In the early years, membership was very exclusive and meetings consisted of approximately forty members, mostly Europeans. In 2011 there were three-hundred and twenty-three members. When I became a member, it was still a rather restricted membership and I had to give a presentation and be voted in by the full membership. The reason was I was not considered a successive member as the previous Cleveland Metroparks Zoo director, Michael Vitantonio, was not a member, although Dr. Len Goss, his predecessor, was a member.

There is not much in my journal about these meeting, but I do remember thinking that I was somewhat out of place at the scientific sessions and workshops at CBSG and found the sessions at IUDZG not up to the quality of AZA conferences. I also remember that we wore earphones as the meetings were translated simultaneously in German and English. As it turned out there were only a couple German members that demanded simultaneous translation even though they actually understood English. Since it was such a huge expense for the host institution, English soon became the official language. Other than that, the only other memory is of going out to Tivoli Gardens in the evening with a group of colleagues.

My second IUDZG meeting was in Singapore and was more memorable as Sarah accompanied me (one of three she attended) and, aside from Singapore, we traveled to Malaysia and Japan. From the moment we landed in Singapore we had many great cultural experiences. After long hours in the air with little sleep, we had terrible jet lag and were up early our first morning and went for a walk. We found a local outdoor bazaar with lots of food vendors. No pancakes for us, we had noodles and fish for breakfast.

Around noon we caught a train to Kuala Lumpur where we checked into the Regents Hotel, which to this day is the nicest hotel I have ever spent the night. My friend, Jim Heck, owner of Explorer's World Travel (EWT), had arranged my African safaris while I was the director of the Sacramento Zoo, arranged the stay. In order to get a reasonable rate, he made business cards for me as EWT's manager of non-profits. It worked, as the daily rate was only one-hundred dollars per night. Of course, we visited the zoo and the aviary, but my favorite memory was a hike in a secondary forest, Templer's Park. What started out as a quiet walk in the forest to see a waterfall and long-tailed macaques, ended as a long muddy hike in the rain. It didn't help that we took a wrong turn and hiked an extra mile or so. Amazingly, the taxi was still waiting for us. We arrived back at the five-star hotel all muddy and walked across its polished marble lobby straight to the bar without even cleaning up and ordered gin and tonics. I have vivid memories of the tall, exotic looking cocktail waitress kneeling down to mix our wonderful cocktails right at our table. Up in the room, I took off my bloody socks and found five leeches. Still it was a great day, as it was the first time I had seen a wild primate on the Asian continent.

Often the best part of WAZA conferences was the people I met and the places I visited. The Dublin conference in 1995 was one example. On the second day of the conference Steve Wylie, Bill Dennler and I took the 7:50 AM train to Belfast, Northern Ireland to see the zoo. At that time the Dublin Zoo wasn't much, so we wanted to see another zoo and others at the conference mentioned that the Belfast Zoo was worth a visit. At the time there were no security concerns in traveling between Ireland and Northern Ireland so there were no check points, soldiers or even passport control. The Belfast Zoo was certainly worth the visit. It was located on a hill above the ocean and had great exhibits and beautiful landscaping. The animal collection included gorillas, chimps, maned wolves, spectacle bears, cheetahs, bongos, Malayian tapirs and many species of tamarins and lemurs.

One vivid memory was a certain night in a very large Irish pub on October 3, 1995. After our small group had a beer or two, all hundred or so people in the pub moved to one small corner where a TV was showing the verdict of the O.J. Simpson trial. The rest of the pub, including behind the bar, was completely empty. When it was announced not guilty, all hundred folks were silent and in a state of disbelief. After thirty seconds of silence, everyone went back to drinking. Later, all our new Irish friends talked to us about how they felt it was an unbelievable verdict.

Three Australian WAZA meetings (Perth in 2001, Adelaide in 2009 and Melbourne in 2012) were some of my favorites. All three were well organized with good speakers and gave delegates a chance to see some of the best zoological facilities in the world. The meetings also gave me a chance to see some beautiful country and unique wildlife.

After the WAZA meeting in Adelaide, Australia, a small group of us traveled to Kangaroo Island. The group included Kris Vehrs (AZA) and her husband John, Steve Wylie, retired from Oklahoma City Zoo and his wife Patsy, Steve McCusker, director of the San Antonio Zoo, his wife Johnnie, Satch Krantz and me. The wildlife and the variety of coastal scenery were largely unspoiled by any development. The island, off the coast of southern Australia, was a two-hour drive from Adelaide through the wine country and a forty-five-minute ferry ride from the mainland. We saw koalas, Australian sea lions, New

Zealand fur seals, echidna, and western gray kangaroos. As for birds, I enjoyed seeing Cape Barren geese, yellow-tailed black-cockatoo, pied oystercatcher, white-faced heron, fairy penguins, superb fairy-wren and many more. At the Kangaroo Island Lodge, staff with the help of guests feed fish to the white pelicans every morning. I have a photo of Kris Vehrs greatly enjoying the experience.

On our last day, Satch felt sick. We returned to the lodge and they called an ambulance. The ambulance arrived and it turned out the EMT on the ambulance was also our breakfast waitress at the lodge. At the local hospital, a South African doctor diagnosed the cause of his pain as a kidney stone. By that time, Satch was feeling better as he may have passed the stone. Leaving the hospital and stopping to pay the bill, the doctor told us just to leave as the paperwork would be too much trouble. When Satch got home, he did get a substantial bill for the ambulance service.

From 1990 through 2012, I felt very fortunate to have only missed four WAZA meetings. I felt strongly that attending these meetings was an important part of my commitment to continual education.

African safaris have been an important part of my life since my first safari to Zimbabwe, then Southern Rhodesia, in August of 1978. Saul Kitchener, the director of the San Francisco Zoo and his wife Barbara, had put together this safari to Zimbabwe, Botswana and South Africa with Joyce Basel of Fun Safaris. Only six clients signed up which meant that Saul and Barbara could not go for free. I happened to be in the office at the time and we agreed that I could go as leader if I paid my airfare. I was the leader of my first African safari and I had never even been to Africa. In fact, I had never been out of the country, except for brief visits to Canada and Mexico!

Since then, I have had had the opportunity to travel to Africa on another 29 safaris. Sarah joined me on seventeen of these safaris.

1. Botswana, Zimbabwe, and South Africa (1978)
2. Kenya (1983)
3. Kenya (1984)

4. Kenya and Tanzania (1985)
5. Zimbabwe (1986)
6. Kenya and Rwanda (1988)
7. Botswana, Namibia and Zimbabwe (1993)
8. Tanzania (1997)
9. Kenya (1998)
10. South Africa (1999)
11. Botswana and Zimbabwe (2000)
12. Kenya walk across Tsavo (2002)
13. Zambia (2004)
14. Kenya Family Safari (2005)
15. Tanzania (2006)
16. Madagascar (2007)
17. Tanzania (2008)
18. Tanzania - 2nd Safari (2008)
19. Kenya/Tanzania (2009)
20. Uganda/Rwanda (2010)
21. Tanzania (2011)
22. Botswana/South Africa (2011)
23. Tanzania (March 2013)
24. Tanzania (June 2013)
25. Tanzania (February 2014)
26. Tanzania (June 2014)
27. Tanzania (January 2015)
28. Tanzania (June 2015)
29. South Africa/Namibia (March 2017)
30. Tanzania (June 2017)

I also traveled to many other ecotourism sites, such as Belize, Costa Rica, Panama, Honduras, Ecuador, Galapagos, Brazil, Peru, India, Borneo, Australia and New Zealand. However, I enjoyed Africa the most.

These safaris had direct implications to my job and they also provided me with some valuable life lessons. For instance, during my first safari to Zimbabwe and South Africa these countries were still under white rule, apartheid. There were whites-only areas of Johannesburg. In Victoria Falls all the European population, about three-hundred at that time, carried weapons, even into the casinos. I remember tripping over some kind of rifle when I left the blackjack table! I felt this experience gave me firsthand knowledge of apartheid in southern Africa.

I learned many other valuable lessons on that first safari. One was how small the world is and how much the rest of the world is interested in America. At the Island Safari Camp near Maun, Botswana, in 1978, the owners, Tony and Yoni, were reading a relatively new *Time* magazine for which they had a subscription. This taught me that people all over the world are interested in America because we have so many resources and America's actions often affect others throughout the world.

In addition, I learned that Africans, and others, could sometimes have a less than complimentary opinion of us. Sitting at dinner one night we invited an African who was sitting alone to join us. He was a government engineer working on a project near Maun. At one point he looked at me and stated that he thought I was a Canadian. I had always thought that not only was I a typical American, but I acted like one. I was a little dumbfounded and asked him why he thought I was a Canadian and for that matter, what does an American look like? He immediately pointed to Fred, one of our participants on this safari. Fred was a sixty-year old retired Marine, a little loud, a lot overweight, and wearing a brightly colored Hawaiian shirt with two cameras around his neck. At that point, I was a little embarrassed for being an American.

This first safari was incredible. We spent a few days camping in the Okavango, several days along the Savuti Channel, several days in a camp overlooking the Chobe River and then finished our safari in Victoria Falls, Zimbabwe. Experiences that I remember to this day include afternoon swimming in the Okavango with an armed guard standing on the boat watching for crocodiles and hippos. I vividly remember tossing bream, a native fish, stuffed with papyrus reed so the fish would float a few yards in front of the boat to entice a fish eagle down from a nearby palm tree. Cameras were all focused on the fish and as the eagle grabbed the fish and we all got great photos. I remember taking the boat into the swamp at night to search for crocodiles and finding several eight footers.

Seeing birds in the wild that I had worked with in the zoo was a thrill. On the boat in the Okavango we observed several pairs of African pygmy goose and well as other water birds. I especially remember one afternoon when I was by myself a few hundred yards from camp; I saw my first African hoopoe in the wild, a bird I still love seeing in Africa.

Our guide was one of the last great white African guides, Doug Skinner. He had spent twenty-five years guiding in Zambia before its independence and his business nationalized. Like many of his generation, he was rugged, hard drinking, had tremendous knowledge of wildlife and ran an exceptional organized safari. Like many safari guides, he told a different story every night. I still remember his story about him being delirious with malaria when several spotted hyenas visited his bedside in camp. He was not sure if it actually happened as he stated it could have been just a dream. Every morning Doug walked through the camp at 6 AM calling out, "waky-waky-waky" to get his clients up in the morning.

By 2020 I had traveled to fifty-even different countries and eight territories. I have found that while there were times when people did not appreciate our government, for the most part, despite my observation in Botswana, they liked Americans. I found that the majority of American international travelers are easy going, fun to be with, genuinely interested in others and less demanding than travelers from other parts of the world.

After becoming director of the Sacramento Zoo, I guided three Kenya and Kenya/Tanzania safaris in 1983, 1984 and 1985. Each of these had approximately thirty participants. My next trip was to Ecuador and the Galapagos Islands, then on a familiarization trip (FAM) to Zimbabwe. FAM trips were offered by travel companies in an attempt to get zoo directors and others to use their companies for safaris. It was the only FAM trip I ever participated in as I thought it was probably inappropriate to participate in these types of free programs, especially for a public employee. Besides I just did not have the time.

My safaris in 1983, 1984 and 1985 were memorable. They all included Sacramento Zoo donors, docents and board members. Several clients from the first safari traveled with me again, even when I moved to Cleveland. I took my 15-year-old son, Travis, on the 1984 safari. I rarely had young people on safari, but Sarah and I did a great family safari to Kenya in 2005. To this day, Travis and I still talk about that adventure. I have vivid memories of Travis bargaining for various swords, knives and shields at Thompson Falls. In those years, elephants came into camp in Amboseli and I can still see him outside our cabin watching the staff chase elephants from the camp. A photo of Travis and me at the Equator sign hung in my office at Cleveland Metroparks Zoo. Perhaps my favorite memory is of Travis ordering a Mai Tai for lunch at the Tamarind restaurant in Mombasa. Several safari clients were aghast. I just thought it was funny. Sorry mom!

While on safaris in the eighties, I saw some great wildlife. And every safari after those added to great moments of wildlife viewing. I never saw a leopard on my first three safaris to Kenya and Tanzania but have seen them many times in later years, although it's still not easy. In the eighties we always saw black rhinos in both Amboseli and the Maasai Mara, but twenty-five years later sightings are very rare. Black rhinos in Kenya can only be found in a few places like Lewa Downs, Lake Nakuru and other protected areas, where they are guarded twenty-four hours a day.

Another difference is the length of time and the amount of time spent flying. Safaris in the eighties were longer and travel was by minibus regardless of the bad roads. I believe people had more time in the eighties. Clients on safaris now have less time and often choose to fly from park to park. On a Kenyan safari, it is now common to fly in and out of both Samburu and Maasai Mara, saving significant time, but adding to the cost.

With son, Travis, age 15 at the equator in Kenya.

The land cost of my 1984 safari to Kenya was one-thousand four-hundred and four dollars, plus the international air was one-thousand five hundred and thirty-one dollars for a total cost of two-thousand nine-hundred and thirty-five dollars. I had thirty people on that eighteen-day safari. In June 2017, Sarah and I took sixteen people to Tanzania for a twelve-day safari. The land cost of that safari was nine-thousand dollars and international air was three-thousand dollars for a total cost of twelve-thousand dollars. While air cost had only doubled in thirty-three years, land costs had increased almost seven times. I find it interesting how people complain about the high cost of airfares.

In May 1986, the safari to Zimbabwe was a special one. First, it was a familiarization (FAM) tour sponsored by Fun Safaris, the tour company that did my first Africa safari in 1978. Mike and Joyce Basil, owners of Fun Safaris, accompanied our group of zoo professionals. Others on the safari included Ted McToldridge director Santa Barbara Zoo and his wife, Don Farst director of the Gladys Porter Zoo in Brownsville, TX and his wife, George Felton director of the Baton Rouge Zoo and his wife, Karen Sausman director of the Living Desert in Palm Desert, Clayton Freiheit director of the Denver Zoo and David Westbrook director of the Little Rock Zoo and his wife. What an amazing group to travel with in Zimbabwe.

Each of the participants brought something different to the safari. Karen Sausman and I were the birders, although she had much more patience than I at identifying African birds. Clayton Freiheit was outstanding at spotting wildlife, often even before the guides. I remember George Felton giving a heartfelt and folksy thank you speech on our last evening. Although George had already had a long career as a zoo director, this was his first safari and he was very grateful for the opportunity.

This was my first and only visit to Zimbabwe, other than visiting Victoria Falls. It was also my first time in open-sided vehicles, common in Southern Africa, but not East Africa. We had some outstanding wildlife experiences including seeing my first and only aardwolf in the wild. In Hwange National Park we watched a single aardwolf for an hour at twilight hunting for insects and small animals. What a treat! In Hwange we saw several large herds of over a hundred elephants and several herds of stately sable antelope.

We spent a couple of nights on houseboats on Lake Kariba adjacent to Mastusadona National Park. Lake Kariba was created in the fifties when a dam was constructed and the Zambezi Valley was flooded. As the lake filled from 1958 to 1964, wildlife was trapped on ever-diminishing islands. The Zimbabwe government, then Rhodesia, organized Operation Noah. Park rangers, led by Rupert Fothergill, eventually rescued over six thousand animals from the islands, including snakes such as the black mamba. While the lake was flooded over twenty years prior to our visit, during our stay we could still see tree trunks rising above the lake. Portions of the lake near the shore resembled a recently burned forest. The trees also provided a healthy population of cormorants excellent structures for nesting.

My next trip, sponsored by the Sacramento Zoological Society, was to Ecuador and the Galapagos Islands in January 1987. To get to Ecuador we needed to fly from Sacramento to Miami and stay the night before catching a three PM flight to Quito. We were worried that our flight might be canceled, as there was political unrest in Ecuador and talk of impeachment of their president. Our flight was not canceled and we arrived in Quito, our base from which we would travel to eastern Ecuador and the Rio Napo River.

In Ecuador we met up with Jim Heck of EWT who would stay with us through the mainland portion of our trip. Travel to the Rio Napo was difficult, as the military rerouted our plane to Coco and we had to land in Lago Agrio, two and half hours from the Rio Napo and our accommodations on the Flotel Orellana. To get to our destination on the Rio Napo from Lake Agrio, we had to take an old school bus. I sat next to Jim in the back of the bus with no air movement and temperatures above 100 degrees. To help matters we were given warm cokes! In was an interesting ride despite the heat and everyone remained in good spirits. In the forest, we saw many of the usual birds including the unique hoatzin, many boat-billed herons and both brown and chestnut jacamars.

Following our visit on the Rio Napo, we stopped in Quito on our way to the Galapagos Islands, arriving at the airport on Baltra Island after a six-hundred-mile flight from the mainland. The Galapagos Islands are a must see for any biologist because of unique and approachable wildlife. Charles Darwin developed his theory of evolution after his five-week visit in the 1830s. Our group of twelve filled the yacht, the Isabella. We were told that the Isabella was once Ecuador's presidential yacht. Although older than some other vessels, it was comfortable except for the lack of air conditioning, which made sleeping difficult. I will never forget many wonderful experiences, including snorkeling with Galapagos penguins and sea lions. We sighted most of the endemic birds including the flightless cormorant and seven of the thirteen Darwin's finches. The most spectacular birds included nesting blue-footed, red and masked boobies, and Frigatebirds. All these birds allowed us to approach them within a few feet.

In the Galapagos Islands at the Charles Darwin Research Station in 1987.

My last trip as director of the Sacramento Zoo occurred in 1988. I took a small group of repeat travelers to Rwanda to see the mountain gorillas, followed by a Kenyan safari to my two favorite destinations to view wildlife, Samburu and the Maasai Mara. At that time, the safari was required to stay a week in Rwanda to be able visit mountain gorillas. That gave us the opportunity to visit Akagera National Park, one of the most beautiful parks in all of Africa, covering about a third of the country at that time. The park's wildlife was sparse in comparison to other parks I had visited. Poaching had been a big problem. We did see one elephant and our driver, John, told us there were only twenty elephants in the entire park. Today the park has been overrun by human settlement and is much smaller, but with the introduction of additional wildlife there is more to see.

We were fortunate to have two days to visit the gorillas, visiting Group Nine and Group Thirteen. It was amazing and like nothing else I had ever done. On the first day we walked about two or three hours to a bamboo forest and I could actually smell the gorillas before we saw them. Male gorillas have a unique smell that I recognized from my days as an animal keeper. Our guides told us to stay where we were while they went to look for the gorillas; however, the gorillas found us and pretty soon we were surrounded by the seven members of Group Nine. At one point we had to get off of the path as two females passed within inches of us.

This was in July of 1988, two months prior to the release of the movie, *Gorillas in the Mist*. We had dinner the first night with Craig Sholley, a scientist who had studied gorillas in Rwanda and former curator at the Baltimore Zoo. He told us then that the movie would not be an accurate portrayal of Dian Fossey's life. She certainly didn't look like Sigourney Weaver, who played her in the movie. I believe Dian's erratic behavior is best described in the 2001 book, *In the Kingdom of Gorillas*, by Bill Weber and Amy Vedders. None-the-less, she does deserve to be remembered for her important role in saving these iconic endangered animals.

This safari then flew to Nairobi, Kenya where we drove north to

Samburu. The weather was desert-like and certain species, such as Grevy's zebra, gerenuk and Beisa oryx were easily viewable. This safari was memorable because it was the first opportunity I had for excellent viewing of a leopard. This male leopard was right out in the open and perched on a rock. The only problem was there were at least twenty other minivans also enjoying this rare opportunity.

When I arrived in Cleveland, it took me several years to start doing African Safaris, although I did do several trips to Central and South America since the zoo was building a large rain forest exhibit. My first ecotourism trip from Cleveland was a ten-day trip to Costa Rica in 1991. I had a nice group of travelers, including Ralph and Ann O'Neil. This delightful couple later traveled several more times with me. Ralph had a great sense of humor and often had me laughing. At the Monteverdi Lodge, after a long day's hike in the mud, Ralph showed up for cocktails stating, "You have to excuse Ann tonight as she had to stay back and clean my boots!" Knowing Ann as I did, nothing could have been further from the truth. This was my first visit to Central America and seeing sloth, spider monkeys, caiman, scarlet macaws and basilisk lizards. Seeing a quetzal at Monteverdi was very special. Another animal I discovered with the help of Rolando, our guide, was the northern ghost bat. In Tortuguero National Park we found these small white bats in the tube-leaf of a *Heliconia* plant.

It also was my first chance to see leaf-cutter ants in the wild, an insect species that is now a mainstay of almost every zoo's tropical building, including Cleveland's RainForest. Seeing these ants in the wild posed more questions than answers and I wrote the following in the journal:

"… these colonies seemed unreal. Where are they going? Why do they work so hard? How can there be so many? How long has this foot-wide trail been in use by the ants? How long have they been working on this particular tree? For every answer there was another question about these intriguing creatures. These ants cut pieces of leaves and flowers and carried

them to their underground nests. Once inside the nest, the pieces are processed by the workers and become a fungus. The fungus provides the ants with food."

While I have learned much about these ants over the last thirty years, they continue to amaze me. Even in 2013, I spent a good deal of time watching leaf-cutter ants at Las Cruses Biological Station in southern Costa Rica.

The last day of our trip in 1991 we were in San Jose and did some shopping and visited the National Museum. Then we went to the Simon Bolivar Zoo with Yolanda Matamoros, who was then part-time at the zoo and part-time at the university. The zoo was awful and Yolanda was very apologetic. Exhibits were dirty and poorly designed and constructed. Aside from native animals, there was a tiger and a chimp. The chimps ten by ten-foot cage was the worst I had ever seen. There was talk back then of moving the zoo to a larger site. To this day, it is still just talk. Years later, I visited again and it was not much better.

One February evening in 1991 we gathered around the TV in the hotel and watched the news that the United States had just invaded Kuwait

In 1993, Sarah and I led our first African safari together. We chose to travel to Namibia, Botswana and Zimbabwe. Since it was the July after our May wedding, people referred to it as our honeymoon safari. This was my first visit to Namibia and Etosha National Park. Etosha means great white place for the large salt pan in the middle of this huge park. The first night at Mokuti Lodge in Etosha, we ran into Gray Clarke, formerly of the Topeka Zoo who now was leading safaris full-time. As only Gary could, he entertained our clients with his humorous stories for a half an hour before dinner.

Viewing wildlife in Etosha was different than in other African parks. We often drove on paved roads to a waterhole and waited for the wildlife. Driving to one such waterhole we observed a spotted hyena running away from the water hole with a large piece of meat in its powerful jaw. Looking at the water hole we noticed two other hyenas in the water. After further investigation we noted a spiral kudu horn above the waterline in the middle of the waterhole. The two hyenas were actually diving for kudu. The water was the color of a weak tomato soup. We learned from others that the hyena clan had chased a young male kudu into the water and killed it.

At that same waterhole the next day we, had another experience that had the lodge guests talking all through dinner. When we drove up, we observed an injured giraffe that could only use three of its four limbs. Within a half an hour the giraffe fell to the ground and lay motionless. The question we discussed was would lions or hyena take advantage of the easy meal. Once it was apparent the hyenas were coming, a senior ranger put the wounded giraffe out of its misery. At the lodge, the discussion concerning the interference with nature went on well into the night.

In February 1995 I went back to the tropics leading a zoo group to Belize. It would be my first visit to the Belize Zoo and since then I have always considered it one of the best small zoos in the world. Sharon Matola, an American, started the zoo with a few animals left in the country by a movie crew. The zoo exhibits native animals in very natural exhibits. The exhibit labels have hand-written poems describing a behavioral trait of that animal. Sharon and her staff have always been very active in conservation efforts throughout Belize.

We also toured the "baboon sanctuary" at Bermudian Landing, obviously not a sanctuary for baboons that only live in Africa, but a sanctuary for howler monkeys. Most of the sanctuary is on private farms where the conservation minded farmers with funding from the World Wildlife Fund and the Audubon Society, had left native fruit trees on the perimeters of their farms, thus providing suitable habitat for over one-thousand native black howler monkeys.

Another highlight of this ecotourism program was a visit to Tikal National Park in Guatemala. One morning we woke up at five in the morning and walked an hour to temple number four to watch a magical sunrise over the Tikal ruins. As the sun rose and the sky cleared, the ruins seemed to rise from the morning fog. The sound of howler monkeys waking up in the morning and keel-billed toucans flying overhead made the morning even more special.

In the small world category, our guide, David Vernon, was the husband of the daughter of one of the Sacramento Zoo docents that I knew very well when I was director at that zoo. I liked David so much that I returned years later with Sarah and we hired David as our guide.

A month later in March 1995 I returned to the tropical rain forest to participate in the Amazon Rainforest Workshop in Peru organized by International Expeditions of Birmingham, Alabama. The zoo had supported the Amazon Center of Environment Education and Research (ACEER) since the RainForest opened in 1992 and I wanted to see this site for myself. I also wanted to learn more about the tropical rainforest. I flew into Iquitos, a city in Peru twenty-four hundred miles up the Amazon River from its confluence with the Atlantic Ocean in Brazil. To get to the ACCER, we had to go down the Amazon and then travel on the Napo River towards Ecuador. Instructors for the workshop were college professors and zoo curators. There were some great lectures in this casual environment and I believe there was even a little competition between instructors to be the most interesting. I remember one lecture by Rob Halpern, then with the New York Zoological Society, on plant reproduction. He made a condescending remark about ornithologists during his talk. Bill Stout, the ornithology instructor, was sitting next to me and leaned over and whispered, "leave it to a botanist to make sex boring."

I also remember Randy Morgan from the Cincinnati Zoo testing a theory that larger square-headed ants could actually glide through the air from the top of the rainforest canopy. He took three different species of live ants, one was a square-headed and one species of dead ant, as a control, and dropped them along a plum-line from the top of the ceiling two stories up in the meeting room. The thought was that the gliding ants would land on the floor further from the plum line. The experiment was inconclusive.

The highlight of the workshop was spending time in the canopy walkway. From the towers in the canopy that were one-hundred and twelve feet above the ground, we observed mixed flocks of many tropical bird species, especially tanagers. I wrote the following in my journal, "There is no way to explain it, unique and wonderful is the best I can do. It's the rainforest equivalent of snorkeling on a tropical reef."

Sarah and I led for our first migration safari to Tanzania that started on Valentine's Day, 1997. Several of our clients had travelled with us on previous trips. Our first stop was at Swala Camp in southern Tarangire, to this day one of my favorite camps in Africa. It was very hot, close to one-hundred degrees, and tse tse flies were a problem. I had so many bites on my legs that in the evening it looked like I was in a knife fight and lost! In the evening I had a temperature but felt better after some sleep. I was disappointed that I had to wear long pants for the rest of the safari. On that same day, my camera broke and Sarah and I had to share her camera and our point and shoot camera. It was a great lesson as not having a camera turned into a blessing as I learned to actually watch Africa and not be so consumed by photography.

Our next camp was in Kusini, in the southern Serengeti. We were able to drive to an area where we were in the middle of the vast wildebeest and zebra migration. It seemed like we saw at least a million animals! Driving along a streambed, we spotted a herd of over fifty impala and then heard the impala alarm call. Curious, we drove closer and saw an adult impala being strangled by a large African rock python. What an incredible site! Unfortunately, our vehicles interrupted the kill and the snake left the scene. While it rarely happens, it's always upsetting to me when observing wildlife changes the outcome of a natural occurrence and I have always tried to avoid it. Sometimes it takes some explaining to clients who want the very best photos possible.

Now that I had seen Tanzania both in the summer and the winter, I knew it would become one of my favorite safari destinations.

In October 1998 I took a small group on a quick safari to Kenya.

Don and Gail Butler and John and Kathy Fraylick were on their first trip with the zoo and remained great zoo supporters throughout the rest of my career. It had been thirteen years since my last visit to Kenya and much had changed. Black rhinos were now completely gone from the Maasai Mara, but there was a program to introduce white rhinos to Lake Nakuru. It was hard to believe, but the roads were even worse than in previous years. And beers were not a dollar, but four dollars. It was great to be back in Samburu, one of my favorite spots in Africa. We saw several leopards and enjoyed seeing a couple of very large crocodiles when they were baited on the front lawn of the Samburu Serena. Grevy's zebra, gerenuk and reticulated giraffe were species that remained easy to observe in Samburu.

In 1999, we planned no zoo sponsored ecotourism program, as there was a WAZA meeting in South Africa. Sarah and I planned a short safari with several zoo colleagues to Cape Town, Kruger National Park and adjacent private reserves. While this was my second visit to South Africa, it was my first to Cape Town and Kruger National Park. Cape Town and its environs now have been a favorite of mine as there is so much to see. On a day drive, one can see penguins at Boulder's Beach and African wildlife at Cape of Good Hope National Reserve and Cape Point. You can also view the place promoted as where the Atlantic meets the Indian Ocean although it's actually a little east of the Cape. In this area one can have a close-up view, and unfortunately smell, of a huge colony of southern fur seals. On another day, one can see what I consider one of the best botanical gardens in the world, Kirstenbosch National Botanical Garden and then visit the wine county, including Stellenbosch, Paarl and Franschhock. There is a cable car ride up to Table Mountain and much more. The view from Table Mountain is spectacular.

It was fun to travel with fellow zoo people, including Mark Reed, Sedgwick County Zoo in Wichita, Kansas, Craig Dinsmore, Hogle Zoo in Salt Lake City and Dave Towne and his wife Chris, from the Woodland Park Zoo in Seattle. We also met up with Jerry and Lois Borin for our tour of the wine country. One of my favorite Mark Reed stories occurred at the Cape of Good Hope sign, a site where just about everyone has a photo of themselves or their group. After our photo, Mark volunteered to assist a young Japanese woman taking a picture of her group. Within minutes the whole group handed him their cameras and I helped Mark take about fifty photos on fifty different cameras! When we finished, the young lady insisted that she get her photo taken with Mark and I took that photo.

Safaris in the private reserves outside of Kruger, such as Sabi Sabi where we stayed for two nights, are luxurious. Sabi Sabi was a beautiful camp with fantastic accommodations, excellent food and wine and expert guides. At the time of our visit, most of the guides were handsome white South Africans, assisted by black South African trackers. Our guide was a very handsome South African rugby player named Brandon. He spoke fluent Japanese having played rugby there for a couple of years and was a top choice for Japanese tourists on safari. He was an excellent guide, and among other sightings he guided us to see painted dogs, a first for Sarah and me. Although we were on a private reserve, the guides tried to stay on the dirt tracks to keep the vegetation from being destroyed. Only when there was something special would they leave the track. Often when they would see lion tracks, they would stop the vehicle, grab a rifle and walk out into the bush to investigate. If they found lions, leopards or dogs they would come back to the vehicle and drive to the areas where the animals were spotted. Often it was nothing and I was never quite sure if they did this just for show. Once Brandon came back with a tiny little frog he picked up along the way and showed it to all of us. I jokingly commented, "My God Brandon, you are an extraordinary tracker to have found that frog!"

In 2000, Sarah and I led a wonderful group of people to Botswana and stayed at three Wilderness Safari camps, Duma Tau, Chitabe and Vumbura, before visiting Victoria Falls in Zimbabwe. Wildlife viewing was spectacular and we saw several families of painted dogs. There actually was plenty of wildlife around our camps. On our first night in Vumbura we woke up hearing lots of splashing in the water that surrounded the camp. Looking out of the tent we could see black silhouettes of fifty Cape buffalo. Also, we knew the camp was the home for many Chama baboons. What we didn't know was at night they slept in the trees above our tent. During the night they would naturally relieve themselves and their dropping fell all night long on the roofs of our tents! Not getting a great night's sleep is a small price to pay for spending a night in a tent in Africa!

It was an extremely wet year in the Okavango Delta that year and the vehicles were routinely in water up to the floorboards. In some places there were wooden log bridges just large enough for one land cruiser at a time. It was on one such bridge, that I thought we might all die! On this one narrow bridge the front tire went over the side and the vehicle came to an abrupt stop hanging over the bridge. We all moved to the high side. I have no idea what kept the entire vehicle from not flipping completely over! We all slowly got out of the vehicle, climbing over the back and walked off the bridge. The driver was embarrassed and wanted to solve the problem quickly before the others would discover it. The driver and the tracker got in the water and under the vehicle. Using a jack and some logs, these two guys bounced the vehicle back up on the bridge just prior to our second vehicle joining us. We were all amazed and happy to get back to camp without injury.

It so happened that while in Botswana, Phil and Alice Alexander were celebrating their fiftieth wedding anniversary. I told the staff that we were celebrating tonight and wanted a cake. I knew they would do something special and they told me about their surprise, but no one else knew about it. After dinner they brought out a beautiful round cake with white icing and a cherry on top. Cutting into the cake Phil eventually realized it was a little unusual. It was elephant dung under the white icing! We all, including the entire staff, had a great laugh and then the camp staff brought out a real cake.

We finished the safari with a wonderful visit to the Victoria Falls Hotel in Zimbabwe and viewed the falls from that side of the river. Some of us played golf at Bumi Hills golf course. Dr. vonThron, the father of one of Sarah's college roommates, did academy awards for each person on the safari. He and his wife, Jane, had purchased a small giraffe statue, the Oscars, and awarded one to each participant on safari. Awards included things such as best actor for pretending to be interested in birds, best director for giving the wrong information, and several others. Ever since then, Sarah and I did something very similar on most of our safaris.

Instead of going to Africa in 2001, Sarah and I led a trip to Australia in October and then I stayed an additional week to attend the WAZA conference in Perth, Australia. Four of six of our clients had traveled previously with us to Africa. I was very happy to be in Australia as Cleveland Metroparks Zoo had just opened Australian Adventure so it was my chance to get first-hand knowledge of Australia and its wildlife. We went to Sydney and visited the zoo and the Blue Mountains. During a picnic lunch I remember having a kookaburra in a tree above our table. No matter where I travel, I always enjoy seeing an animal in the wild that I had worked with for many years in zoos. We then went to Lamington National Park and stayed at O'Reilly's Guest House where we saw some great birds, including regent and satin bowerbirds, lyrebirds and many others that were a first for me. We also hand-fed a seed mix to wild king parrots and crimson rosella. We visited the Daintree rainforest and snorkeled on the Great Barrier Reef.

On our boat trip to the Great Barrier Reef, not all our clients wanted to snorkel and some stayed in the boat and then were given a ride in a small glass-bottom dingy where then could look below at the reef with its magnificent corals and tropical fish. These folks were already back on board when the snorkelers returned. On our arrival, Jack Thompson, who always had a joke, stated that, "I hope it's OK, but I just sat on someone's camera." Jack Bramen, another jokester, answered immediately, "I don't want those photos when they are developed!"

We flew to Tasmania and up to Crater Lakes where there was in two-feet of snow. The cold did not stop dozens of Bennett's wallabies and Tasmanian pademelons from coming to the lodge in the evening for treats from the kitchen.

One day in Tasmania we had scheduled a boat trip from the Freycinet Lodge to see marine mammals, but unfortunately, we had to cancel as it was windy and the ocean was too rough. No problem as it gave four of us an opportunity to play golf. We went to the local post office to rent clubs, purchase tees and balls and pay our green fees. We drove five miles to the 9-hole public course that had great views of the ocean below. There wasn't a soul there although there was a run-down red barn that I guess served as a clubhouse. Ironically there was a sign on the door of the barn that read, "Dress Code Strictly Enforced." While it really wasn't a well-maintained course, it was a great fun. We returned the clubs in the afternoon and realized that we didn't even leave a deposit. I am not sure anyone would steal the awful rental clubs anyway. After dinner that night we got a real treat when we walked along the beach to view fairy penguins come ashore. After Tasmania, the group went on to New Zealand, Sarah flew home to Cleveland and I went to Perth to the WAZA conference.

This trip occurred just after 9/11/2001. Every Australian we met was very supportive of America and we felt very welcome. The Los Angeles airport was still closed to traffic and close in parking and it was very surreal flying through that airport.

Tsavor Tsavo

One unique safari occurred in January 2002 when Satch Krantz and I got four friends to take a two-week walking safari across Tsavo National Park in Kenya. The following is the account of that special two weeks that I wrote on my return home.

A couple of years ago, I read a book by adventure writer, Rick Ridgeway, entitled, In the Shadow of Kilimanjaro. The book chronicled a thirty-day walking safari from the top of Mount Kilimanjaro in Tanzania, through West and East Tsavo National Parks in Kenya, and finishing with a swim in the Indian Ocean. I shared the book with my friend and colleague, Palmer "Satch" Krantz, director of the Riverbanks Zoo in Columbia, South Carolina. In the summer of 2001, while Satch and his wife were visiting in Cleveland, we discussed the book over a couple of glasses of wine in my back patio. We had both been to Africa many times leading zoo-member safaris, but we had never been on a walking safari. In fact, neither of us had known that it was even possible. While the idea of climbing Kilimanjaro did not appeal to us as it was too cold, too little oxygen and not enough wildlife. We both thought that a walk in Tsavo would be a great adventure. Our wives were surprisingly supportive, probably because they did not think we would actually do it!

After returning to work the next week, Satch found the walking safari company, Tropical Ice, on the Internet and he started e-mailing the owner, Iain Allan, immediately. Iain guided the Ridgeway group four years earlier and was interested in doing a similar safari again. It would only be the second time an organized group walked completely across both Tsavo West and Tsavo East.

After getting details on the cost, approximately $8000 each, and the dates (January 28 – February 11, 2002), Satch and I looked for a couple of friends to share the experience. While several friends initially expressed interest, most had to decline for a variety of reasons. Satch found Dan Love, a doctor from Columbia and I found Tony Lesh, the Cleveland Metroparks Zoo's consulting veterinarian, and Jeff Campbell, a dentist and friend of mine that had traveled to Botswana with Sarah and me in 2000. Satch and I both asked Gary Lee, a Philadelphia based zoo architect that had done work in both of our zoos. For safety, six was the ideal number of clients for this walking safari.

Tsavo East and Tsavo West are two different National Parks with two different National Park wardens and staffs. Together they are just over eight-thousand square miles in size, a little larger than the state of New Jersey. Tsavo means place of slaughter probably coming from the fact that Maasai raiding parties would come into this area, killing the more peace-loving inhabitants. In 1948, Tsavo became the second

National Park in the system (Nairobi National Park was first in 1946) when the powers of the colonial government felt that the area had few human inhabitants and was worthless for anything but wildlife.

We needed a full two weeks to walk the one-hundred and twenty miles from Mzima Springs at the west end of Tsavo West to the Sala gate on the east end of Tsavo East. Each morning at 5:45 AM we were awakened by one of Iain's staff members with a friendly "Jambo." We would dress and have a light breakfast of coffee, toast, cereal and fresh tropical fruit. We started the walk at seven AM sharp. We walked four to six hours through a variety of African bush habitats. All one-hundred and twenty miles followed two rivers, the Tsavo River in West Tsavo and the Galana River in East Tsavo. Camps were moved each night for the first eight nights and we used a permanent tented camp as a base camp for the last five nights. At the permanent camp, we were transported by Land Rover each morning back to the spot where we had stopped the previous afternoon.

Each day was a different walk. In Tsavo West, we hiked through thick Commifora and thorn tree scrub forest. We followed hippo trails and often climbed over large rock outcroppings. Mountains, such as Ngulia, rising up to six-thousand feet, were always in sight. In Tsavo East, we walked along the Galana River and the habitat was much more open, especially when we left the thick saltbush that covers the river edge. While the occasional overcast sky provided a welcome relief from the hot African sun, most days were sunny and warm. At the end of each walk, there was always a cold drink, usually a Tusker beer. Those welcome drinks were the best drinks any of us had ever remembered.

A foot safari is a very different type of African safari. Peter Matthiessen in his book, The Tree Where Man Was Born, wrote, "On foot the pulse of Africa comes through your boots. You are an animal among others, wary of the shadowed places, of sudden quiet in the air." We always walked alert, not so much because of any danger, but because we did not want to miss anything. We kept our binoculars handy for birds as they would appear with no warning and some *would be new species for us. Scenery changed amazingly fast, even while walking. Each turn of the river seemed breathtakingly beautiful and required another photograph.*

But there was something else very special about walking in Africa. It takes one back in history where one cannot help but compare themselves to early African explorers. While the first Europeans to East Africa had none of the luxuries we enjoyed during our walk, like cold beer and support from a fleet of four-wheel drive vehicles, they did feel the same hot sun, crossed the same muddy rivers, and saw the same wonderful wildlife. As my mind wandered a little during the walk, I had to admit that I at times thought of myself as a contemporary of Denys Finch-Hatten or another famous early settler.

On our safari, lunches were substantial and, like the dinners, we never had one repeated. On most days we rested after lunch before the game drives which started at 5 PM. Even if we would have had the energy to walk in the afternoon, it was just too hot. For the most part the wildlife is inactive during that part of the day so walking would not have been that interesting. Game drives from both the four-wheel drive Land Rover and the Toyota Land Cruiser were always rewarding. Iain's Land Rover had a CD player with stereo speakers. Returning from the drive at sunset to music from either Out of Africa or Jimmy Buffett was a very surreal experience. Simon drove the Land Cruiser that was called "GH". George Harrison of the Beatles had owned the vehicle prior to it being brought to Kenya by a British dignitary assigned to the British embassy. The vehicles allowed us to see all the wildlife we did not observe during the walk. The animals were wary of us on foot. In addition, the vehicles allowed us to see three times more of the Park than if we just walked.

The movable camps differed from the permanent camp in that we slept in individual yellow and blue pup tents. In the permanent camp, we each had a large safari tent. It was nice to be able to stand up in the tent and not crawl on our hands and knees to get to bed. In both types of camps, delightful hot showers were provided each night by the camp staff. While our drinking water was pure borehole water that was boiled and filtered, shower water was directly from the river. But by the end of a hot day, even the brownish river water made us feel clean. Water can be a health problem in Kenya, indeed in all of Africa. However, the Tropical Ice camp staff provided excellent drinking water and we all stayed healthier on this trip than on any previous African safaris.

Another wonderful surprise of this safari was the food, or more properly, the cuisine. We had the best and most diverse meals that any of us had ever experienced in Africa. Kihue, a very accomplished bush chef, regularly read American and European cookbooks. Stuffed bell peppers, chicken Kiev, eggplant, grilled tilapia, and even roast turkey perfectly cooked were some examples of our gourmet meals prepared in a metal box over a wood fire. Wonderful South African wines were served with every dinner.

The six of us fifty something hikers were in good hands with the Tropical Ice crew, about fifteen in all. Iain Allan was born in Scotland but was a Kenyan citizen having lived there since he was eight years old. Iain's twenty-year-old daughter, Jodie, named after Jodie Foster as Iain is a big movie fan, was home from school in Melbourne, Australia and she joined the safari. She seemed to enjoy her time with her father and managed being fathered to death by all of us. Two armed (Belgian semi-automatic rifles weighing twenty-two pounds) Kenya Wildlife Service (KWS) rangers, James and Joseph, accompanied us on the hikes. Other than rangers, no one else was allowed to have a firearm in a Kenyan National Park. Mohammed, a six-foot six-inch Samburu and a retired KWS ranger was the undisputed lead guide through the bush. He pointed the way and we all followed in single file. During our hikes, James was in front, but took direction from Mohammed. Mohammed, carrying only a traditional Samburu spear, was second, followed by Iain. The six of us followed Iain, but in no particular order. Then came Jodie, followed by Joseph. James was young, probably in his twenties. His youthful demeanor seemed to suggest that everything was a joke. He found great fun in calling Gary various names in Swahili. Joseph was about fifty years of age and had a smile that suggested that life was always quite wonderful. He was a delight.

The camp staff was well trained and for the most part stayed out of sight unless they were doing something for us. They worked about fifteen hours a day, especially when we were moving the camp every day. Ngeroge was the camp manager, and his name became very familiar as Iain was always calling him about something. Like Radar in in the TV series Mash, Ngeroge was usually ahead of Iain so if wine was ordered it was there the moment Iain asked. He and about four assistants set up the camp, served the food, cleaned tents and prepared the showers. Simon drove the Land Cruiser. Simon was an accomplished guide, and knew animals, including the birds, quite well. If he didn't know a bird, he would stop and attempt to find it in one of his books. Wildlife common on the game drives included impala, dik dik, gerenuk, hartebeest, common waterbuck, lesser kudu, Cape buffalo, elephants, hippos, Peter's gazelle (a sub-species of Grant's gazelle), and zebra. We also managed to see klipspringer a couple of times. While we saw lions on several occasions, including twice on foot, we never saw leopard, cheetah or hyena. However, there was a hyena in camp on the second night and we all heard his unmistakable call. Iain felt that wildlife sightings could have been better, but East Africa had a particularly good short rain this year. With water available throughout the parks, game was not concentrated at river's edge. We still saw plenty.

Bird life on walks and drives was typical of any African safari. We enjoyed watching carmine bee-eaters and saw those most evenings as we drove near the Galana River. Their striking reddish color combined with the bee-eater behaviors, made them easy to recognize. Other common birds spotted during the walk included grey-necked kingfishers, martial eagles, European rollers, African fish eagles, blue-napped mouse birds, Namaqua doves, Bateleur eagle, and several species of hornbills including Von der Decken's hornbills. Some unusual birds, at least for all of us, included a variable sunbird, paradise flycatcher, Verreaux's eagle, straw-tailed whydah, Vitelline's masked weaver, woolly-necked stork, and goliath heron. In total, we spotted about one hundred different species of birds.

The trip was just plain fun! We all had such fun with each other. Since we were relatively the same age, we had lots to talk about during the afternoon or during meals. We started making a couple of silly lists of things that we discussed during the walk. First, there was the "wines of Tsavo." While we stated "wines", we really meant whines. They are as follows:

- *"My legs are too short for a walking safari in Kenya."*
- *"God, my feet hurt."*
- *"It's hell getting in and out of those pup tents."*
- *"My tent is hotter than your tent."*
- *"It's not a _____, until I say it's a _____."*
- *"Where did the breeze go?"*
- *"Your snoring kept me (us) awake."*
- *"Who ate all the brie and the paw paw chutney" (Yes, we really had that for lunch)?"*
- *"My blisters are bigger that yours."*
- *"My socks have more burrs on them than yours."*

The second list of items reflects some exaggerations and embellishments that developed after we had been together for a while. We titled this list, "the biggest crocs in Kenya!"

- *"That (rock) got to be a croc."*
- *"It's only fifteen more minutes to camp."*
- *"The biggest croc I have ever seen just slipped into the water."* This was also used for a snake on at least one occasion.
- *"We do not see snakes on walking safaris."*
- *"It's only a two-hundred-meter walk to the car."*
- *"I couldn't possibly have one more _____."* (beer, dessert, or whatever)
- *"No thanks, one Tusker will do for me."*

- *"It is not safe to wade or swim in the rivers."*
- *"It is not safe to drink water or eat veggies and/or lettuce."*
- *"You can't possibly get gourmet food in the bush, so just tough it out."*
- *And the biggest croc of all was used by Iain to win a scrabble game. "The cowcatcher on a locomotive is a phuntil."*

When we were hot, tired and sweaty after our walks, we enjoyed using the line from Norm in Cheers, "A beer, yes, that sounds like a refreshing drink!" Norm used that line when he didn't want his new boss to know he was a regular in the bar.

Friends have commonly asked if we were ever frightened. Other than the horrific ride on the highway from Voi to Nairobi which I will never do again! I have to say that I felt very safe the whole time. There were times when we could have been frightened, but these incidents were over before we realized that there was danger. For instance, we all walked within eighteen-inches of a five-foot puff adder. We would not have known, but the last in line spotted the very camouflaged snake in the six-inch deep grass. If someone would have been careless and walked through the tall grass, which we had to do on many occasion, instead of on the sand, it could have been disastrous. Along the Tsavo River on one walk, the first three hikers ascended a ten-foot high riverbank, only to turn around immediately, and quickly retreat. The looks on their faces told us immediately that there was danger. They had surprised a sleeping hippo out of the water. Fortunately, the hippo did not follow them and we simply chose an alternate route. My favorite incident took all of about four seconds. We had just left a clearing and were walking into a lugga (dry riverbed), when I heard a very loud sound that reminded me of the sound I would hear if I unlocked the rear door of the lion building at the zoo and surprised the lions. Within seconds I looked to the right a saw one lioness already hundred-feet across the Galana River and another animal about one-hundred and fifty feet the other direction. I felt bad that we had disturbed these peaceful animals. When we started our walk, Iain gave us instructions on moving towards the rangers when there was danger. While we never would want to shoot an animal in a national park, on the rare occasion it is necessary. Iain said that in twenty years of doing walks, his staff only had to shoot a couple of hippos. We were fortunate that we did not even fire a warning shot.

On any African safari, a most enjoyable activity is watching elephants. This safari was no exception. In the sixties, Tsavo was home to forty thousand elephants. Drought and uncontrolled poaching in the eighties reduced the population to just a few thousand. Today there is a healthy population of about eight-thousand animals and there is room for more. Tsavo is fortunate that it is such a large park with very little human pressure on its borders. Joyce Poole, an American who has spent much of her adult life studying elephants in Kenya, feels that the Tsavo elephants are some of the largest. This may be because Tsavo has such good vegetation and elephants have always had plenty to eat.

We saw elephants just about every day on our walk. Perhaps our most interesting encounter occurred along the Tsavo River on our second day of hiking. We had just walked down a lugga and there they were a hundred-feet ahead enjoying a morning bath in the shallow mud along the river. It took them a few minutes to notice our presence and by then we had managed to move up the lugga wall and out of immediate danger. We watched these cows and calves for fifteen minutes until they decided to leave the river and move up the lugga and out of sight. Along the Galana River we saw large herds of elephants, some thirty or forty strong. One wonderful evening we watched one of these large herds cross the river just after sunset. I particularly enjoyed watching elephants in the tall saltbush along the Galana River. Once in the saltbush, the only visible part of the huge elephant was the top their backs. It looked like a group of large smooth gray boulders gliding magically over a sea of green vegetation. One never tires of watching elephants.

I considered this safari a fifty-fifth birthday present to myself. I am not certain that I could have chosen a better present. I feel fortunate *that everything worked out perfectly and the adventure was all that I hoped for when scheduling this trip..*

MORE INTERNATIONAL TRAVEL

In May 2003, Sarah and I joined Mary Healy, director of the Sacramento Zoo, and her friends on a birding trip to the Asa Wright Nature Center in Trinidad. Due to some scheduling conflicts, we joined the group about halfway through the trip and then we stayed extra days to travel to Tobago where we stayed at the Blue Water Inn. On our first morning standing on the wooden deck of the nature center, we saw twenty bird species before breakfast. On nearby hiking trails we watched the golden-headed manakin's elaborate courtship display at their courtship area (leks) and also visited Dunstan's Cave, one of the few roosting spots for a breeding colony of oilbirds. Oilbirds, related to nightjars and owls, are actually distinct enough to be in their own family, Steatornithidae.

Aside from the great birding, Mary, her husband Steve and Sarah and I were driven by our guide to St. Andrews Golf Club outside of Port of Spain and played a round of golf.

One evening we traveled to Matura Beach and watched six-foot long female leatherback turtles lay eggs. It was amazing to watch the female dig a very deep hole using only her back flippers. When her first hole started to cave in, she left it and started another one and eventually laid her eggs there. On another evening we all got in a small boat at Caroni Swamp and watched several hundred scarlet ibis fly to a stand of trees to roost for the night. As great hosts, Steve and Mary provided the cocktails.

Our next zoo sponsored ecotourism program wasn't until 2003 when we led a small group to Costa Rica, just prior to the WAZA conference in San Jose. Pat and Amy Mullin and Sarah and I played golf at a beautiful course at the Marriott overlooking the Pacific Ocean. There were large iguanas on the course and toucans flew overhead. We had two carts and one caddy for the four of us. By the second hole he knew our rental clubs better than we did.

At the end of the trip, I said goodbye to the group in San Jose and I stayed to attend the WAZA conference. Our icebreaker was at the San Jose Zoo and there were protestors at the gate. Many delegates were appalled at the shape of the zoo. I remember Lewis Greene, then at World Conservation Society (WCS), was very upset as the AZA's tapir advisory group (TAG) had sent the zoo money for an improved tapir exhibit and nothing had been done.

After Costa Rica, Jim Heck of EWT surfaced at the annual conference of AZA and was promoting Hoopoe Safaris, a Tanzanian-owned safari company that he was representing in the United States. However, as always, he could do other destinations and I was interested in Zambia, having heard great things and never having been there. In August 2004, along with our friends the Koncals and Fraylicks, Sarah and I traveled there.

Our first camp in Zambia was Mfuwe in South Luangwa National Park in the eastern part of the country. I have wonderful photos of Sarah enjoying a wonderful cool afternoon swim in the pool while watching elephants approach the small river below the pool. One of my favorite African photos occurred at this park during our sundowners. As our drinks were poured and the sun was setting, we watched in awe as a herd of elephants crossed the river between us and the setting sun. This beautiful photos has been my screen saver since then.

From South Luangwa National Park, we flew on a charter plane to the lower Zambezi National Park and Chiawa Camp. Here we were offered several great experiences, including a walking opportunity and canoeing on the Zambezi among hippos and elephants. And, of course there were sundowners every evening. One evening we were on a small houseboat cruising the Zambezi and just after the gin and tonics were poured the two-way radio came on with instructions to return to camp immediately. As usual in Africa, the cause remained a secret. We dumped our cocktails and sped to shore. Once there, we jumped into a vehicle and drove three kilometers to find two adults and seven six-month old wild dogs, a rarity in any part of Africa.

The next day Sarah and I decided to take a break from the usual afternoon drive and stay in camp and relax. The camp staff did not seem comfortable with this saying that we might miss something special, but we were insistent. After a nice relaxing afternoon, we dressed for dinner and staff took us to a vehicle instead of the dining room. They took us a few kilometers away to a special place in the bush where the others had already arrived from their afternoon drive. A hundred lanterns surrounded the fire and grill for a surprise bush dinner. It was a memorable evening in the bush.

One of the reasons we wanted to stay in camp that afternoon was there was always wildlife in the camp, especially elephants. The day before during the midday break a herd of elephants came to visit the camp around 1 PM and didn't leave until we were loaded in the vehicles for our afternoon drive. In fact, one large female fell asleep for about two hours with her trunk rested on the railing of the porch at the Fraylick's tent.

Leaving the camp on our way to Livingston, Zambia and Victoria Falls we had to drive to an airstrip about an hour away. We got there on time for our charter flight. When the pilot emerged from the plane he asked for Sarah Taylor and he had a fax from America. Of course, we thought the worst and that something had happened at home. Not so. Kathleen, of EWT, sent a fax that said the Cleveland Indians, Sarah's employer, had an historic win by beating the Yankees 22 to 2!

The most unique adventure of this safari was a trip to Livingston Island and a swim to the edge of Victoria Falls. For ninety-five dollars each we took a small boat to Livingston Island and got good views of the Victoria Falls from the Zambian side. Then we had a delightful lunch with wine under a canopy. After we changed into our bathing suits in the "loo with a view," the fun began. We actually swam one hundred feet from the shore to a rock just a few feet before the water dropped three hundred feet to the river below. Then we entered a small pool of standing water just above the drop. We have pictures and video that documented the whole experience. Our two guides carried our cameras in plastic bags so we could document the incredible experience. One guide took Dave's video camera and did a half an hour documentary of the whole experience, complete with his narrative about "Zambia being a wonderful country and we would one day return." I assume someday the wall of the pool will fall away and a few tourists will plunge to their deaths. I am just glad it wasn't us.

In 2005, some friends asked us to do a family safari and we chose Kenya. We had seven young people ranging in age from nine years to twenty-one. We had three birthdays on that safari, including our friend Kay Muller's fiftieth. We celebrated that birthday at the ARC in the Aberdare Mountains.

Sarah and I learned several valuable lessons on that safari that served us well on future safaris. First, there was a thunderstorm in Cleveland on the day we left and our plane was delayed and we missed our connection in Newark. With Kathleen of EWT assistance, we found the last room available in Newark and stayed at a Knight's Inn located in a not so nice part of town. After about five hours of sleep, we returned to the airport and we were rebooked on a flight to London and then through Brussels to Nairobi. When we arrived in London, we verified our flights for tomorrow and went to a very over-priced Sheraton Hotel and had a light dinner in the hotel's sports bar for eighty dollars.. The only sport on TV was darts! Welcome to London! We made it to Nairobi one day late, only missing the city tour. What we learned was to never have a short connection departing overseas from the United States? On all my future safaris, I always scheduled a minimum of a four-hour layover at the departing airport.

With all the changes in our airline schedule, Sarah lost her bag. No surprise! She had just enough to get by as she could wear my shirts and she purchased some safari clothes along the way. Shoes were a problem as she only had sandals. From then on, she always wore her boots or running shoes, which were much more versatile, on the plane. Due to a miracle and Jim Heck and his Kenyan staff's hard work, she got her luggage about two thirds of the way through our safari. We were in Samburu and when our plane came to fly us to

Governor's Camp in Maasai Mara, her bag was delivered. Amazing! Lesson two: Since we got one of our two checked bags when we arrived in Nairobi, we always equally divide our belongings between the two bags.

This was a great safari with great friends and the wildlife viewing was excellent. In Governor's Camp, Sarah was very well dressed in clean clothes. At Governor's Camp we met with Dr. Richard Estes, author of several books on mammals of Africa including, *The Safari Companion*, a book that has always been important to me when leading safaris. Dr. Estes accompanying us on a couple of drives, including one to the Mara River where we hoped to see wildebeest or zebra crossing the river, but to no avail. Jim Heck really wanted us to see the entire migration so the next day we drove sixty kilometers towards Keekorok Lodge on the other side of the Mara. After lunch at the lodge we drove out and did see a good portion of the migration, a beautiful sight. When we woke up the next day and went to breakfast, we looked out over the plains and the migration had arrived at Governor's Camp!

Going home was not easy either. Our evening British Airline's flight to London was cancelled and we were put on a flight the next evening. After some negotiation, we were able to get a free room back at the Norfolk Hotel where Jim was still staying. Since we missed the city tour on the first day, we took advantage of the delay and went to Giraffe Manor and Karen Blixen's house. We also visited Kuzuri beads. This jewelry has been our all-time favorite item to purchase as gifts. Our route home had also been changed and was problematic as there was not much time for transfer in London and we had to go to JFK and take a limo to Newark for a 2:30 PM flight. In the end, it all worked out as we made our flight to JFK from London and British Airlines got us a limo ride to Newark. We got to Newark on time only to find out that our 2:30 PM flight to Cleveland had been cancelled and we were put on a 4:10 PM flight. We got home at 6 PM. After this safari, I knew I could always handle any delay. Sarah and I helped each other and whenever one of us got frustrated, the other stayed calm.

In 2006, the Cleveland Zoological Society sponsored Safari Ndovu (Elephant Safari) to Tanzania as the zoo had begun raising funds for a new elephant exhibit. Liz Fowler, the Cleveland Zoo Society's executive director, accompanied Sarah and me. Jim Heck was also with us and we went to the Ngorongoro Crater and Tarangire National Park and then went south to the Selous Game Reserve and Ruaha National Park, both new destinations for me. We ended the safari in Zanzibar. It was also the first time I met Tumaini Meishaa who would be my head driver/guide on many subsequent Tanzania safaris.

Sarah and I at Swala Camp in Tarangire National Park in 2006.

This was my only safari where someone had to leave early. Don and Eileen Morrison, great zoo supporters, were on this safari and Eileen injured her arm getting out of the vehicle on the first day in Arusha. Later in the Selous she slipped and she and Don began to realize it was probably better that they go back to the United States. Jim arranged for their transfer to Dar es Salaam and then home. Since they flew business class, changing the flights was not too difficult. The Morrisons remained very supportive of the zoo and once we returned to Cleveland, Liz managed to get them to commit to a substantial gift to the African Elephant Crossing.

We had planned to celebrate Eileen's birthday at Vuma Hills Safari Lodge in Mukumi National Park, a stop between the Selous and Ruaha, and had even ordered the cake. So as not to disappoint the lodge staff and avoid a long explanation, we appointed Amy Mullin to act as Eileen. When the cake was delivered with Happy Birthday Eileen spelled out on the cake, Amy did an Academy Award performance as Eileen!

We ended this African safari with a couple of days in Zanzibar where we toured the old town and a spice farm. At the end of the day, Jim surprised us with a sunset cruise on the Indian Ocean. After the cruise we went back to the Zanzibar Serena and had a three-hour roof top dinner. On the cruise, Sarah and I presented our academy awards to our travel companions. An obvious award went to Amy Mullin as best actress for her portrayal of Eileen Morrison!

As it was Labor Day weekend, the Mullins and us had decided to spend the weekend in Amsterdam. While we each went separate ways during the days, we got together every evening for wonderful dinners and a review of the day's events. One day Sarah and I took a train to Emmen, where I finally got the opportunity to see that wonderful zoo. Colleagues had been telling me to see that zoo for years. We enjoyed our visit.

One of my most interesting safaris occurred in 2007 when five of us traveled to Madagascar. Betsi Morris and Emily Alexander, both east siders who I convinced to go to Madagascar at a breakfast at the Botanical Garden, joined the Koncals and me. Like the Galapagos, I had read much about Madagascar and its unusual endemic (found nowhere else) fauna and flora. We saw about two dozen reptiles and amphibian species, all endemic except for the Nile crocodile. We spotted over 50 different species of birds, half of which were endemic including blue coua, hook-billed vanga, lesser vasa parrot and a few more. Mammal viewing was especially interesting as we saw a tremendous amount of diversity, especially with the endemic lemurs, sighting fifteen different species. The Verreaux's safaka were all over Berenty and they danced up and down the dirt paths we shared with them. Ring-tailed lemurs were abundant in Berenty and they were very accustomed to the lodge's guests. We got great photographs of us with lemurs. I used one photo on my Facebook page for years. Tracking the huge indri (largest lemur) in Andasibe-Mantadia National Park (Perinet) by listening for their amazingly loud call was a great adventure.

And then there were the people we met. One of the rock stars of wildlife conservation was Alison Jolly She passed away in 2013. After getting a PhD from Yale in the early sixties, Dr. Jolly first came to Madagascar. Her first book, *Lemur Behavior – A Madagascar Field Study* contributed greatly to the world's knowledge of these unique primates. In 2004 she wrote a wonderful autobiography entitled, *Lords & Lemurs – Mad Scientists, Kings with Spears, and the Survival of Diversity in Madagascar.* Our small group was fortunate to have lunch with the seventy-year-old Dr. Jolly who happened to be in Berenty during our visit. After fifty years working in Madagascar, her excitement for the wildlife was evident and contagious. I enjoyed watching her work with Malagasy students, something she obviously still enjoyed after all those years. We met with others active in Madagascar conservation, including Dr. Steve Goodman of the Field Museum in Chicago and Karen Freeman, of Park Ivoloina Conservation Center and Zoo. Ivoloina is an out of the way facility that the AZA's Madagascar Fauna Group has been supporting for years. It was nice to see the Cleveland Metroparks Zoo on a sign listing major donors.

We also met other interesting people, including the former Governor of Mississippi, John Mabus and his new wife. They were there on an around-the-world honeymoon. Of course, the three women in our group had to have an extensive conversation on the age difference. They agreed that he was in his sixties and she was in her forties. After the lengthy discussion, my normally quiet friend Dave

Koncal had had enough and addressed the three women, "You can't spot a God damn bird, but you can see wrinkles on the Governor's wife's face. That is amazing!" We all later Goggled the governor and found out he had been divorced for some time and his new wife had had a very successful career as a nurse.

When the Governor found out we were all from Ohio, he volunteered that he was Governor of Mississippi at the same time Dick Celeste was Governor of Ohio. He jokingly stated, "I don't know who President Clinton liked less, me or Dick Celeste. He appointed me Ambassador to Saudi Arabia and appointed Dick Ambassador to India." He further stated, "If you want to be an ambassador, find a country that has no standing army and puts colorful paper umbrellas in its drinks." Part of the pleasure of travel is the people you meet and the stories they tell. Years later, John Mabus became President Obama's Secretary of the Navy.

In 2008 and 2009 I was fortunate to have two more Tanzanian/Kenyan safaris. Actually, the 2008 safari was two safaris, the first was a special safari that included the opulent Crater Lodge and travelled the usual route before ending in the Northern Serengeti. The second safari, arranged by Travis's mother, Shannon (yes, my ex-wife), started at Migration Camp in the Northern Serengeti and ended in Tarangire National Park. My friend, Tumaini would joke with me for years that I was a Maasai as I had two wives!

I was gone a total of twenty-four days and had many great experiences and stayed in several great camps and lodges and some marginal ones. It was my first time to visit Dr. Charles Foley's research camp in Tarangire. Charles and his family were there and he gave us a great introduction to his work with elephants. I remember his three and five-year old daughters pulling up their small child's chairs and joining the group. After about five minutes of their father's talk, they pulled their chairs away and continued playing with their toys. They were always under the watchful eyes of two nannies as in the bush one never knows what is lurking in a nearby thorn bush. A leopard or puff adder are two of many possibilities. Dr. Foley had done elephant research for fifteen years in Tarangire and discovered some amazing things about these magnificent creatures. My favorite piece of information I learned during that visit reinforced the fact that elephants do remember. From 1992 – 1994 there was a terrible drought in Tanzania and forty percent of the infant elephants died. As Charles and his team studied the family groups, they found that those with the female matriarchs over thirty-five-year old had lower infant mortality than those with younger matriarchs. Looking at past weather patterns, he found that there had been a similar drought in the late fifties. He therefore suggested that the older matriarchs remembered where the water was in a drought and were able to lead their families to the scarce water. Amazing! Most of his research involves studying the migration patterns of elephants and other wildlife in and out of the park. The elephants come into the park in the dry season as the Tarangire River always has some water and they go out of the park for phosphorous, especially necessary for the lactating cows.

Other highlights of the 2008 safaris included driving cross-country north from Shifting Sands and to where we had lunch on an isolated kopje. As soon as we arrived and got out of the vehicles, some young Maasai appeared around a kopje about a half-mile away and started walking towards us. As we ate our lunch, we were surrounded by about a dozen Maasai. These were not the Maasai that one visits as part of an organized tour. These were Maasai that rarely encountered tourists. Fortunately, Tumaini spoke to them in their native language. The group that visited us was composed of women and young men. The moremi (warriors) would be too proud to be bothered to visit us outsiders. I remember giving some of our food to one of the women and a young man took it from her, certainly an accepted behavior for a Maasai. Tumaini was not happy with that behavior and in his fluent Maasai gave the young man a lecture on how modern Maasai men should treat women. As I had gotten to know Tumaini, I realized that he had little patience for some of the old ways of the Maasai.

Our 2009 safari was like most of our Jim Heck safaris as there were several itinerary changes from when folks signed up until we left. This one was to be another total Tanzania safari, but was changed to be a Tanzania and Kenya safari. Jim had severed his relationship with Hoopoe Safaris so we needed to change some properties. Since then Jim has gone back to using his original company, Explorers World Travel (EWT), to book safaris and other travel.

My favorite memory of the 2009 safari occurred during a morning drive in the Ngorongoro Crater. I was with Dave and Hope Koncal when we stopped and observed some vultures on a kill, probably on a wildebeest, a hundred yards away on the crest of a hill. Then we noticed several female lions lying quietly near the kill, obviously resting from their recent feast. After about ten minutes, one female stood up and walked slowly towards the kill. As she got near the kill, the vultures started to stir and then the lioness ran forward as the vultures flew. The lioness leapt ten-feet in the air and grabbed the last vulture to leave the scene. We were all amazed when a few minutes later the vulture flew off, obviously not seriously hurt. The best part was that Dave got it all on video.

For my twentieth African safari in 2010, I Sarah and I took a small group of zoo supporters to Uganda and Rwanda. This was a primate safari as we had two hikes to see chimps and two hikes to see mountain gorillas, one in Uganda and one in Rwanda. All four of these unique visits with great apes were limited to eight people and we could spend only one hour with the animals. Getting to the chimps or gorillas can take an hour or much longer. Guides know where the troops are the night before, but the apes can travel a long way in the morning before the tourists arrive. Aside from these two species of great apes, we observed a half a dozen other primates and ten species of non-primate mammals, including thousands of the ubiquitous Uganda kob. There was excellent birding as these two countries sit between the rain forests of West Africa and the savannas of East Africa. The birding highlight for me was the shoebill and the great blue turaco.

At the welcome center for gorilla treks in Rwanda, all the safari leaders met with the staff of the facility to get assigned one of eight troops. According to Jim Heck, who was leading our group, all the leaders greatly exaggerated the lack of physical abilities of their clients in an attempt to get assigned a troop that was easy to reach. One guide said there was a woman in his group with a broken leg and another group leader said a man in his group was one-hundred years old. The conversation was part in Swahili, part in French and part in English. Jim did his best and got us assigned to one easy-access hike and one a little more difficult. Those of us willing to take a more difficult hike, included Jim, Sarah and me and the others, including Dave and Hope Koncal took the supposedly easy access group. Well either the gorillas had moved or Jim misunderstood the directions. Our group had relatively easy access to the Sabyinyo Group and we were back at Sabyinyo Silverback Lodge in time for lunch. The others had a long and difficult hike and did not return to the lodge until 3:30 PM! However, they did see a much larger family group of about twenty individuals, including many youngsters.

I will never forget the look on Sarah's face when she turned to me and whispered, "A female (gorilla) is right there." Sure enough, twenty feet in front of her was our first gorilla quietly munching on bamboo shoots. It wasn't until I got home that I realized that the Sabyinyo troop was one of the two troops I had seen in 1988. The silverback male, Guhondo that we viewed in 2010 was a young teenager in 1988 as my journal verified.

As stated previously, most of our safaris end with academy awards. These are awards Sarah and I give in jest to best birder, best actor and so on. Bill Barzhaf suggested we all do limericks and we agreed. Several of these were quite clever.

"Trekking for gorillas ain't cheap.
Descent in Bwindi was steep
Tho the going got tough
And the effort was rough
We rode home in a comfy jeep". Bill Banzhaf

"At last we found the gorilla.
He charged, but not like Godzilla.
So close an attack
I jumped our guide's back.
Indeed, it was quite a trill-a." Margo Vinney

"To Uganda went a group from Cleveland
With a zoo director they couldn't believe in
Roads bumpy, trails long
Birds identified, many wrong
None-the-less, they stayed, as none would leave him".
Steve and Sarah

In February 2011, I took six clients on a migration safari to Tanzania, my first time traveling to Tanzania that time of year since 1997. It is the best time to travel to Tanzania, as the wildebeest and zebra migration is most likely to be in the southern Serengeti during those months. Leaving Cleveland in a snowstorm made this February safari even more special. All six clients were very compatible and all were taking a bucket list adventure. Anne Kirby, a neighbor, was the last to sign up and she and I flew together out of Cleveland Hopkins airport. We had a day in London that we used to visit the London Zoo, which I hadn't visited since 1985. Paul Price-Kelly, the curator of invertebrates, who I knew from past CBSG and WAZA meetings, met us at the entrance. He got us in the zoo, took us to the tropical building and even gave us umbrellas as it had started to rain. Aside for the tropical house we saw the gorillas, the aquarium, the Komodo dragons and a few other exhibits before we left the zoo for the train back to the airport.

Anne and I arrived in the morning and went directly to the Hatari Lodge just outside Arusha National Park. The lodge was named after the John Wayne movie from the sixties. Hatari means danger in Swahili. We had a nice game drive in the afternoon and then I went with Tumaini to the airport to pick up the other clients. The next day we had two separate game drives in Arusha National Park, although the highlight for most of us was the small herd of giraffe that were around our cabins at the lodge. We also stopped in town to exchange money. I used the ATM and there was no problem, but others, went into the bank where each transaction seemed to take hours! Ken, a dentist in Florida, tried to exchange several fifty-dollar bills. One was not a new bill in full color and the teller took the bill, said it was counterfeit and punched about thirty holes in the bill before giving it back. I am sure that Ken was able to exchange it once he returned to the United States and I can just imagine the story he told his local bank teller.

This was an excellent safari for game viewing as we saw fifty-five different lions, six cheetahs and five leopards. In addition, staying at Ndutu Lodge in the southern Serengeti we were in the middle of the migration and the greatest concentration of wildebeest and zebra was in the savanna between Lake Ndutu and Niabi Hill. There were many great experiences but the highlight for me was seeing the famous Manyara tree-climbing lions actually resting in trees. This was something I had read about for years but had never seen. We also saw leopards in trees, somewhat common, and even watched a cheetah jump into a tree, not so common.

In August 2011, Sarah and I returned to South Africa and Botswana with a great group of zoo supporters, including Jim and Muffy Boland and Tom and Kathy Leiden. It was our first visit to the Kalahari Desert. Aside from the Kalahari Desert and the Okavango Delta in Botswana, the safari also included Cape Town, South Africa. Because of the diversity of habitats on this safari, my animal count for the entire safari included over one-hundred and seventy bird and forty mammal species, including four different leopards.

As with any safari, we visited some new places and had some great new experiences and we repeated visits to some of our favorite places. The wonderful repeated experiences included the penguins at Boulder's Beach and a walk through the beautiful Kirstenbosch National Botanical Garden. Sarah and I vowed to spend at whole day at Kirstenbosch when we have more time. As far as new experiences, there were many. Tom Leiden, who is a major supporter of an NGO (SACCOB) working to protect seabirds in South Africa, especially the penguins, had arranged for Margaret Roestoff, development director for SANCCOB, to show us around the Boulder's Beach penguin colony and then stay with us as we visited Cape Point. Sarah and I also visited the District Six Museum, which we both found fascinating. District Six was a vibrant mixed-race community in Cape Town that was declared a "White Group Area" by 1982. Sixty thousand people were forcibly removed to the Cape Flats, twenty miles away and their houses and businesses were flattened. This is one of many tragic stories of the apartheid era.

In Botswana we stayed at five different Kwando Safari camps and they were all first-class. They also had staff members that were as good as any we have had on any African safari. One driver/guide, Jacob, on our first evening in the Kalahari grabbed one of our I-pads that had an astronomy application and wouldn't give it up. He knew all the constellations but had such a thirst for knowledge that he could not help using technology to improve his skills as a guide.

The highlight of this safari came on one of the last mornings when we left camp before sunrise and had a very chilly one-hour drive to a painted dog den. Its location was well known to the guides. The guides wanted us to get there early so we could see the adults wakeup and call the pups from the den. Our timing was perfect and when we drove up, the adults were just starting to move. After about fifteen minutes, one female, most likely an older sister, put her muzzle down a den and called the pups. Within seconds, nine pups emerged. The female dog regurgitated food for each of the pups. We stayed for an hour watching the dogs and then went off for morning coffee.

During that safari, Tom and Gail Bunn, who Sarah met through Wake Forest University alumni events, taught us a new phase when they ordered a glass of wine to take to their room or tent prior to dinner. From that time forward we used the term "dresser" whenever we took drinks to the room or tent prior to dinner.

Our 2012 safari was to the Pantanal in Brazil, the world's largest wetlands, twenty times larger than the Everglades. Our fellow travelers included our friends and frequent travelers, the Fraylicks and the Koncals. For this trip, we used Terra Incognito Ecotours, a small one-man company owned by Gerald "Ged" Caddick, a British citizen married to an American and living in Tampa. Before starting his travel company, Ged had worked in several zoos including the Jersey Zoo in the English Channel, the Belize Zoo and the Lowry Park Zoo in Tampa, Florida. He had led a successful tour to Borneo for the Cleveland Zoological Society with Liz Fowler, executive director. His Pantanal program looked like a perfect alternative to an African safari. We saw wildlife that I never thought I'd see in my lifetime, including giant anteater, Toco toucan, Hyacinthine macaw, giant otters, jaguar and much more. Jaguars were attracted to the shade near the river in the heat of the day so it was very easy to spot jaguars in the Pantanal.

PLANE RIDES

Most people complain about the long air trips to faraway places. While there is no doubt at times, they could be a huge hassle, for the most part I enjoyed the long flights. I used flights as time to reflect on my life. I watched movies that I never saw in the theaters. I relaxed the best I could. After many years, I even learned to get some sleep on planes. If I didn't have my computer or it was just too crowded, I wrote long hand. Below is the reflective piece I wrote while flying to Madagascar in 2007.

MY LIFE

October 9, 2007 – Somewhere over the African Continent

If anyone would have told me forty-years ago that my life would be this full, I would not have believed them. I have a wonderful job as zoo director in a large midwestern zoo. I enjoy the Cleveland Metroparks Zoo and feel I have accomplished much and have much more to do. I have been married to Sarah for fourteen years. She has her almost perfect job as controller for the Cleveland Indians. We both enjoy this community and have many friends here.

I have a wonderful thirty-eight-year-old son, Travis, and a wonderful daughter-in-law, Karen. Travis and Karen have three children, my grandchildren, Shae (6), Henry (4) and Ainsley (3). The Mastersons, Karen's parents, are great folks and they are very kind to Travis and spend lots of time with the grandchildren. They have several lovely homes, one in Long Beach (Neutra – architect), one in Sun Valley, Idaho and one beach cottage overlooking the ocean in Laguna Beach. Shannon, Travis' mother, and I have a fine relationship and in fact I am taking her and some of her friends to Tanzania next summer.

I met Sarah eighteen years ago on a United Airlines flight from Cleveland to Chicago while I was returning to Sacramento after my first interview for the director's position. Sarah turned fifty last April. She is intelligent, beautiful, conscientious, loving and very hard working. She encourages my travel. She is dedicated to her family, even when they don't do what she thinks they should. She adores her nieces, Emma and Ava. I enjoy her father, Don, her sister, Donna, and her brother, Jay, and their significant others and we regularly spend time with all of them.

While my parents have long since passed away and my older sister joined them last year, my sister Jean and brother Ray are still part of my life. I am probably closer to Ray now than I have ever been in the past. We travel together and still celebrate holidays together. I have many friends, none closer than Satch Krantz, director of the Riverbanks Zoo. We have much in common, including love of TV shows such as Seinfeld and West Wing. We talk daily and share our zoo problems. Other friends like Kay and Carl Muller and Paul and Theresa

Koomar keep Cleveland interesting.

When I land in Madagascar, I will have visited forty-one different countries. I have visited all but four states. As of this summer I have seen one-hundred eighty-two of two-hundred and sixteen AZA accredited zoos and aquariums.

Our annual income from our two salaries is substantial; Sarah's a bit more than mine. When we retire we will have nice pensions and have considerable savings. We own our own home in Rocky River, Ohio and always pay cash for cars and household appliances. We are unique in that we have zero debt! All this puts us in the top two-percent of all Americans and much higher than that worldwide. Never-the-less, we have many friends that are even better off than us. We seem to surround ourselves with very successful people.

While I do take several pills each day for the usual senior ailments, I am healthy. I exercise either at the Tennis Club or by running. We eat healthy most of the time. I am five-feet ten-inches tall and one-hundred and seventy pounds and I would like to lose ten pounds. I worry about my memory loss, baldness and hearing loss, but it doesn't preoccupy me.

Sarah and I play golf. Sarah plays tennis one or two times a week. We cook dinner together. We eat outside any time the weather cooperates. We love good wine. We go to Indians games. We go to concerts, museums and community benefits.

Staff and friends gave me two parties this year. One was for my sixtieth birthday and a second for being a zoo director for twenty-five years and for being in this wonderful profession for thirty-five years. It was great to have friends help me celebrate these milestones.

Yes, I never would have thought that I would be this well off at sixty!

Like a leader in any profession, there can be no question that a zoo director must also work harder and smarter than everyone else on the staff. However, it was equally important that I had other interests. Golf and travel were two of my interests, but it could just as well been woodworking or opera. It does not matter what your outside interests are, just that life cannot be all work. The vast majority of successful people have an exciting balanced life.

While most of my international travel had something to do with being a zoo director, Sarah and I did have other vacations. To help celebrate Mary Healy's, director of the Sacramento Zoo, fiftieth birthday we traveled to Trinidad and Tobago in 2003. We took a Barefoot Caribbean cruise in 2004 were we visited several islands near St. Maarten. We traveled to Italy in 2007, Bermuda in 2008 and the Bahamas in 2012 and traveled extensively around the United States whenever we had the opportunity. I also accompanied Sarah to the Dominican Republic when she traveled there to review accounting procedures of the Cleveland Indian's baseball team's operations in the Dominican Republic. While she worked, I visited the zoo, aquarium and the botanical garden. And to be completely transparent about this travel, during these vacations we did go bird watching and we also visited the local zoos.

CHAPTER 6

ADVENTURES IN RETIREMENT

PLANNING & THE FIRST YEAR

My friend and colleague, Ken Redman, had this amusing story upon his retirement from the Honolulu Zoo in 2008.

"Finally, one of my treasured memories is when a zookeeper came into my office with a concern that she felt was not being addressed. During the course of our conversation, she blurted out – I am sure there are many zoo directors who are worse than you are. Let it be known that she has never worked at another zoo, so she didn't have anyone specifically in mind. I'll leave it to your judgment".

On June 18, 2012 I gave the executive director of Cleveland Metroparks a letter stating that I intended to retire at the end of the year

After telling the zoo's senior staff of my decision, I sent this letter by e-mail to my friends and colleagues.

To my friends and colleagues,

I would like you to know that I am retiring from my position as director of Cleveland Metroparks Zoo and moving on to the next phase of my life. My last day at the zoo will likely be December 31, 2012. Some call this retirement, but I do not. I know I will be very busy in the future with projects I have in the works and others I do not know of myself.

Some of the things I do know about include continuing to take people to Africa, and other destinations, as I have a couple trips in 2013. I will continue to be involved in the Cleveland community as Sarah and I do not plan on moving. Sarah is not planning on retiring. I think she wants to make sure that there is enough money to find me a nice old folks home, not that I will know where I am anyway, but I appreciate her sweet thoughts!

I plan to spend more time with the things I enjoy, like traveling, birding, hiking, riding bikes, gardening, and a little more golf. I plan to continue leading safaris for my good friends, Jim Heck and Kathleen Morgan of Explorers World Travel and maybe for other ecotourism companies. Scott Schultz, Schultz and Williams, has said that he might have some consulting work for me from time to time. I also plan to finish a self-published book on my forty years so far of zoo work and my travels. I am doing this not for publication, but to pass on to my three grandchildren. It's about half written, but as those of you that know my writing acumen realize I still have lots of work ahead of me.

My many years in this amazing business have provided me with incredible opportunities. My forty years as an AZA member and twenty-two years as a WAZA member have provided me with treasured memories and many lifelong friends. Every zoo and aquarium visit and every conference and meeting has been very special, always learning and always providing a laugh or two. Whatever I was able to accomplish for AZA or WAZA, it was never in anyway equal to what I gained from the experiences, as a committee member, officer, or as accreditation inspector. I still hope to be involved as it would be difficult to give up the fun!

I still plan to visit new zoos and aquariums. For those that have followed the contest, I am currently at two-hundred and twelve of two-hundred and twenty-four AZA accredited institutions and I plan to get a couple more this year.

I must thank Cleveland Metroparks for the many opportunities I have had over the past twenty-four years. The successes we have had are largely due to the fact that I was able to surround myself with people much smarter than myself. I worked for two very intelligent and hard-working executive directors that answered over the years to ten different dedicated park commissioners appointed by three different probate judges. I worked with seven different presidents of the Cleveland Zoological Society, and I consider all seven to be friends. A couple even traveled to Africa with Sarah and me. I am especially grateful to all our team members here at the zoo and the zoo society, both those that have left and those still here. Their collective energies, enthusiasm, and expertise in their particular fields have served this zoo extremely well. For those very talented staff members currently at the zoo, I believe I am leaving them a pretty good place with a solid reputation, both locally and nationally. However, there are challenges and I know they will overcome these challenges and create an even better zoo.

Fortunately, even though I am technologically challenged, there are many ways to stay in touch. You know, even Mike Dee is on Facebook every day! Sarah is taking me to the Apple store very soon and I will distribute all new numbers prior to my leaving the Zoo.

I thank you all for your friendship and much good advice over the years and hope we continue our friendship for many years to come.

Cheers, STEVE

Prior to my announcement, I conferred with my friend and colleague, Satch Krantz, and asked him to read a couple of letters/announcements. He knew right away what they were about and said he was sorry to lose a colleague. I responded by saying that I would still be around and we would continue to talk regularly. He immediately responded with, "Why would I talk with you, you won't have any good gossip." We zoo folks do love our gossip!

My announcement was followed by six months of finishing some final projects such as performance reviews, 2013 draft budget and working on projects that were part of the 2012 zoo work program. I also had a huge list of things I needed to do personally prior to my retirement, such as buying a car, first new car in over twenty-four years as I had a company car at Cleveland Metroparks Zoo, and purchasing and learning to use Apple computers, I-pads and phone.

What was very humbling to me was all the e-mails, cards and letters I received from friends and colleagues. I was very deeply touched by all those that took the time to write and the many large and small gifts I received.

One note I received was particularly touching to me. This note was from Dr. Kristen Lukas, curator of conservation and science at Cleveland Metroparks Zoo, a position she had had for about ten years. Kristen had gained a certain amount of notoriety, even fame, while at Cleveland Metroparks, for having such knowledge of gorillas that she was appointed chair of the AZA gorilla SSP, the committee that manages all the gorillas in AZA zoos. With the exception of maybe being chair of the elephant SSP, there is no more difficult task in AZA than being chair of the gorilla SSP. Many zoos want gorillas and all want breeding troops, which is impossible as the zoo populations have almost as many males as females. Therefore, some well-known zoos, including Cleveland Metroparks Zoo, kept bachelor groups.

Anyway, Kristen wrote a very nice hand-written congratulatory note accompanied by a typed insert entitled, "What I've learned from Steve Taylor". Here it is:

- Be succinct
- Don't take yourself too seriously
- Pick up trash
- Care about individual people
- Have a plan
- Be an understanding boss
- Arrive early
- Travel to Africa as much as you can
- Have fun with your friends
- Show emotion
- Conserve with a big "C"
- Love your spouse

Wow! I think that is who I am, but it was great to hear from someone else, especially from someone that I respect.

My longevity as zoo director for Cleveland Metroparks Zoo had set some interesting records. First, when I retired after twenty-four-years I had been zoo director at Cleveland Metroparks Zoo, formerly Cleveland Zoo, longer than any other leader in the zoo's one-hundred and thirty-year history. Secondly, during my tenure as zoo director, I saw many colleagues in local attractions and cultural institutions come and go. For instance, the Rock and Roll Hall of Fame and Museum had four CEOs, the Natural History Museum had four CEOs, the Art Museum had five CEOs, and the Cleveland Botanical Garden had three CEOs. Much of my longevity had to do with the organizational and financial stability of Cleveland Metroparks and Sarah's interest in staying in Ohio. Oh yes, and no one else wanted to hire me!

I was very pleased when the Board of Park Commissioners of Cleveland Metroparks appointed Dr. Chris Kuhar, one of the zoo's two curators, as the new director, soon to be called executive director. Chris had worked in the zoo's conservation department early in his career before working at the Atlanta Zoo and then Disney's Animal Kingdom. I would like to say that I was his mentor, but quite frankly I did not realize he had the interest in being a director (certainly my fault) as his main interest was science. Not only did he want to be the director of the zoo but once he was appointed, he has done a fantastic job. He also has been very kind to me and we have lunch together a few times a year to talk zoos. In 2019, he became chair of the AZA board of directors, being the fourth director from the Cleveland Metroparks Zoo to hold that position.

I never planned to retire from working, just retire from being a full-time zoo director. I still had much I wanted to accomplish and skills I wanted to improve upon. When Pablo Casals reached ninety-five, a young reporter threw him a question.

"Mr. Casals, you are ninety-five and the greatest cellist that has ever lived. Why do you still practice six hours a day"? And Mr. Casals answered, "Because I think I'm making progress".

And that's how I felt about my retirement.

During my first few weeks of retirement, while there certainly were some lifestyle adjustments, I did joke that my life had not really changed that much.

- I get up every morning at 6 AM and make coffee for Sarah and me.
- Have some breakfast and read the newspaper.
- Go to my basement office read e-mails. Answer e-mails.
- Review my personal annual work program to see if I am on track.
- Do paperwork; write thank you notes, etc.
- Manage capital improvement projects, new toilet, basement carpet, painting, etc.
- Prioritize work orders such as fix toilet, fix lock and repair a lamp.
- Manage capital equipment purchases such as printer, bookcases and TV.
- Horticulture program such as winter/spring cleanup and plan for summer gardens.

- Manage staff, including housekeeper, mechanics, gardeners, painters and plumbers.
- Plan ecotourism programs by answering e-mails and questions. Choose lodges/camps for upcoming safaris.
- File paperwork and other documents
- Organize photos and power points
- Schedule speaking dates
- Review budget and finances
- Plan for dinner and exercise
- And I still wake up for an hour or two at night and worry about all the work I have to do in the morning.

What had changed? Well, one thing – every day was now blue jean Friday!

While I felt fortunate to have traveled the world during my work years, this world traveler still had many places to visit. While I had been to forty-nine states, I still had not been to Alaska. There are many places in the United States I hadn't visited, including Yellowstone. I had visited Australia three times in conjunction with three different WAZA conferences. However, I had not traveled to New Zealand or the Northern Territories of Australia. Sarah and I traveled to several Caribbean islands but there were more to visit, including the Virgin Islands, the Cayman's, Cuba and Puerto Rico. Most of Asia was still unvisited, including great wildlife adventures in India, Borneo and Indonesia. I had seen both gorillas and chimps in Uganda and Rwanda, but not orangutans in Borneo or Malaysia. I had visited many of Europe's great capitals, but there are many more to visit including Lisbon, Athens, Warsaw and Stockholm. By traveling before and after WAZA meetings, I had visited many of the great zoos of the world, but still planned to see ones in Chester, Munich, Hamburg, Jersey Island and the Nordon's Ark.

When I retired, I reread the words of the comedian George Carlin on how to stay young and I tried to live up to those words. They were as follows:

1. Throw out nonessential numbers. This includes age, weight and height. Let the doctors worry about them. That's why you pay them.
2. Keep only cheerful friends. The grouches pull you down.
3. Keep learning. Learn more about computers, crafts, gardening, whatever. "An idle mind is the devil's workshop." And the devil's name is Alzheimer's.
4. Enjoy the simple things.
5. Laugh often, long and loud. Laugh until you gasp for breath.
6. The tears happen. Endure, grieve, and move on. The only person, who is with us our entire life, is ourselves. Be ALIVE while you are alive.
7. Surround yourself with what you love, whether it's family, pets, keepsakes, music, plants, hobbies, whatever. Your home is your refuge.
8. Cherish your health: If it is good, preserve it. If it is unstable, improve it. If it is beyond what you can improve, get help.
9. Don't take guilt trips. Take trips to the mall, even the next country; to a foreign country but NOT to where guilt is.
10. Tell the people you love that you love them, at every opportunity.

    And always remember:
    Life is not measured by the number of breaths we take, but by the moments that take our breath away!

Similar to Carlin, my life's journey has taught me a few things about life. I believe that these are ten important concepts on living a great life and dealing with whatever life throws at you.

1. Be nice! If you slip up – apologize immediately.
2. Stay healthy. If you have health issues, deal with them.
3. Don't worry about the things that are out of your control such as the stock market and difficult bosses. Don't obsess over

systemic constraints such as teamster contracts, complicated purchasing rules. Acknowledge and move on.

4. Don't put off making a tough decision or doing an unpleasant task. It's much better to get it behind you.
5. Relax more. Don't worry as much. As they say, "No one on their death bed ever says, I wish I would have worked harder."
6. Always be learning new things. Travel is one method.
7. Tell those special people that you love them.
8. Thank people often and do it each day at work and with neighbors and friends.
9. Enjoy the simple things, including walks after dinner, meals at home, sunsets, gardens, birds, oceans and much more..
10. Don't let the things stupid people do affect you. In fact, whenever possible stay away from people that do stupid things.

During 2013 I often joked with people that I had a perfect retirement plan. I married someone ten years younger that was gainfully employed! And yes, Sarah kept on working. Most days she was fine with it even though her job could be stressful. When she came home after a ten-hour stressful day she would talk about some of the problems and some people that caused her stress. Then she might ask, and how was your day? Believe me, there was no right answer to that question!

The year 2013, first year of retirement, was wonderful for me. I had done all that I planned. Highlights for 2013 included two flawless Tanzanian safaris for EWT with my guide and friend, Tumaini. I exercised each day, either by running three and a half miles, going to the gym, practicing yoga (I usually attend the 12:30 PM class for all levels, although I am not sure there is a level to describe my yoga), riding my bike and even lost a few pounds. I went bird watching in Costa Rica with friends and had a great experience. I felt I was able to use my zoo expertise by consulting with the Audubon Park Zoo in New Orleans, consulting with the Greater Cleveland Aquarium and completing two AZA accreditation Inspections, the Butterfly House in St. Louis and the Buttonwood Park Zoo in New Bedford, Massachusetts. I kept active in the zoo profession by attending two AZA conferences and one WAZA conference. I helped Schultz and Williams by attending two pre-bid meetings for two very interesting projects. I visited four AZA accredited institutions that I had not visited previously, including The Maritime Aquarium in Norwalk, Connecticut and Shark Reef at Mandalay Bay in Las Vegas, Sea Life Aquarium in Kansas City, and the Mesker Park Zoo in Evansville, Indiana. That left only nine more to reach one-hundred percent. I visited Cleveland Metroparks Zoo many times and attended several fund-raisers. I managed to do a number of important renovations to our home in Rocky River, including a new back fence, a complete renovation of the basement, first floor painting, repaired the window wells, completed extensive improvements to the landscaping and orga- nized the garage. Sarah and I played golf all summer, including a week- end in Oglebay Park. I only played about the same number of rounds that I had played in previous years, somewhat unusual for a retiree. We bought bikes and I rode mine often on errands instead of driving my car and Sarah and I rode them throughout Cleveland Metroparks and in Cuyahoga National Park in the summer months. Sarah and I celebrated our twentieth wedding anniversary at the Commander Palace in New Orleans. I visited the Long Beach Taylors in August and saw lots of soc- cer as well as celebrated my granddaughter Shae's twelfth birthday on the Queen Mary.

I became a member of the Board of Directors of the Akron Zoo and I have enjoyed my time on the board for many years. After Pat Simmons took a job as director of the North Carolina Zoo, I felt I was able to give the new director, Doug Piekarz, some useful advice. I was able to facili- tate a meeting with staff on their conservation programs. When I came to Cleveland in 1989, we referred to the Akron Zoo as a zoo with a "duck and a chicken." Pat Simmons worked hard and got a county property tax levy to help fund the zoo and the zoo took off. By the time I was ap- pointed to the Akron Zoo board, the zoo was doing extremely well.

In all, my 2013 travel took me to seventeen different states. And, most importantly, I thought I had finished this book, but I had not as there are a few stories still to tell.

CONSULTING

Zoos and Aquariums were more to me than a great place to work, they were my hobby. I was not about to just leave the zoo world and I stayed active by reading news about zoos and aquariums every day. From 2013 to 2020, I attended six AZA National Conventions, five Regional Workshops and three Director's Policy Conferences. I also attended WAZA Conventions, one at Disney and another in Puebla, Mexico and a Zoos and Aquariums Committed to Conservation (ZACC) conference in Denver. I felt honored that Denny Lewis, vice-president for accreditation felt I was still valuable as a chair for visiting committees for ten different AZA institutions.

My first day of consulting was January 30, 2013 and I got up at four in the morning as I had a 6 AM flight to Syracuse, New York through Washington, D.C. Just prior to going out the door I went up to the bedroom and announced to Sarah that "I was going to work." In a sleepy stupor she said, "it's about time." Heck, I had only been retired for thirty days! I had signed a consulting services contract with Schultz and Williams, Inc., the major planning and management firm working with AZA zoos and aquariums. Rick Biddle and I were in Syracuse to interview for a strategic planning project for the Rosamont Gifford Zoo. I arrived at the zoo in the morning and had a couple of hours to walk around by myself. It was an unusual day for January in upstate New York as it was over fifty degrees and no snow or rain. The cab driver told me that they had over sixty inches of snow in a twenty-four-hour period two weeks ago.

After a giant sandwich at the zoo's only food facility, we started our interview at 1:45 PM. Rick gave a fifteen-minute opening power point about Schultz and Williams and I added a comment where appropriate. By 3:30 PM we were in a cab on our way back to the airport. My flight direct to Cleveland was two hours late so I did not get home until after 10 PM. It was the bumpiest flight I had ever been on and I literally had to hold on tight to the armrests.

I had to think that as good as I thought consultants had it, maybe it wasn't for me. My eighteen-hour day included an hour and a half interview, ten hours in airports or on planes, three bad sandwiches and three terrible glasses of cheap white wine!

With that said, I really did want the job. It was a great medium-sized zoo. They had just opened a huge new Asian elephant exhibit. The zoo had a great animal collection and much of it was indoors. Many of the other animals were winter hardy, including snow leopards, red pandas, Andean condors, white-lipped deer, penguins and Amur tigers. I immediately liked the staff and the board members I met. The fact that both the county and the society were very open to giving the zoological society management responsibilities made our team well positioned. This is an area where Rick Biddle was a national expert having worked in the last twenty years with many other zoos that had privatized. Also, this was an area that I was well versed in having worked in four government-run zoos with non-profit support groups. Unfortunately, after all that we didn't get the job!

Shortly after that we did get a consulting job assisting the Buffalo Zoo in creating a comprehensive plan. I knew Donna Fernandes, the zoo's CEO, very well having first met her when I was an instructor at the AZA Management School. In a weird coincidence, I ran into her in the pool in Captain Morgan's Retreat in Belize in 1998. We looked at each other about the same time and said, "I know you." That day Donna and her future husband, Robert, got engaged.

One of the oldest zoos in the country, the Buffalo Zoo had a good reputation for an outstanding animal collection. It's biggest challenge was that it was only twenty-four acres and had minimal parking. The zoo was completely surrounded by a popular city park and efforts to expand the zoo were met with community resistance. There were unsuccessful efforts to move the zoo outside the city, but those efforts failed. By the time Donna became CEO, the decision was made to do the best they could on the current site. Since Donna had been president/CEO of the zoo, she had done a great job of raising funds and creating a new entrance complex and several new modern exhibits, including an indoor rainforest exhibit. The Arctic Edge exhibit for polar bears was under construction when I visited and opened in 2015.

I enjoyed working with Rick Biddle and Jill Macauley from Schultz and Williams and the Buffalo team, including both staff and board. The zoo had a 2008 Master Plan completed in 2008 by PJA, an excellent zoo design group and it was still valid. We did the usual benchmark studies, analysis of strengths and weaknesses and did interviews with key players in the community. We worked with the staff and the board on vision, mission and values and created four strategic goals, each with objectives and action steps with a timetable and cost. It was great fun for me and believe Donna was able to keep the momentum going until she retired in the Spring of 2017. When she left the Zoo after sixteen years, the board showed their appreciation by naming a major renovation the Donna M. Fernandes Amphibian and Reptile Center.

In May of 2013, Ron Forman, CEO of the Audubon Institute, invited me to come to New Orleans to evaluate their elephant programs. They had had some issues with their recent accreditation inspection as they were still not in protective contact with their elephants. Sarah and I used this as an opportunity to celebrate our twenty-year anniversary in New Orleans, so before my work with the zoo, we spent a couple of days touring this wonderful city and playing golf. The evening of our anniversary, we had dinner at the famous Commander's Palace. Prior to my work at the zoo, Ron and his wife, Sally, took us to dinner at Clancy's, one of Ron's favorite restaurants. I was delighted when Ron introduced me to his friend, James Carville, Bill Clinton's campaign manager.

I had asked David Hagan from the Indianapolis Zoo to partner with me on the evaluations as David knew much more about hands on management of elephants than I did. The evaluation was easy as they had already made some changes as they were no longer walking the elephants through the zoo. They were under construction on a new elephant facility that would allow for protective contact.

Another project I enjoyed very much was helping my friend, Beth Heidorn, executive director of the Racine Zoo, by facilitating a board retreat in January 2016. I had known Beth since she was the education curator at the Minnesota Zoo in the nineties. I had followed her career and was delighted see that she was hired as executive director at the Racine Zoo, a small AZA accredited zoo in Wisconsin on the shores of Lake Michigan. I had last visited the Racine Zoo in the summer of 2001. Even in the winter of 2016, I could see there had been some improvements. Beth had big plans. At the board retreat we were able to work with the board on a Strengths, Weaknesses, Opportunities and Threats (SWOT) document. Since that time Beth has done a great job creating enthusiasm for the zoo by greatly expanding the number and types of community events. It has resulted in increasing attendance from 80,000 to 125,000 guests.

BIRDING

My trip to Costa Rica in April 2013 was different for me as it was with five friends focusing on bird watching. After all, aren't retired folks supposed to work on their hobbies! Steve Wylie, former director of the Oklahoma City Zoo, had organized these annual birding trips since 2005. He and I had been good friends even before we were on the AZA Board together in the early nineties when he was president-elect when I was president. I had never found time in the past to travel with this group while I was working as I had other priorities. When I knew I was about to retire, I asked Wylie if I could join the group. Somehow, the group agreed to let me join them! I realized that they were all more accomplished birders than myself, but I knew I would learn much by being with this group. I joked that I thought that I probably did not fit in with these serious birders, and then I worried that I would!

Steve Wylie, Bruce Bohmke (Woodland Park Zoo, Seattle), Tony Vecchio (Jacksonville Zoo) and Ted Stevens (retired ornithologist and husband of Beth Stevens, Disney's Animal Kingdom) were tremendous birders and Gary Lee was there to get the photographs. I had had an interest in birds all my life and spent time birding in whatever part of the world I happened to visit; however, I was only a graduate of the pre-school for birders compared to my four friends. I did my best to keep up and at least show interest, but I never had the patience to intensely watch birds and identify the difficult and confusing ones. I realized then that my difficulty was the fact that I did not have great vision, I was colorblind, I did not hear that well and, most importantly, I had the attention span of a kindergartener! The real birders were very kind to me and tried very hard not to make me feel like an idiot. And I did learn much from them.

I guess I didn't do too bad as I was welcomed back for more birding adventures. I was able to go to Honduras, Colombia and Panama with this group, all countries new to me. We went to Honduras in April 2015 and our guide was Robert Gallardo, an American that graduated from Humboldt State in California before joining the Peace Corps going to Honduras where he now lives. He had just published, *Guide to the Birds of Honduras*. The birding was excellent and we also had an opportunity to visit the amazing Mayan ruins. Copan is the southernmost main city of the of the Mayan civilization. From the fifth to the ninth century AD it is believed that twenty-thousand Mayans lived in the area. The ruins are well preserved and there was a wonderful museum that added to the experience. It was also a site for the reintroduction of scarlet macaws. These macaws had become endangered in Central America due to poaching of young chicks for the pet trade.

In April 2016, the group went to Colombia. I got there ahead of the group so I could visit the Cali Zoo, one of the international members of AZA and one of the best zoos in South America. When the others in the group arrived, we visited several very different habitats as we drove up the Cauca Valley between the two main mountain ranges, the Eastern and Central Cordilleras of the Andes. I saw over two-hundred bird species, including trogons, motmots, several species of toucans and over twenty species of tanagers and honeycreepers. The experienced birders in the group saw many more. However, even I saw forty different species of hummingbirds. My favorite was the four and one-half inch bearded helmetcrest with its black and white crest and shaggy white beard that we found twelve-thousand feet up in the Andes Mountains.

In 2018, the group traveled to Panama. Rudy Zamora, our guide in Costa Rica, was our guide in Panama. During our visit south to the Darien, we had a local guide that was very familiar with this region. For most of us this was our first chance to see a harpy eagle. On March 13 we were up at 4:30 AM and after a quick breakfast we headed south as far as the Pan American high-way would go. From there we took dugout canoes to a small vil-lage in the Darien where we boarded two well used pickup trucks and drove forty-five minutes into the park. We hiked with local villagers, one probably didn't weigh one-hundred pounds and he carried our ice chest with our lunches. After about one hour we arrived where the harpy eagle was usually seen. No eagle. We relaxed while our guides walked the muddy and slippery trails searching the surrounding area for the harpy eagle. After two hours they found a young eagle about two-hundred yards from where we had stopped. We all felt extremely fortunate to have seen this mag-nificent bird in the wild. The rest of our Panama tour was around the canal zone. During this birding trip we actually saw thirteen species of mammals, including northern tamandua, three-toed sloth, Geoffroy's tamarin, mantled howler monkeys, Panamanian night monkeys, white-faced capuchin, paca, Central American agouti, white-nose coati and jaguarundi.

LEADING SAFARIS

In my first year of retirement, I had two Tanzania safaris. The first one was assigned to me by EWT when a group of six wanted Jim to lead them on safari in February/March, but he was already booked. He asked me to lead it and I did. This was a very high-end safari I enjoyed it very much and hoped I added something to the client's experience. One unique experience was on the first day in Arusha when we visited a local school with a 4-H Club. David Epstein was a member of the National 4-H Board and wherever he traveled in the world he scheduled a visit to the local 4-H club. We had prear-ranged with Tumaini to take us to the school on the first day and once we arrived, hundreds of young students entertained us. After singing and dancing we were taken to the 4-H garden plot and the students showed us their projects. David and his wife, Paula, presented the club with a generous one-thousand-dollar donation.

This was also one on my best visits to Lake Manyara. First, we drove in the back way from Tarangire National Park that was much more interesting than taking the normal highway through Mto-wa-Mbu Village. We stayed for three days at the very beautiful &Beyond Tree Lodge. Because of the location of the camp near the southern end, in the evening we were able to have sundowners just outside the park overlooking the Lake Manyara. This still is an unique experience on an East African safari. We had great views of the famous tree-climbing lions of Lake Manyara National Park. Later I learned that there was only one pride of fourteen lions in the park. Two weeks after we left, the park flooded, completely destroying the visitor center at the entrance and many bridges.

The remainder of our safari was excellent as we were in the middle of the migration near Ndutu Lodge and we observed a cheetah chase and catch a young gazelle. Near Serenera we watched a lion pride for an hour stalk and chase wildebeest. They were unsuccessful due to the fact that there were more than seventy vehicles watching the event.

Sarah and I then led a similar safari in June 2013. It was originally a Zoological Society program, but no one signed up and we almost forget about it until Craig Donnan, managing partner of the Cleveland office of Deloitte, asked Sarah if it would be possible for us to take his family of five. We put the safari together and later added another couple. The Donnan's daughters, ages fifteen, eighteen and twenty-two, were a delight. It was wonderful to see Africa through the eyes of young people. The sisters were extremely close although they had the usual arguments, especially about who got the first shower. In several camps, the third shower only had cold water! Throughout the safari we saw about seventy different lions, a record for me at that time. We had great weather, except for on the rim of the Ngorongoro Crater that was so foggy that you couldn't see ten feet in front of the vehicle. We caught the end of the migration just north of Soroi Lodge in the Grumeti area of the Serengeti.

Sarah and I had an unusual experience in Dunia camp in the central Serengeti. Coming back from dinner one night our canvas tent porch was covered with army ants. Getting into our tent was tricky as we hurriedly rushed forward, opened the zipper and jumped into the tent. Immediately we got naked, as ants were everywhere on our bodies biting us at will. After recovering, I took the Doom, an insect spray in Africa and probably not legal in America and sprayed the canvas porch killing thousands of army ants. Fortunately, they never got in the tent that night. In the morning I found a trail of ants moving freely under our tent. I told Peter, the camp manager, he should take care of the ants prior to the next clients using the tent. Sarah and I were just glad it was our tent, not the one with the three girls who had often worried about mice, lizards and insects in their rooms or tents. The invasion of army ants at their tent would have been a major disaster that may have been heard all the way to Arusha!

Jumping with Maasai warriors in Tanzania in 2013.

The next two years (2014 and 2015) I had another four safaris in Tanzania. Some experiences were similar, but there were many new experiences. The February safaris would start in Arusha and end in the Serengeti and the June safaris would fly from Arusha to the northern Serengeti and drive back to Arusha. In this way, both safaris would have the best chance to see the great migration. Again, as Gary Clarke would say, "Your best safari is your next safari." So true.

On most northern Tanzania safaris there are certain places that I consider a must see and certain ways that make them the best possible experience. Tarangire National Park is the land of elephants and baobab trees. As I mentioned previously, Dr. Charles Foley has done his very significant research from his research station within the Tarangire National Park.

On a couple of safaris, I was able to introduce my clients to Derek Lee and Monica Bond, two Americans doing research on giraffe. Giraffe are now more endangered than elephants. There are about three-thousand giraffe in the Lake Manyara/Tarangire ecosystem and these two scientists have identified about half of them. Their research is significant as giraffe can also migrate in and out of these two national parks and it's important to keep wildlife corridors open for their migrations.

Leaving Lake Manyara and before heading up to Ngorongoro Crater is the town of Karatu. I love touring people through the local market where you can purchase anything from reconditioned running shoes to fruits and vegetables and anything else you would need. I usually bargained for inexpensive necklaces with a simple carved African animal. If I buy them by the dozen, I can usually get them for less than a dollar each. I give one to each of my women clients and also bring some home for small gifts. About three miles up the hill from Karatu is our favorite Tanzania lodge, Gibbs Farm. It is a working coffee farm and much of the food served at their restaurant is grown on the farm. The tropical gardens throughout the lodge are beyond beautiful and full of birds. The spacious rooms are a delight with indoor and outdoor showers, fireplaces and a desk overlooking the garden.

Another must see in Tanzania is the Ngorongoro Crater. When we would arrive at the gate at Ngorongoro Crater there is a small museum that has a twelve by twelve-foot relief map of the crater and the Serengeti. I would gather the group and give them an orientation of where we were headed. The Ngorongoro Crater is the best place to see east African wildlife and the only problem is the hundred square mile crater floor can get very crowded. We always drove down into the crater as early as possible to get the best possible viewing of wildlife. We stayed and had a picnic lunch and usually did not leave until the late afternoon. The crater was also important to my clients as it was the only place in Tanzania where one was likely to see black rhinos, although sometimes at a great distance. There were as few as thirty-two black rhinos in Tanzania in 1995 and with increased security the number was above one-hundred by 2010, including animals being introduced into the central Serengeti.

Although a long ride, one of my favorite days on safari was the ride from the crater to Serengeti National Park through the Ngorongoro Conservation Area. Leaving early in the morning our first stop would be the famous Olduvai Gorge where in 1959 Mary Leakey, wife of the famous anthropologist, Louis Leakey, discovered fossils of Nutcracker Man. Louis and his wife had found many interesting fossils in the gorge but finding evidence of the one-million seven-hundred thousand-year-old Nutcracker Man after twenty-seven years of digging was probably their most significant finding at the time and an important breakthrough in the understanding of human evolution. Visits would include a short visit to the small museum (a new much larger museum opened in 2018), created with assistance from the Cleveland Museum of National History and a short lecture from a staff scientist. We would then a ride down into the gorge to see the site of the discovery. We would continue driving out on the opposite side of the gorge to head towards a unique phenomenon, Shifting Sands. Shifting Sands, as the name implies is a fifty-foot high crescent-shaped mound of sand that moves with the wind across the savanna about seventeen meters a year. From there we would often head overland and have lunch in the middle of nowhere under a large isolated fig tree the locals called the "Devil Tree."

After lunch we would start our game drive through the Conservation Area towards Serengeti National Park. If it was February, we would have a good chance to catch up to the migration shortly after leaving the devil tree. If it was a June safari, we were more likely to view the migration from the northern parts of the Serengeti. Viewing migration of one and a half to two million wildebeest and zebras is one of the greatest wildlife adventures in the world and the highlight of a safari in Tanzania.

My thirtieth African safari (Sarah's fourteenth) in June 2017 was one of my best. Sarah and I knew most of the group for a while. My friend, Mike Benz, was CEO of the Cleveland United Way. Gigi Benjamin, traveling with her husband, Phil, was chair of the Cleveland Zoological Society when I retired in 2012. Betsi Morris, traveling with her husband, Warren and son Stephen, traveled with me in 2007 to Madagascar. Jeff Heinen, traveling with his wife Nancy and son Jake, was the owner of a Northeastern Ohio's successful grocery chain. Seven others gave us a full group of sixteen. We saw a total of seventy-five different lions, seven cheetah and three leopards. As this was a June safari and everyone wanted to see the migration, we started at Chaka Camp in the northern Serengeti almost on the border of Kenya. On our first game drive we caught up with much of the great migration of wildebeest and zebra. We stopped for lunch on a hill looking out at what I would guess would be a hundred thousand animals.

A new experience for me was having a special catered lunch in an isolated forest by Ngoitokitok Springs on the floor of the Ngorongoro Crater. This was very different from the usual, but adequate, box lunch in the parking area of the springs with fifty other safari vehicles nearby. To make it even more special, only Sarah and I knew of this surprise ahead of time.

PERSONAL TRAVEL

2014 was the year for me to check-off another of my bucket list items, visiting all fifty states. Sarah and I, along with Satch and Becky Krantz took a two-week tour of Alaska in July. Before the Krantz's arrived, Sarah and I drove to the town of Seward and visited the Alaska Sealife Center, an AZA accredited facility. The director, Tara Reimer, arranged for us to have an interesting behind-the-scenes tour. After spending the night in Seward, we drove back to Anchorage and then the next day flew to Fairbanks. There we met up with our group and Jim Heck, who was our guide for the rest of the trip. While most of Jim's business is Africa, he also loves Alaska and tries to have one or two tours there each year. As it was my first trip to Alaska, I was glad to have Jim as our guide and with no responsibilities myself, this really was a true vacation.

Jim's itinerary was excellent and allowed us to visit several of the most interesting places in Alaska. In Fairbanks we visited the Museum of the North, saw a section of the pipeline and had a tour of the Alaska University's Large Animal Research Center for caribou and muskox. From Fairbanks, we took the train, Goldstar Service, to Denali National Park where we took a Bluebird bus, named Charlie, for a six-hour drive to Kantishna Roadhouse with our very enthusiastic driver/guide, Christine. Sarah and I had a great guided hike on the tundra to Friday Ridge and Wickersham Dome. Walking on three-foot deep spongy tundra was a unique experience as we felt we might fall through with each step. From there we flew in a small plane to the charming town of Takeetra passing the incredible Mt. Denali. We flew so close, it felt like we could reach out the window and touch it! In Takeetra we caught the train to Anchorage.

From Anchorage, the four of us flew to Gustavus so we could go halibut fishing. None of us were fishermen, but since we were in Alaska, we felt we should give it a chance. We were not disappointed. A mile or so from the dock, we had to fish for our bait. We each dropped a line in the water with five hooks and no bait and after a few minutes, while watching humpback whales in the distance, we caught twenty to twenty-five herring and pollack. Halibut fishing was different. Captain, Steve Miley, showed us how to drop the line approximately one-hundred and fifty feet and within seconds of my line hitting the bottom, I hooked a huge halibut, probably weighing one-hundred and fifty pounds. Alaska fisheries are well regulated and you can keep one halibut and that can be either a young fish under forty-two-inches or an old fish over sixty-inches. Those in between are the breeders and they are left in the ocean to produce more halibut. My fish was just under sixty-inches so had to be thrown back. We all caught a legal fish and came back with four nice ones that we took to a place that cleaned them and prepared them for us to take home.

The rest of our trip was cruising Glacier Bay on a converted World War II mine sweeper, called the SeaWolf. The owner and naturalist was Kimber Owens and she was a wealth of knowledge. We saw lots of wildlife from the ship, including grizzly bears, wolves, humpback whales, Steller's sea lions, sea otters and harbor porpoise. Every day we got off the ship for hiking and kayaking. Kayaking close to a giant glazier, especially when a large chunk fell to the sea, called calving, was especially exciting.

Also, in 2014, Travis's mother called me and said that I should do another father/son trip since the last one was thirty-years ago. I thought it would be a good idea and when Travis and I talked, we decided Argentina would be a good destination. Travis and Karen had lived there before they had children and I wanted to see Temaiken Bioparque, an international AZA accredited zoo, plus travel to Patagonia to see wildlife.

After an overnight flight we arrived in Buenos Aires on Monday, October 13. For four days we visited many of the major sites of Buenos Aires and visited Travis's former office and their former house. It was a great help that Travis spoke Spanish. We had great lunches and dinners, most of which were either fresh fish or steak. Of course, with dinner we had Argentina's Malbec wine. A highlight for me was walking and birding in the three-hundred and fifty-hectare Reserva Ecologica Nature Preserve. There was a good variety of birds including white-faced whistling ducks, Coscoroba swan, red-fronted coot and Guira cuckoo. Another highlight was the great tour of the Tamaiken Bioparque with Damien Pellandini, zoo director, and his staff. Opened in 2002 by one of the wealthiest families in Argentina, the zoo was as good as friends had described. Even more interesting was a special area a mile away from the zoo for breeding endangered birds, and a few mammals, including giant anteaters.

On Friday, October 17 we flew to Puerto Madryn where we had arranged tours of both Peninsula Valdes and Puerto Tombo. Our trip to Peninsula Valdes was a two-hour drive and during the drive our guide, Claudia, talked about the history of Puerto Madryn and Peninsula Valdes. On the peninsula, sheep shared the brush habitat with guanaco, lesser rhea, mara and other South American wildlife. On the beaches we saw southern sea lions and elephant seals. Leaving the peninsula after lunch we stopped at a village on the Gulf of Nuevo and went whale watching where at that time of year the southern right whales enter the gulf to have their calves. The next day, Claudia took us south to Punta Tombo to see a huge colony of Magellanic penguins. After being at sea for several months off the coast of Brazil one million penguins return in September to Punta Toma to lay their eggs and raise their chicks.

The father/son trip was a great idea and both of us had a great adventure with few disagreements. Travis was not so keen on me stopping to look at every bird. In fact, at one point he mentioned if he never saw another bird again, he would be happy! He also felt that I did not do a very good job of picking our two-star accommodations, as the rooms were very small. When we returned to Buenos Aries, we checked in to a very nice Hilton. It was a good choice because on our last day we could use the locker room in the hotel to shower prior to taking our overnight flight back to the United States.

Sarah retired as the controller of the Cleveland Indians Baseball team on December 31, 2016 after the Indians lost the World's Series to the Chicago Cubs in seven games in October. Her retirement gave us more opportunity to travel.

The trip of a lifetime occurred from January 10 through April 4, 2017 when Sarah and I went around the world. In eighty-three-days we visited ten countries, took twenty-five flights, slept in forty beds, never lost our luggage and stayed healthy. How did we do it? We planned well and had all our one-way airline tickets ahead of time. We had four prepaid adventures. Those included a bike ride in New Zealand, wildlife tour in Borneo, a tour of India to see tigers and other wildlife and safari in southern Africa. The other half of the trip we planned as we went, using the internet to arrange accommodations the day before we landed in a new location.

We stayed in the southern hemisphere to enjoy the warmer weather, going east to west. We went to New Zealand, Australia, Thailand, Malaysia, the island of Borneo (Malaysia), Singapore, India, Seychelles, South Africa, Swaziland and Namibia. While there are many stories with each country, in the spirit of this book I will try to keep it to one or two zoo or wildlife adventures from each location.

New Zealand was very special to both of us. I always felt that Australians were the nicest people I had ever met. We found that New Zealanders (Kiwis) were even nicer. Our first stop was Christchurch where we explored the city and the surrounding area. It was still re-covering from a large earthquake two years prior to our visit. We did manage to visit the Orana Wildlife Park. One unique guest experi-ence we observed at the zoo was loading guests in a cage in the back of a pick-up truck and driving the truck into the lion exhibit! We did not participate!

From Christchurch we joined ten others for a five-day bike trip through surreal mountain scenery of the Molesworth and Marlborough Wine Country that included a unique overnight at the thirty-three thousand-acre Upcot Merino Sheep Station. Back to Christchurch we took a bus to the southern tip of the island, where we took a ferry to

Steward Island to explore for a couple days and observe native birds, including the weka, a flightless rail and several other species.

Next we flew to Wellington on the north island and the capital of New Zealand. We visited the botanical garden, Te Papa Museum, the Parliament Building, called the beehive, Zoolandia and the zoo. At the zoo, we met up with the director, Karen Fifield, who I had known from several WAZA meetings. At the zoo we were able to see some of New Zealand's iconic native species that we had not been able to observe in the wild, including kiwi, kea and the tuatara, a prehistoric lizard-like reptile. Like Cleveland Metroparks Zoo, the Wellington Zoo had a window between guests and the animal hospital and Sarah and I watched the veterinary staff perform a procedure on a tamarin. In the evening after our zoo visit, we had a delightful dinner with Karen at a restaurant across the street from our hotel.

Our time in Australia was spent in and around Melbourne, Australia. I had been to Melbourne twice before and loved the area. At a WAZA conference in Puebla, Mexico in September 2016 I mentioned to Jenny Gray, director of Zoo Victoria, that Sarah and I would be visiting Melbourne the following January. She cautioned me to get reservations quickly as we would be there during the finals of the Australian Open. It had always been a bucket list item for Sarah to attend the Australian Open. We did not get tickets for the final match just in case our plans changed and we were unable to get to Melbourne as scheduled. As it turned out it was a reasonable expense to get passes for the grounds. These passes worked out beautifully as on the day of the finals, we could watch it on a live screen in the Margaret Court Arena. When Federer beat Nadal, he came through a tunnel to the arena and held up the trophy for all of us to see. It was a wonderful experience.

We enjoyed Melbourne and went to the zoo and had lunch with Jenny Gray. We walked around the very cosmopolitan city, enjoying the unique public art and dined at some fabulous restaurants. We biked to the beach for a seafood lunch, played golf at Albert Park

Golf Course and ran the tan, a hardpacked dirt running trail around the Melbourne Botanical Garden. One day we took a guided tour of the Great Ocean Road, one of the must-see attractions of this part of Australia. At one point we stopped to hand feed wild king parrots and crimson rosella. While there, we also observed mating koalas. The main attraction of the Great Ocean Road is a rocky shoreline, the Twelve Apostles. Why the name Apostles? We were told that if they just called them the twelve rocks sticking out of the ocean, no one would come to see them!

One place I was excited to visit again was the Healesville Sanctuary, one of three institutions of Zoos Victoria. It is out of town and since we do not like to drive in foreign countries, we took two trains and one bus to get there. We stayed two nights in the historic Healesville Hotel. The sanctuary is the home of native Australian wildlife and has conservation programs for some of the most endangered, including the Tasmanian devil. There is a very clever bird show that highlights their rehabilitation and conservation programs. There is also a unique demonstration with the duckbill platypus, Tales from Platypus Creek. Jenny had arranged for us to participate in feeding the echidna.

Leaving Healesville, we caught a public bus to start our journey back to Melbourne. We asked the driver if it would be possible if we could get off the bus and visit a local winery. He assured us that the buses run regularly and we could flag one down and it would stop and we could continue our ride back to Melbourne. We had a nice wine tasting at the Yering Station Winery. After the tasting we went out to the highway and waited for the bus. After a while the bus approached and we waved as it went right by! We ended up going back it the winery and they called a taxi from the nearest town that was ten miles away. One of the greatest things about travel is improvising when things do not go quite as planned.

On February 5 we flew to Bangkok, Thailand for four days. On the first day we explored the city, including a visit to the Grand Palace. Sarah was wearing shorts so I had to purchase her a long skirt for one-dollar. While we had not planned any wildlife experiences, we did have an idea of two activities that we had read about in the *USA Today*. The first was to spend a couple of days at Hua Hin Beach. Sarah got on the internet and discovered it was three hours away. No problem as the three-hour taxi ride only cost fifty-four dollars. It was relaxing to spend two days in a nice small hotel on the beach. Our second activity was attending the Amita Thai Cooking School. A boat took us on the polluted Chao Phraya River through a lock and up a canal to a complex of houses, one of which had a teaching kitchen for the cooking school. After a tour of the herb garden, we prepared chicken wrapped in banana leaves, pork with basil, prawn soup and coconut pancakes. It was great fun and we tried the recipes when we returned home, but we did not quite duplicate the experience.

From Bangkok we flew to Kuala Lumpur, Malaysia. This large metropolitan city had certainly changed since our visit in 1991. The eighty-eight-floor Petrones twin tower dominated the skyline and there were many other skyscrapers. We were told that there would be three hundred more new buildings in the next four years, including one with one-hundred and eighteen floors. After a day of site seeing on our own, we went on the internet and found a guide, Tony Khong. Tony was a great guide and we saw many sites we would not have seen if it wasn't for Tony, including the changing of the guard at the Presidential Palace, Chinatown and tasting food in three different ethnic restaurants. When Tony found out we were interested in nature and wildlife, he agreed to take us the next day to Kuala Selanger, a beach town where the river joins the ocean. We first went to a park-like area near the lighthouse where silver langurs were gathering for public feeding. While I am not a huge fan of this type of tourism, it was great to get a close-up view of these beautiful primates, especially their bright orange babies. After visiting the primates, we got in a small boat and headed to the mouth of the river where we fed fish to Brahminy kites, gulls and a few white-bellied sea eagles. Near the dock we were treated to a fabulous dinner called a shell out. We were given bibs and plastic gloves and a huge pile of shellfish was placed in the middle of the table. It was a great way to end a very interesting day.

While planning our world tour, Ged Caddick of Ecotours told us of Caroline Pang who provided tours of Borneo. We arranged with her a tour of the Sabah in the Malaysian portion of this island, the other portion is Indonesian. We flew from Kuala Lumpur to Sandakan on the northeast coast of the island. Our guide, Ben Duncan and his driver, Wilford, picked us up at the airport and took us to the Sheraton hotel. After a little rest and walk around the town, Ben picked us up at 7 PM for dinner. We were taken up into the hills to an old colonial house, the English Tea House and Restaurant, and left there. It was a wonderful experience. At first, we were the only ones there and later a few others also came to dinner. It was a beautiful warm night with dinner outside and Frank Sinatra music playing in the background.

The next day we drove an hour to our first stop, the famous Sepilok Orangutan Rehabilitation Center. Guests were in two large glass-fronted rooms that looked out at what appeared to be a zoo exhibit complete with a climbing platform. Only this exhibit had no back wall or barrier of any sort. The center was surrounded by the rainforest so when young orphan orangs were ready, they could just leave the care of humans. Most young orangs come back and forth for a while and some for much longer. Graphics at the center stated that one-hundred and sixty orangs had come to the center since 1964 and sixty-six percent had been successfully released back into the rainforest.

Next to Sepilok was the Bornean Sun Bear Conservation Center. I was surprised to see the Cleveland Metroparks Zoo logo on the list of donors. I guess we supported this center years ago when we worked on bringing sun bears to the zoo. We discovered that they had forty-two bears at the center but have not had much luck with reintroductions.

Our next stop was Gomantong Caves. Aside from several species of bats, the cave had nesting swiftlets. The swiftlet nests are harvested by the locals for bird nest soup. Ugh. The walkway in the cave was full of bat guano and it was very slippery. On the walls were thousands of cockroaches. While interesting, it wasn't our favorite experience. Leaving the cave, we were fortunate in observing a troop of beautiful red leaf monkeys.

We continued our drive past the village of Sukau to the Kinabatangan River where a boat took us a mile upriver to the Sukau Rainforest Lodge, branded by National Geographic as one of the unique lodges in the world in 2015. On walks and on a boat on the river, we saw amazing wildlife. While we only caught a glimpse of a male orang, we had many opportunities to view the amazing proboscis monkeys. Other mammals including sambar deer, pygmy squirrel, Malayan flying lemurs, long-tailed macaque and provost squirrel. Bird watching was also fantastic, especially seeing a half dozen species of hornbill, including the black, Oriental pied, white-crowned, wrinkled, bushy-crested and rhinoceros.

Not far from the lodge was the headquarters for a conservation organization, HUTAN, headed by Dr. Mark Arcanez. Mark was in Kota Kinabalu at a conference on proboscis monkeys, but we met with the organization's program director, Datu Md Ahbam Abulani, or Bam, who had visited the Cleveland Metroparks Zoo in 2012. I was proud to see a poster on their wall thanking the Cleveland Metroparks Zoo for our support of their conservation programs. HUTAN has been successful working with owners of palm oil plantations by convincing them not to plant palms within fifty meters of the river. This allows some of their land to provide homes for native wildlife.

The lodge encouraged everyone, both men and women, to wear a sarong to dinner. I think it was the first time I ever wore a skirt! Going native was great fun.

Sarah and I on the Kinabatangan River in Borneo in February 2017.

On February 21 we took the boat down the river to find our driver, Wilford, who was waiting to take us to Danum Valley through the town of Lahad Datu, a total drive of four hours. We saw lots of signs of forest elephants on the drive, but never saw an elephant. When we were a few hundred yards from the Bornean Rainforest Lodge, we did find a male and female orangutan and got great photos. The lodge had elevated rooms and an elevated walkway which was necessary as it rained heavily at times. One critter we got to unfortunately see close up was the tiger leech. This six-inch leach has orange stripes, thus the common name. Sarah came to dinner one evening and sat down and it looked like she had been shot! Somehow a leech had got her in the chest and there was a large blood spot on her white t-shirt. I was proud of her as she calmly excused herself and went back to the room to change.

Our flight from Lahad Dutu to Kota Kinabalu was cancelled due to storms, but Ben took care of us and we stayed overnight in Lahad Datu. This was the only flight we missed during our entire eighty-three-day trip. The next day we flew to Kota Kinabalu and then on to Singapore.

Like Kuala Lumpur, Singapore had changed dramatically since our visit in 1991. The twenty-six hundred room Marina Bay Sands hotel with its three fifty-five floor towers connected on the top by the Sky Park with its infinity pool dominated the bay. From the hotel we viewed the iconic Gardens by the Bay. Both the hotel and the gardens were built on a landfill.

We had arranged to meet Caroline Pang in the morning for what we thought would be for coffee, but she spent the entire day guiding us on a wonderful tour of the city. Her travel business was a non-profit which supported wildlife conservation. She is a professional photographer for Reuters. We had a great tour and learned all about Singapore. She even found us a laundromat in Chinatown and stayed with us until our laundry was done.

The second day we went to Sentosa Island where I had arranged with AJ Penny for a tour of Dolphin Island and the Aquarium, two of AZA's international members. Dolphin Island allows guests a variety of different activities to interact with the dolphins. In the aquarium, I enjoyed seeing giant spider crabs, the huge moray eel exhibit, sea-horses, jellyfish and a large sawfish that AJ said was eating some of their specimen fish.

In the evening, we headed to the unique Night Safari, adjacent to the Singapore Zoo. It was a fantastic complete zoo experience with over a thousand animals. We experienced this unique zoo, both on the open-sided tram and also taking advantage of the walking trails. The night safari had all the mega-vertebrates such as Asiatic lions, Malayan tiger, Asian elephants, sloth bears and many more. I really enjoyed seeing the smaller nocturnal animals such as mouse deer, palm civets, fruit bats, golden cats, leopard cats, slow loris and hog badgers.

From Singapore we flew to New Delhi, India where EWT had arranged a full itinerary with Akorn Tours which included some of the must-see sites in Delhi and Agra and a week in two National Parks, Bandhavgarh and Kanha. On arrival we were picked up by our guide, Heri, and driver, Devender. They took us to the Holiday Inn Express, adjacent to an indoor shopping mall. We were impressed with the security as we went through metal detectors and our luggage through x-ray prior to entering the hotel. In and around Delhi we saw may historic mosques built from 1500 to 1700 by several different Mughai Emperors. The Mughai Empire ruled India from the 1500s until it was dissolved by the British in 1857. Many of the UNESCO World Heritage Sites, including the Taj Mahal, have been described as the jewels of the Muslim architecture of India. It was almost too much to comprehend and frankly I got a little bored of visiting these amazing historic structures.

After Delhi, we were driven to Agra and visited the Taj Mahal. Our guide, V. J. Singh, not the golfer, grew up in Agra and he stated that as a child the Taj was his playground. I read somewhere "the Taj is like the Grand Canyon, one of the few things that never disappoints you." We visited in the afternoon and again in the morning and because of the difference in natural lighting, the Taj changes colors at different times of day. Another highlight in Agra was a rickshaw birdwatching tour of Keoladeo Ghana Bird Sanctuary. It had been a hunting preserve for the royal family. A plaque showed the success of various hunting trips, including one of a United States Senate delegation on November 18, 1949 that bagged two-hundred sixty birds. With our guide, we saw some great birds, including painted stork, open-bill stork, white spoonbill, Indian common moorhen, white-breasted waterhen and much more.

Sarah and I at the Taj Mahal in March 2017
as part of our 83 day around the world tour.

The first thing we noticed when we entered Bandhavgarh National Park was a park ranger riding an elephant. We saw spotted deer, also called chital, sambar deer, muntjac and blackbuck. I was particularly excited to view a herd of the world's largest cattle species, the guar. After spending most of the time looking for tigers, we finally got a good view of a large male. We were not alone as there were at least twenty other vehicles with us and all were jockeying to get the best view for their clients.

After a hundred and eighty-mile, six hour drive we arrived at Kanha National Park. Here we had a troop of Hanuman's langurs visit our room every day. This park was famous for its effort in saving the Barasingha, also called southern swamp deer, from extinction. The guides stated that there were approximately seven-hundred and fifty Barasingha in the park during our visit. We were very fortunate to find a sloth bear on one of our drives and also have a quick sighting of a leopard.

I was impressed with the management of both of these large parks as they were divided into four or five sections and every day each vehicle was assigned to one section. This kept each section with a reasonable number of vehicles and visitors.

From Kanha we flew to Mumbai, the business center of India, stayed two nights and then flew to the Seychelles. A week later when we were in Namibia and we met some folks that had also traveled to India. They asked us if we knew what India stood for? They said, "**I'll Never Do It Again!**" I am not sure that would apply to us as we only visited a small portion of the country. There are many countries we have to explore before we return to India.

Our original plans called for us to fly from Mumbai to Cape Town, South Africa, on Ethiopian Airlines through Addis Ababa. In New Zealand, I mentioned to EWT that we were uncomfortable with the quick turnaround in Addis, plus the airport is one of our least favorite in the world. Jim rearranged for us to fly to the Seychelles and spend a few days before going to Cape Town. The Seychelles were a perfect place for us to relax on the beach and gave me a chance to get over a cold I acquired in India.

After a four-hour flight from Mumbai, we arrived on the main island of Mahe before transferring to the island of Praslin where we arranged to stay at Cote d'Or in a small cottage on the beach. The beach was beautiful with white sand and at each end there were iconic rock structures that are unique to the Seychelles. We were within walking distance of a small town with several wonderful restaurants with incredible seafood. We had heard of a small restaurant, PR's, down the beach past town and near the Raffles resort. On the map it looked like it was only a mile or so along the beach. It turned out to be three miles and much of our walk was on the main road. It was worth the walk and for lunch we had a delicious shrimp and rice dish. As it started to rain hard, we took a taxi back.

The next day, we flew from the Seychelles through Joburg to Cape Town, South Africa and met up with our friends, Dave and Hope Koncal at the Victoria and Alfred Hotel on the Waterfront. I got my first haircut in seventy days. After seeing the sites in and around Cape Town, already mentioned in this book, we flew to Windhoek, Namibia. Sarah and I had visited Windhoek and Etosha National Park in 1993, but this time we were going to the famous Namib Desert. Jimmy Gariseb, our driver and guide, picked us up at the airport and took us to the office of Ultimate Safaris where we stored some of our luggage as we planned to fly back to Windhoek on March 23 on a small charter plane.

It was a five-hour drive to the Namid Dessert and the Sossusvlei Desert Lodge. In the middle of the desert our vehicle got stuck in the only mud hole for miles around. Fortunately, a local landowner happened by and was able to help us get our vehicle out of the mud. It was March 18th, Dave's sixty-ninth birthday and my seventieth birthday. We could not have found a more beautiful and luxurious place to celebrate. Like all lodges in Africa, staff helped us celebrate with champagne, cake and singing. It was a birthday I will always remember.

The next morning, we left before sunrise for the Namid Naukluft National Park to explore the desert pans (dry lakes) and the dunes. We did a short nature walk through the desert and saw signs of desert life, including very dry dung pellets from gemsbok (conserving water). The highlight was climbing up the rim of a large dune and then walking, and sometimes sliding, down a steep slope. Back at the vehicle, I took a full cup of sand out of each boot.

The next day we drove all morning to the coastal town of Swakopmund and stayed overnight at the Hansa Hotel. Then the next morning we drove five hours along the Skeleton Coast and passed the Tropic of Capricorn to Damaraland.

Mowani Mountain Lodge was another fabulous all-inclusive lodge with individual luxury chalets tucked in between many rock outcroppings. There were many animals to view around the lodge and on game drives, including springbok, black-backed jackal, red hartebeest, steenbok, rock hyrax, dassie rat and several species of desert birds and reptiles. Two animal sightings were very special. One afternoon we went looking for desert elephants. Jimmy had heard they were at a seasonal pond in the morning. They were not at the pond, but after a half an hour on a rough rocky road we found a young male. Soon we found the herd of ten elephants of various ages. The elephants were very calm and came quite close to our vehicle. These elephants are not separate species, but elephants that have adapted to living in this harsh desert environment by knowing where to find water and feeding on desert plants. A second species I was excited to see was the Hartman's Mountain Zebra. This subspecies of the mountain zebra is only found in Angola, Namibia and northern South Africa. It is a species I worked with when I was a keeper in the seventies at Los Angeles Zoo.

Sarah and I enjoying sundowners in the Damaraland, Namibia, in 2017.

From the Damaraland we flew an hour and a half in a small charter plane back to Windhoek. It was an extremely bumpy ride and we had thought it may have been better to do the long drive. We got to the airport, glad to be on the ground and an Ultimate Safari employee was there with the rest of our luggage. From Windhoek we flew through Joburg and then on to Skukuza, just outside Kruger National Park.

The historic Kirkman's Camp is in the Sabi Sabi private reserves, outside Kruger National Park. There are several private reserves west of Kruger and there are no fences between the park and these reserves. We had a very knowledgeable guide, Josh, and a great tracker, Jerry, with us on all our game drives. Wildlife was plentiful and if there was something very special, such as a lion kill, the vehicles would drive off the road, something not allowed in the Kruger National Park. One of those special events was the viewing of a female leopard with two ten-week old cubs. Seeing young leopard cubs in the wild was a first for me and Josh and Jerry were very pleased that they were able to find them for us.

From Kirkman's Camp we drove through Kruger and then through the entire length of Swaziland, staying there one night at the Foresters Arm's Hotel. From here we continued south where we again entered South Africa. Our first stop was the St. Lucia estuary where we had a scheduled cruise. The two-hour boat ride was a little disappointing as we only saw a few hippos, crocodiles and birds.

The next day we arrived at the Phinda Mountain Lodge, owned by &Beyond. Our spacious air-conditioned chalet was beautiful inside and out. The secluded outdoor deck had an outdoor shower, a plunge pool and overlooked Phinda Private Game Reserve. Wildlife was usually on view from the deck and plunge pool, especially nyala. Warthogs were also common around the lodge and one afternoon Dave and Hope Koncal couldn't get to their chalet as two warthogs were sound asleep on their doorstep. We had a wonderful guide, Richard, and an eagle-eyed tracker, Jomo. Like other southern African safaris, the tracker rides on a seat on the left front fender and drivers are on the right side of the vehicle. Our first game drive was very successful with views of cheetah, both black and white rhinos, lion cubs and much more.

On one drive we noticed some water plants with masses of white foam attached to the plants above the waterline. It turned out that they were eggs of foam frogs, something I do not think I had seen on previous safaris. This Reserve is eighty-five square miles and it's completely fenced, but large enough to have most of the wildlife safari goers desire. All the wildlife had been reintroduced since 1991 when the park was established. Elephant were plentiful as were giraffe, lions and even leopards. It was easy to see the Big Five, elephant, rhino, buffalo, leopard and lion, in one day. After seeing most of these animals we went to look for some of the more elusive ones. It took a while, but we did catch a glimpse of a red duiker and a suni antelope, both new species for me.

One evening the manager told us we might want to bring a sweater. This was a hint to us that we would be having a bush dinner, a delightful feature of these luxury camps. We didn't say anything and when we stopped for cocktails out in the bush, we thought we may have been wrong, but we were not. After cocktails we drove a little farther and joined everyone from the lodge for a wonderful bush dinner. The next day we started our journey home.

While we were gone for eighty-three days, we were not that anxious to come home. We could have kept traveling!

In January 2018, Sarah and I traveled to Panama for an interesting short tour. From Panama we traveled south and joined our friends, Satch and Becky Krantz on a trip to Ecuador, the Galapagos Island and Machu-Picchu in Peru. We met them in Quito, Ecuador where they were staying with their son's in-laws, Marcello and Marie Eugenia Moncayo.

In Panama, Sarah and I had arranged with Ancon Expeditions of Panama to have Rich Cahill as our guide. He is an American citizen living in Panama. His parents came to the Canal Zone in 1948. We knew many of the same people, including Ged Caddick and Rudy

Zamora. On our first day, Rick picked us up and he had his twelve-year old son, Willy, with him. Willy turned out to be nice addition. He was interested in everything and we enjoyed his company. The first day included a tour of the Chagres River, source of water for the canal, and a visit with the Embera people, one of seven indigenous tribes of Panama. After that we returned to Panama City and had a tour of the Gehry Biodiversity Museum and then a bike ride, partially in the rain, along the Amador Causeway.

The next day was dedicated to wildlife and the canal. Rich has encyclopedic knowledge on the Panama Canal. We visited the Soberania National Park where we hiked the pipeline road and visited the Panama Rainforest Discovery Center and Observation Tower. There we saw chestnut-mandible toucan, keel-billed toucan, mealy parrot and several species of hummingbirds and tanagers. Of course, I wanted to visit the Summit Municipal Garden and Zoo. I had heard that Ron McGill of ZooMiami helped them set up a display for harpy eagles. It was a large aviary with one eagle and an extensive indoor interpretive area, much of it featuring Ron. Staff were working on several of the primate exhibits and instead of locking the spider monkeys up in holding during the construction, they simply let them loose on the grounds. We then toured the Miraflores Locks and watched several large and small ships go through the locks. The fifty-one-mile canal was opened in 1914 and a third lock to accommodate the larger cruise ships was opened in 2016. Rich had attended this second opening.

On the third day of our visit we explored the city ourselves and walked along the Cinta Costera, a park next to the bay. Our last day in Panama, before our evening flight to Ecuador, we made arrangements to visit Barro Colorado, home of the Smithsonian Tropical Research Center. Anyone studying tropical biology reads references from this research center. I really wanted to see this famous facility. This six square mile island was formed when the lake flooded to create the canal. Our Panamanian guide, Milva, was one of the staff scientists on the island and she studied bats. We learned that the center had forty staff scientists working on three hundred and fifty scientific projects. While the tour was rather basic, we did see both spider and howler monkeys, agoutis and several birds, including the great tinamou.

After stopping in Quito, Ecuador and meeting up with Satch and Becky, we flew to the Galapagos Islands. I had visited the island in 1986 and was anxious to see the changes over the last thirty years. First change was the itinerary as in 1986 we were able to visit more of the islands in one tour. Now most tours pick the northwest or the south and central itinerary. We chose the northwest that started at Baltra where the airport is located, and then went to Las Bachas on Santa Cruz, Genovesa and Prince Phillips Steps and Puerto Egas on Santiago. We then sailed north across the Equator and around Isabela stopping several places on the west side of Isabela and on Fernandina. Sailing south we stopped at the Puerto Villamil where we went to the Arnaldo Tupiza Breeding Center for Galapagos tortoises. From there we returned to Santa Cruz and drove across the island to catch a ferry to Baltra and the airport. On my 1986 tour, we also stopped at the southern island of Floreana, Espanola and Santa Fe.

Our ship on this tour was the one-hundred ten-foot sailing yacht, the Beagle, although it only once utilized it's sails. There were six passenger rooms and aside from the Krantz's and us there were two other couples, one room for two women that knew each other in high school and reconnected to travel, one room for a single woman that loved to travel and one room for two men that separately booked the cruise. All were well traveled.

There were many highlights on this tour. On the way to Isabela we spotted a very active group of three-hundred common dolphins that swam alongside our ship for about a half an hour. Different from my first tour, this tour had full wet suits for everyone and we snorkeled at almost every destination seeing an amazing variety of tropical fish, sea lions, green turtles and Galapagos penguins. The wet suits were essential as the Humboldt current brings colder water to these islands. Penguins like colder water and that is why there are Galapagos penguins on the equator, the northern most species of penguin. Being in the water very close to sealions and green turtles was a special experience. As one passenger noted, "the sea lions don't seem to understand the concept of personal space." On my 1986 tour I remember seeing many more land iguanas. While on this tour we only saw them near Urbina Bay on Isabela. In 1986, we went by horseback up into the hills on Santa Cruz to see a dozen of Galapagos tortoises. On this tour we only saw one tortoise and that was on a hike on Isabela and that huge tortoise was deep in the brush.

Comparing my wildlife list on my two tours of the Galapagos revealed that I basically saw the same species. On this tour I did add the Galapagos owl to my bird list. Galapagos is famous, not for the large numbers of species, but for its unique species and the ability of visitors to get very close to most wildlife.

On January 20 we flew from the Galapagos to Guayaquil, Ecuador for an overnight before flying on to Peru and our visit to Machu Picchu. The Hotel du Parq in Guayaquil was near the airport and was a great place to relax, although it did not have a much-needed washer and dryer. As an added bonus there was a zoo on the property, although it was closed. We actually were able to walk in through an open gate and there were great exhibits of peccary, tapir and other native animals. We had a wonderful dinner outside in a courtyard of the hotel before going to our room and watching President Trump's State of the Union Address.

From Guayaquil we flew to Peru, stopping in Lima before connecting to Cusco. Our plane was late and then had to circle Cusco as weather was an issue. We felt relieved when we finally landed safely. We were met by our guide, Oswaldo, and taken to the beautiful Palacio Nazerenas. Oswaldo was our guide throughout our visit. The elevation of Cusco is eleven-thousand feet and it takes some time to get adjusted to the altitude. Drinking coco tea and doing everything, walking, eating and drinking, slowly helped to get us adjusted to the high altitude.

We spent a few days touring around Cusco and the Sacred Valley with its Inca cities of Pisca and Ollantaytambo. On February 4th we boarded the Vistadome train from Ollantaytambo to Aquas Calientas, which was just below Machu-Picchu. The next day at 6:30 AM we took a bus up the mountain to the entrance of Machu-Picchu. Oswaldo did us proud by having us go in one direction and pointing out all the highlights. We were amazed at the completeness of this ancient city with its domiciles, meeting areas, cultivation areas and religious buildings. How the Incas were able to precisely place the giant stones to create this city can never be fully understood. The Incas built Machu-Picchu between 1438 and 1472 and it was inhabited until the Spanish conquered the Incas a century later, although they never saw Machu-Picchu. This most important archaeological site was not known to westerners until Yale Professor Hiram Bingham "discovered" it in 1911. With nearly a half a million tourists a year, it is now the single-most visited tourist site in South America.

For the remaining portion of 2018 we did some local and US travel, including a wonderful trip to Arizona that included a visit to the Grand Canyon. We were all set to lead some friends on a South African safari in September, but then I was diagnosed with HPV throat cancer and Jim Heck took our group.

By 2019 I was back among the living and ready to continue life and travel. Our first major international trip was with the Krantz's to Europe, into Paris and out of Stockholm. It included a week Seabourn cruise from Copenhagen to Stockholm via Tallinn, Estonia, St. Petersburg, Russia, and Helsinki, Finland. None of us, despite being senior citizens, had ever taken a cruise. We did enjoy the spacious rooms, the great food and wine and the nightly entertainment. We toured Tallinn and Helsinki on our own but had arranged for a guide in St. Petersburg. Sarah heard about Nikolay Yermolayev from friends that toured St. Petersburg with the Cleveland Museum of Art and he arranged for his wife, Tatiana, to tour us for two days.

Prior to our cruise we toured northern France, including Normandy. It was a highlight of our vacation. We traveled from Paris by train to Bayeux which was one of the beautiful small towns where we stayed in northern France. On our first night we had a wonderful dinner at Le Volet Quie Penche where the owner was quite a character. When we asked him to take our photo he readily agreed. Then he reversed my I-phone and took a photo of himself. He shared the photo and we all had a great laugh.

Satch had arranged for us to have a two-day tour of Normandy. Our guide, Adrian, was excellent and first took us to Utah Beach and Omaha Beach. We observed Utah Beach and how it was relatively easy for the Allied troops to take. Omaha Beach was different and troops were pinned down on the large beach for a long time and took heavy loses. Looking at the beach it was easy to see that the four-mile beach was wide and Allied troops were easy targets. We then went to Saint Mere Eglise where one American paratrooper fell on a church and hung there before being captured and then rescued when the Americans took the town. This historic moment was played by Red Buttons in the movie the Longest Day. Point du Hoc was a fortified cliff where two-hundred and fifty American rangers climbed the cliff to take out a series of guns and they were relieved after two days of heavy fighting.

After visiting Normandy, we were taken to Mont Saint Michel. This was a beautiful island church and village and we were told by Adrian that it attracts ten-thousand guests a day. It certainly was crowded, but we were able to negotiate the walkways and got to the top. Despite the crowd, Adrian was able to find us a café for lunch. That is why you have a guide!

Adrian drove us to St. Malo, a walled city in northern France. We had the afternoon to explore this beautiful walled city. Sarah even found a very nice striped sweater. After some wine in the hotel we had dinner at L'Ansrage restaurant. We choose St. Malo as it provided us a departure port for a ferry to the island of Jersey, one of the Channel Islands that are part of Great Britain.

Why Jersey Island? The Jersey Zoo was a bucket list item for me. The founder, Gerald Durrell, was an important influence for my career as a zoo professional. I started reading his books in junior high school. The first one was a *Zoo in My Luggage* about his adventures in Cameroon collecting animals for zoos. Other books, and a TV series, were about his growing up on the island of Corfu in Greece and about his establishing a zoo on the island of Jersey. I think I have read all of his twenty or more books and even got to meet him on two separate occasions. At one meeting I was able to tell him that he was responsible for me working in zoos.

We left the ferry and caught a taxi for a short ride to our hotel. The very friendly taxi driver told us four very raunchy jokes. We got to our hotel and the first order of business was to find a laundromat. Satch had come directly to Europe from Tanzania so he was desperate for clean clothes. Staff at the hotel told us there was a laundromat just three blocks away. The staff at the laundromat took our laundry and did it for us for ten dollars each.

Lesley Dickie, director of the Jersey Zoo, met us at the gate. Both Satch and I knew Lesley from WAZA meetings. The zoo was celebrating its sixtieth anniversary. Gerald Durrell and Jeremy Mallinson were directors for the first forty years and then there were three other short-term directors until Lesley became the sixth director a few years ago. The zoo did not disappoint us. Exhibits for gorillas, orangs, lemurs, meerkats and others were large and well landscaped. Often the animals were difficult to observe, but the zoo was not concerned as it was all about animal welfare and conservation. Golden lion tamarins and pied tamarins were loose on the grounds and were locked up in their night quarters in the evening. Lesley took us all in a huge fruit bat exhibit and we fed bats bananas. I especially enjoyed the small museum that highlighted the life of Gerald Durrell.

Next we flew through London to Copenhagen where after a two-day visit we boarded the Seabourn's Ovation. After a day at sea and a short visit to Tallinn, we arrived at St. Petersburg. Tatiana ("Tana") picked us up in the morning for our tour. Using this tour company meant that we didn't need a Russian visa, otherwise we would have had to get a visa ahead of time. Our first day started at the Hermitage, the largest art museum by size in the world. The Louvre in Paris has more objects. When we arrived at 9:30 AM there was a huge crowd waiting to enter. Our driver, Sav, said "welcome to Chinatown," as the majority of those in line were Chinese. Tana had arranged for us to have early entry and we entered quickly and spent two and a half hours in the museum and it overwhelmed us.

After the museum we went to a nice riverside restaurant but were denied access as Satch and I had on shorts. Who knew? However, Tana found a local restaurant that featured typical Russian dishes and we felt like we were in someone's living room. A short tour took us through what looked like a refrigerator but was actually a speakeasy with its own still. They used it for small groups. The rest of the day we visited the Faberge Museum (I was not overwhelmed) and then a very nice canal boat tour in a small boat.

Our second day was spent in the country to tour the Tsar's Village and Catherine's Palace, presented to the Tsar's wife in 1710. The highlight was the Amber Room where the entire room was lined in amber. This was not the original Amber Room as the Germans took all the amber during the siege of St. Petersburg in World War II and it was never recovered. The gardens and fountains on the grounds were breathtaking. All the fountains worked on gravity as there were no pumps.

Tana was very knowledgeable and very Russian. She reminded us that the Russians lost more lives during World War II than any other nation. During the 900-day siege of St. Petersburg, formerly Leningrad, over a million Russians died, mostly of starvation and disease. She felt that Putin was doing a great job. She also stated that America had nothing to fear from Russia as they were a relatively small country compared to America. She also commented that those countries that left the Soviet Union years ago were not doing very well on their own. She obviously hadn't been to Estonia! One of the best reasons for travel is to get different perspectives of the world.

After St. Petersburg we had a few hours in Helsinki, Finland. After a long walk and seeing much of the city, I took Sarah to a dress shop where I had seen a zebra striped dress in the window. She tried it on and we both loved it. When we got back to the ship, we realized that the plastic security device was still attached. It wasn't until we got back home in Cleveland and googled how to remove security tags, did we get it off. We used a rubber band and just kept moving it back and forth until the device came apart.

Our last stop was Stockholm and after we left the ship and took our luggage to the hotel, we took a ferry to the Vasa Museum. A huge building enclosed the Vasa, one of the largest wood warships ever built. It was top heavy and when launched in 1628 it sunk even before it left the harbor! It was pulled out of the bay in 1960 and reassembled. The museum did a wonderful job of telling its story.

I had arranged to see Skansen-Akvariet, an indoor zoo inside the Skansen Open Air Museum. Skansen has a farmyard, exhibits of native wildlife and many historical exhibits. I had known Jonas Wahlstrom, the owner and director of Skansen-Akvariet, for years as we both regularly attended WAZA meetings. As a young man, Jonas worked at the Skansen Open Air Museum and he talked the management into letting him have an empty building for his reptile collection and that was the beginning of his zoo. Aside from reptiles, amphibians and fish, the zoo had a fine collection of small mammals, including ring-tailed lemurs, meerkats and Titi monkeys. There was a special exhibit of breeding Cuban crocodiles that Jonas had received from the Moscow Zoo. Young crocodiles hatched at this zoo had been returned to Cuba with great fanfare, including a visit with Fidel Castro.

Unexpectedly, Jonas invited us to his country home for lunch. After an hour drive we arrived at his delightful home. The first thing we saw was a troop of nine free ranging ring-tailed lemurs. There were also a series of aviaries, including three with pairs of breeding Hyacinthine macaws. There was a spur-thighed tortoise that was content mowing the front lawn. In the house, Jonas's wife, Christina, was busy making a lunch that including crayfish and vegetables from their garden. Of course, we had schnapps and wine. After lunch, Jonah had his caretaker drive us back to the city.

The twenty-two-day European trip was delightful and it was great to share it with our good friends, Satch and Becky Krantz.

Sarah had visited all but seven states so in the late summer of 2019 we decided to visit five of them. We flew to Bismarck, North Dakota, then went in a counterclockwise circle to Montana, Wyoming, a corner of Nebraska and ended in South Dakota. It was a great chance to see Yellowstone, Grand Tetons, Theodore Roosevelt National Parks, Mount Rushmore and much more. Our first stop was Theodore Roosevelt National Park where we took a wonderful hike among dozens of prairie dog towns before watching a large herd of bison from a safe hundred yards away. Our first day in Yellowstone it was raining and then the first snow of the season started. We managed to see most of the sites in the northern portion of the park and lots of wildlife including pronghorn, big horn sheep, elk, a mother grizzly bear with cub, a black bear and bald eagles. We got a room in the Lake Hotel, but the dining room was full for dinner and there was nowhere else to eat for miles around. We were put on a waiting list and got a table around 7:15 PM. Then the next day, we visited Old Faithful and other major attractions in the park. After that we headed south and spent the day in Grand Tetons. We did a nice three-mile hike near the Jackson Lake Lodge where we only saw one other couple. We noticed they were carrying bear spray. We stopped by Jenny Lake, one of the most beautiful spots in the Grand Tetons, before heading to our room at the Antler Inn in Jackson.

The next day we stopped by the visitor center on the way into Grand Tetons and asked if we should have had bear spray when we hiked yesterday. The answer was a definite yes! We found out that instead of paying fifty dollars for our own bear spray, we could rent it for nine dollars a day. No problem. We did the four-mile Taggard Lake hike before having a picnic lunch in Teton Village.

We were concerned that we may have weather issues for the remaining portion of our trip even though we were moving east and south. The rangers at the visitor center told us that the pass going east from Grand Teton would be icy, but the roads were clear going south towards Casper, Wyoming. While there was a small amount of snow on the roads, it was relatively easy driving. We got the last room at a

Quality Inn in Casper, next to what appeared to be a nice restaurant called the Fort. It was a real cowboy bar. Silly us, we asked for a wine list. The waitress said, "we don't sell much wine by the bottle here" and she bought over two twenty dollars bottles and I chose the Italian Pinot Grigio.

From Casper, we headed east towards Nebraska where we had lunch before turning north towards Rapid City where we checked into the historic Alex Johnson Hotel. We walked through town to see all the life size bronze statues of the Presidents of the United States. It seemed a little strange to me that George Washington was right outside a Starbucks. We spent the next morning at Mount Rushmore which is never disappointing. We did one more forest hike in Custer State Park. When we calculated our hikes, we ended up with around twenty miles. We had driven eighteen hundred miles. We also saw forty-eight license plates, an obsession with Sarah, only missing New Hampshire and Hawaii.

For a year I had been working with a firm that booked speakers on small cruise ships, under a 1000 guests, and in December 2019 I was scheduled to give four natural history lectures on a Crystal's Symphony cruise that started in Costa Rica and ended in San Diego, California. My four lectures were (1) The Jaguar, the True King of the Jungle, (2) Monkey Business, (3) Adventures in Birding in Central America, and (4) The Good, the Bad and the Nasty – Reptiles of Central America. It took a whole year to create these power points, but during my research I actually learned many new things and enjoyed the process. Our stops included San Juan Del Sur, Nicaragua, Acajutla, El Salvador, Puerto Vallarta, Mexico and Cabo San Lucas, Mexico. Visiting Nicaragua and San Salvador meant that I had travelled to all eight countries in Central America.

Prior to boarding the Symphony, we spent a couple of days in San Jose, Costa Rica with our friend Gary Lee, zoo architect and one of the members of the "Wylie Birding Group." Gary and his firm, CLRdesign worked on several Cleveland Metroparks Zoo projects, including the African Elephant Crossing. Gary and his friends, Ernesto and Margie Arias, share an amazing house in the hills above San Jose with two separate suites, plus guest rooms on the lower floor. Gary arranged for us to have a tour of Poas Volcano, which I had visited in 1993, and La Paz Waterfall Garden. The Garden had great exhibits for butterflies, hummingbirds, toucans, frogs, reptiles and other native animals of Costa Rica.

On the cruise, Sarah and I enjoyed visiting all four coastal cities on the itinerary. In El Salvador we hiked the Cerro Verde National Park nestled between three majestic volcano cones. El Salvador is the land of the volcanos as there are one-hundred and eighty-seven of which twenty-two are active. In San Juan Del Sur in Nicaragua we spent some time visiting the town. Then we walked along the beach and through a lagoon to a road leading up to a hill that offered a beautiful view of the entire crescent-shaped bay. On the top of the hill was a small church and on the top of the church was a statue, Christ of Mercy, one of the tallest Jesus statues in the world. Coming up the Pacific coast we stopped for a day a Puerto Vallarta. I had been there about forty-years ago but didn't remember much. The town was full of Americans, many of which lived there. We had lunch at Oscars, overlooking the river where brown pelicans were fishing. Sarah got some fantastic photos. Cabo San Lucas, the southernmost tip of Baja California is where the desert meets the sea. We spent two days enjoying this beach town. On the second day we took a tour boat to Los Arcos, an arch on the rugged coast. We got off the boat and spent a few hours on the beach. We ended our cruise in San Diego and flew home from there.

After visiting the Krantz's in Kiawah Island, South Carolina in January 2020 and attending the midyear AZA meeting in Wilmington, North Carolina, Sarah and I took a week to visit Grand Cayman. We stayed at an Airbnb on the far end of the island. As we don't like to drive in foreign countries, we took bus vans everywhere for five dollars a ride. We explored the entire island and really enjoyed the Queen Elizabeth Botanical Park with its endangered blue iguanas, the Cayman Island Turtle Center, walking on the volcanic Mastic Trail and walking around downtown Georgetown. We also went to Hell, a volcanic tourist trap that some marketing genius thought resembled Hell. We also took a tour with Captain Morgan's Watersports of a reef where we snorkeled with tropical fish and then spent an hour at Stingray City where everyone got off the boat in waist deep water and interacted with stingray. It was a little touristy, but it was fun.

At the beginning of March we attended my daughter-in-law's surprise fiftieth birthday party in Long Beach, CA. We then flew to San Jose, CA to celebrate Ray's eightieth birthday with some of his friends at Tamra Restaurant. We were then planning to fly to San Antonio for a family wedding, but with the warnings about Covid-19, we flew home instead.

When Covid 19 hit the United States and the rest of the world, travel came to a halt. About ten months into the Pandemic, I wrote the following description of our activities:

1. We hiked all eighteen parks of the Cleveland Metroparks, most (thirteen) of the Lorain County Metroparks and some of Lake County Metroparks and two times in Cuyahoga National Park. Visited the Holden Arboretum.
2. We biked Lorain/Oberlin bike path, several times through the Rocky River Reservation and Canal Way to Peninsula and back.
3. We visited Presque Park in Erie, PA.
4. We kayaked Rocky River and Hinckley Lake.
5. We cleared out house of unwanted items that were picked up by Volunteers of America.
6. We got take-out from Thai restaurant and dined outdoors at several Rocky River and Lakewood restaurants.
7. We played golf, more than ever. Sarah played in a Tuesday league and I played in a Thursday league. I played thirty-five rounds in 2020.
8. We had backyard social distancing evenings with finger food and wine, usually once a week in the summer.
9. We regularly Zoomed with relatives and friends.

10. We spent time in the garden almost every day. Spring planting and fall clean-up.

11. We played six hands of gin most evenings after dinner, March - December (forty-nine games to five-hundred). By December, I was ahead by one game.

12. I digitized all the slides that were in focus. No more slides in the house.

13. I continued my autobiography and added all our activities in retirement.

14. I created a power point, "Adventures of a Safari Leader."

15. I cleaned out my desk and reorganized.

16. Sarah purchased a new desk and we set up an office on the second floor.

17. I cleaned out workbench in garage and organized all nails, screws, etc.

18. We walked every day. Sarah walked 12,000 steps every day. I walked or ran most days. I did stretches, twenty pushups and forty sit ups every day.

19. We did yoga every Sunday and often one other day. Did yoga at Rock and Roll Hall of Fame one Tuesday evening.

20. From July through October we watched baseball and golf on TV.

21. Watched various Zoom presentations from UCI, Wake Forest University, Cleveland Clinic, Cleveland Zoological Society and the City Club.

22. We had wonderful dinners together, mostly outside in summer, every night.

23. I watched Netflix. Occasionally we found something to watch together.

24. Sarah did several thousand-piece puzzles, some were done in a day or two and some took a week.

25. We attended an outdoor Helen Welsh concert on July 27.

26. We shopped at Heinen's once every ten days and in the summer we picked up food from Fresh Fork weekly.

27. Sarah did accounting work for her friend Kay's business, Experiential Learning.
28. I attended Zoom board meetings and committee meetings as a board member of the Akron Zoo.
29. We walked through Cleveland Metroparks Zoo and Akron Zoo. Attended a meeting for donors of Cleveland Metroparks Zoo on plans for gorilla exhibit. Attended the Asian Lantern Festival.
30. We visited Sarah's family in Granville, OH. Stayed overnight at the Granville Inn and ate dinner outside with the family at the Buxton Inn.
31. Went to Maumee Bay, played golf, hiked and stayed two nights in the lodge. Went to Mohican State Park in January 2021 and spent two days hiking.
32. I read thirty-five books, both fiction and non-fiction.
33. I worked on identifying thirty to forty common Eastern US trees.

With all of that, we were still bored. Like just about everyone else in the world during the pandemic, we missed going out to dinner in a restaurant, visiting with friends and relatives, traveling outside Ohio, going to the movies and other social activities. We were very cautious and because of that we stayed safe and healthy.

None-the-less Sarah and I felt extremely thankful for all we had. We knew that many others in the world were not so fortunate. We both had had great jobs that we loved and they gave us resources to do whatever we wanted in our retirement. As we continue with our lives, we know we will have many more adventures.

"Choose a job you love, and you will never have to work a day in your life."
Confucius

ACKNOWLEDGEMENTS

I would like to acknowledge all the dedicated staff that work in AZA accredited zoos and aquariums. Their collective efforts to help save wildlife and wild places goes beyond commendable. I was fortunate to work with many of them.

I was also fortunate to work for five years or more in four different zoos with different leaders who taught me valuable lessons and supported my career. Dr. Warren Thomas at the Los Angeles Zoo had an encyclopedic knowledge of wildlife and he was able to use it as an enlightening and entertaining public speaker. Peggy Burks at the San Francisco Zoological Society introduced me to setting measurable objectives ("what gets measured, get's done"). Bob Thomas at the City of Sacramento monitored the zoo's progress but was never a micro-manager. Vern Hartenburg at Cleveland Metroparks supported me as an officer of AZA, a member of WAZA and allowed me to travel the world on behalf of the zoo and it's conservation programs.

My wife Sarah deserves a special thanks for all the hours she spent editing this book and correcting the numerous typos and poorly worded sentences. Any that are still in the document are solely my work, not hers. It was wonderful to share many of the adventures in this book with her.

CPSIA information can be obtained
at www.ICGtesting.com
Printed in the USA
LVHW081353061121
702620LV00024B/188